1	2	3	4	5	6	7	8	9	10	11	12	13
14	15	16	17	18	19	20	21	22	23	24	25	26

CHABE
RHACRE
ODPOR
EVIREG
NOBYE
SUCRIT

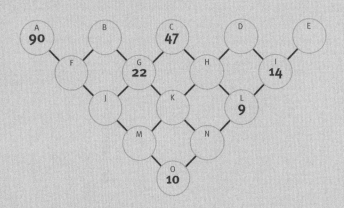

A 90
B
C 47
D
E
F
G 22
H
I 14
J
K
L 9
M
N
O 10

6	20	27	4		31	13	4
				19 / 6			
		8			4		
13			12			12	14
	5			20			
				20	9		

Boost Your
BRAINPOWER

Boost Your
BRAINPOWER

OVER 400 PUZZLES, GAMES, AND BRAIN TEASERS TO BOOST YOUR MIND

JACKIE GUTHRIE AND TIM PRESTON

CHARTWELL
BOOKS

Quarto is the authority on a wide range of topics.

Quarto educates, entertains and enriches the lives of
our readers—enthusiasts and lovers of hands-on living.

www.quartoknows.com

This edition first published in 2017 by:
CHARTWELL BOOKS
an imprint of Book Sales
a part of The Quarto Group
142 West 36th Street, 4th Floor
New York, New York 10018
USA

ISBN-13: 978-0-7858-3546-2

Editor: James Bennett
Designer: Mark Batley

FOR PUZZLER MEDIA
Design: Wilson Hui, Martin Edwards
Additional Contributors: Roger Prebble, Trevor Truran, Mark Whiteway, Lizzie Purcell, Jenny Anstruther
Artwork: Andy Hamilton, Jill Wadsworth, Mark Beeton

10 9 8 7 6 5 4 3 2 1

Printed in China

Contents

Improve Your Brain Power

These days, we're constantly reminded of the need to keep physically fit so that our bodies stay healthy. What we often forget is that our minds need similar care and attention to stay in peak condition. By giving our brains a regular workout, we can improve our mental capabilities, because the more we exercise the mind, the better it functions. In fact, brains thrive on exercise, and as you're about to find out, a good brain workout can be a lot of fun!

GOOD HEALTH!

So just what are the advantages of exercising the brain? For a start, experts tell us that people whose brains are highly stimulated are less susceptible to brain disease and deterioration. Use it or lose it, they say. In addition, mentally active people appear more likely to live longer. So keeping our minds working as we grow older could pay off handsomely!

ENJOY YOURSELF!

Fitness trainers tell us we're much more likely to stick to an exercise routine if we enjoy it. In the same way, a brain workout should be something to look forward to, and that's where this book comes in. But what makes puzzles so enjoyable? Finding the solution to a difficult problem is very satisfying and leaves us with a great sense of achievement. Meanwhile, the more we struggle, the more we're working those brain cells, giving us a better chance of solving the next, more difficult problem. In other words, the more the brain is challenged, the better it will face the challenges to come.

PUZZLE POWER

We've included a huge variety of puzzles in the following pages that are designed to challenge all your problem-solving capabilities: from straightforward logical reasoning to creative and lateral thinking. Tackling the puzzles will improve your brain power in ways you might come to notice in everyday life: your memory will be sharper, you'll think more quickly, you'll be able to concentrate more easily and for longer, and you'll be thinking on more than one level at a time.

BEFORE YOU BEGIN...

The book has been divided into five sections, each of which presents a particular type of challenge to your brain, as explained on the opposite page. Within each section, there are four levels, starting at the relatively simple Level 1, and moving gradually up to the most challenging Level 4. As your brain power will be improving with every puzzle you solve, we strongly recommend that you start at the beginning of each section, and work your way through. So don't waste any more time: flex those brain cells, turn the page and begin your workout.

As we grow older, staying active—in mind as well as body—could help us live longer.

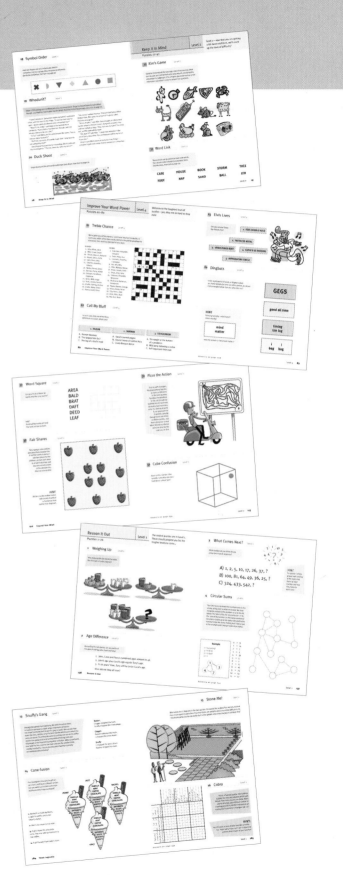

Keep It In Mind
Pages 8–49

Some people accept failing memory as an inevitable sign of aging. In reality, your memory simply needs to be kept in shape. Here, we test your ability to remember words, shapes, images, and the tiniest details. You'll see an improvement in your powers of recall by the end of the chapter!

Improve Your Word Power
Pages 50–91

You'll probably be familiar with a lot of these puzzles—crosswords, arrowwords, codewords—but there'll also be a few you won't have seen before. These problems challenge the side of the brain concerned with language, and there's a fair bit of general knowledge thrown in for good measure.

Expand Your Mind
Pages 92–133

Does your mind ever deceive you? In this section, you'll face many visual and spatial challenges, including a variety of optical illusions to set your head spinning. You'll also be fitting shapes together, both mentally and by hand, conquering tricky mazes and even convincing your brain to see what isn't there.

Reason It Out
Pages 134–175

How quickly can you spot a pattern or crack a tricky code? Your deductive powers will be tested to the limit here with a mixture of number, word and sequence puzzles. Mental arithmetic will come in handy, but most important will be your ability to reason your way out of a complicated problem.

Think Logically
Pages 176–215

Look at all the facts, put them together and find the logical conclusion. It sounds simple enough, but you might just change your mind when you tackle this lot. There's no trial and error involved—you will need strategic skills, great reasoning powers and, in many cases, a good deal of persistence.

Keep It In Mind

In the digital age, it might seem natural that we've come to rely on devices to help us remember things. Diaries have been replaced by Personal Digital Assistants (PDAs). Information on almost every subject is available at the touch of a button. Why bother to remember complex facts if you can look them up on the Internet? Maybe technological progress is one reason why many people in the modern world feel that their memories are deteriorating.

HELP YOURSELF

Computers are very clever, but they can't solve all of life's problems. They can't tell you where you left your door keys, for example! If you'd like to be able to remember your wedding anniversary, your children's birthdays or your own cell phone number, this section of the book should help.

STARTING OUT

Most of the puzzles in this section are in two parts. First, you'll usually be presented with a situation. You'll then be directed to questions on a different page (labeled with the same puzzle number, but preceded by Q for Question).

Focus is very important when it comes to remembering things.

The puzzles are interspersed with tips, tricks and strategies to improve your memory. With the right attitude, we believe you'll be able to tackle all of the challenges in this section. When you begin, put this thought at the front of your mind: according to Einstein, the brain is a muscle, and it can be trained. What it needs is regular exercise.

STAY POSITIVE!

Your brain chooses what to remember and what to forget. How it makes these decisions is something to consider. It sounds like an automatic process, something over which you have no control, but plainly, that's ridiculous. Can you imagine this scenario? "I'm sorry I didn't call on your birthday; my brain chose to forget it. I really must have a word with that organ!" The problem is that if you don't make a conscious decision to commit something to memory, you are liable to forget it. Quite often, what you remember turns out to be something that interests you, and that you have focused on intently. This means that if you want to remember something, you must accept that it's necessary to concentrate, to pay attention. The more positive your approach to the subject matter, the more easily you'll remember it. This should encourage you to tackle the puzzles with the knowledge that, if you focus on the tasks, you'll find them a lot easier.

IN THE PICTURE

How to memorize varies from person to person. There appear to be four main methods: auditory (hearing and speaking), visual (images), abstract and verbal (formulae, definitions), and physical experience (touch, smell). If you can work out which method works best for you, you'll probably find it easier to remember things. If you're not sure, begin by using visual techniques. The key is often to create an association between a picture and the thing you want to remember. Expert memorizers often work with a fixed location, and mentally place things to be remembered in different places at this location. For example, imagine the location is your house. Let's pretend your house consists of an attic, a bedroom, a bathroom, a kitchen, and a lounge. Now consider this list of groceries: spaghetti, bread, milk, eggs, beef, potatoes, oranges, ketchup, salt. The expert memorizer would mentally place the items around the house.

COME DANCING QUESTIONS (see p9)

1. How many stars did you see in the picture?
2. How many points did each star have?
3. How many fingers did you see on the man's right hand?
4. How many buttons were there on the man's jacket?
5. Was the woman wearing a necklace?

He or she might put the spaghetti and the salt next to the rocking horse in the attic; the oranges and the ketchup on top of the laundry basket in the bathroom; the milk and the eggs on the bed; the potatoes on the kitchen table; the beef and the bread on the TV in the lounge. Visualizing the items in this slightly surreal way helps to compartmentalize and organize them in the mind. How we store memories, then, determines how easily we can access them.

Seeing things perfectly does not mean we will remember them!

SEEING THINGS

We don't necessarily need a house to put all our memories in. Sometimes just grouping items together in one bizarre image will be enough to help us remember them all. For example, in puzzle 1 on page 10, the pictured items in the group include a snake, a car and a telephone. So concentrate on a picture involving all three: perhaps a snake driving a car while talking on the phone. Then start adding the other images to your picture: perhaps the car is having to swerve because a dinosaur slips on a banana skin in front of it; sometimes, the more ridiculous the image, the more likely it is to stick in your head!

As individuals, we'll always find it easier to remember some things than others. For example, somebody who feels comfortable with numbers, when asked to remember the number 796316, would probably form an immediate pattern in their head involving these digits. Here, they would easily recognize that 79-63=16, and the number would be fixed in their memory. If we can recognize a pattern in something, we'll be unlikely to forget that sequence.

So, in order to improve our memories, we must look for patterns, create recognizable images and learn to sift relevant information from that which is unimportant. The following puzzles are full of exercises that will help you to do all of these things, and many hints and tips are given as you go through. By the time you're finished, you'll have no excuse for forgetting a friend's birthday ever again!

COME DANCING!

Here's your chance to take a practice run with a memory puzzle. Look at the picture at right for a few minutes, taking note of the details. Then, cover the picture and attempt to answer the questions on the opposite page without looking back. Then check the answers at the bottom of the page to see how you did.

YOU CAN SAY THAT AGAIN!

Visual memory techniques, as described on this page, are certainly useful, but tricks alone won't always work. Sometimes there is no substitute for hard work. Repetition, for example, does help imprint certain things in our minds. If we say something over and over again, we stand a good chance of remembering it. This is the way that many of us learned our multiplication tables in elementary school.

COME DANCING SOLUTIONS
1. Four 2. Five 3. Three fingers and a thumb 4. Two 5. No

1 Kim's Game | Level 1

To get you started, here's a simple example of a popular challenge. Examine these few objects for no longer than thirty seconds, then turn to page 12. To help you remember the objects, try to make some association between them in your mind.

2 Word Links | Level 1

Some people find it easier to remember words than images. Have a look at the words below, then turn to page 12.

**HORSE
FLUTE
TREE**

**FLOWER
RABBIT
GUITAR**

**DOG
SHOE
CHEESE**

**JACKET
BISCUIT
HAT**

3 Me and My Pa | Level 1

There are people who are brilliant at remembering trivial details...the shape of a vase, the name of a distant relation, the taste of a particular cookie. Test your own powers of retention of trivial facts. Consider this list of famous people and the professions of their not-so-famous fathers. Then turn to page 12.

PERSONALITY	FATHER
Elizabeth Taylor	Art dealer
Nancy Reagan	Car salesman
Jerry Hall	Truck driver
Will Smith	Refrigeration engineer
Robert Redford	Milkman
Jon Bon Jovi	Hairdresser
Greta Scacchi	Artist

4 Before and After | Level 1

Study the picture of the goldfish bowl for one minute, then turn to page 12. Can you spot the six differences between the picture on this page and the one on page 12?

5 Family Tree | Level 1

Family trees provide highly structured information, which makes them easy to understand, but it isn't always so easy to assimilate structured information. Consider the following, then turn to page 12.

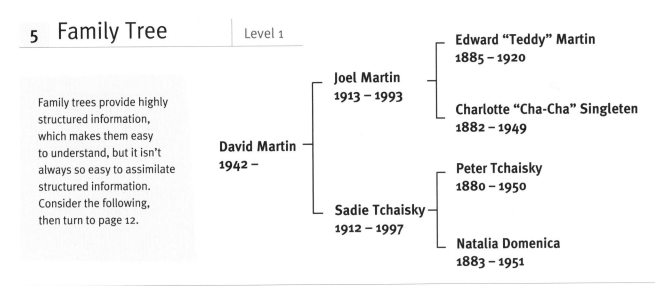

David Martin
1942 –

Joel Martin
1913 – 1993

Edward "Teddy" Martin
1885 – 1920

Charlotte "Cha-Cha" Singleten
1882 – 1949

Sadie Tchaisky
1912 – 1997

Peter Tchaisky
1880 – 1950

Natalia Domenica
1883 – 1951

6 Jimmy O'Brien and the Knoblings | Level 1

How good are you at picking up facts? Read the following story through twice, then turn to page 12 to answer some questions without looking back.

On a sunny June morning, Meera looked out of her window and saw a grotesque blue creature in her garden. It had four eyes, one on each side of its perfectly cuboid head, and four fingers on each hand. Three spindly arms and three spindly legs sprouted from its square body. Its feet were webbed, like a duck's. The creature was entirely hairless, except for a single bushy eyebrow over one eye. This eyebrow was raised, because the creature had noticed Meera.

"Can you help me?" it said, in a strange, croaky-squeaky voice.

"I'm heading for Thenon but seem to have lost my way." The creature sat down on a red toadstool and looked at her expectantly.

"I'm afraid not," said Meera. "But I do know where Herion is," she continued in a rush, "because Jimmy O'Brien told me. He goes to Herion High School with my sister. It's just past that tree and through the park."

"My dear child," the creature sighed, then smiled with an air of suffering patience. "Herion is the land of the Knoblings. They are bright pink! I have no wish to associate with such ludicrous creatures."

"Right," said Meera, as if she understood. "Well, is there anything I can do to help you?"

"It seems not," said the creature, and it disappeared.

Meera stood still for a few seconds, trying to understand what had just happened. Had she imagined the whole thing? She went into the garden to investigate and discovered that the toadstool on which the creature had been sitting had turned bright blue. Smiling to herself, she went inside and started to get ready for school.

After a few minutes, Jimmy knocked at the door to call for her sister. When Meera opened the door, it was clear Jimmy had been running. His face was bright pink.

Q1 Kim's Game | Level 1

The questions on this page relate to puzzles from pages 10–11. The three questions below refer to puzzle 1.

a) How many of the objects were capable of powered flight?
b) How many items were there altogether?
c) Can you name them?

Q2 Word Links | Level 1

Look back to puzzle 2. How many words were connected with:

a) Animals? Name them.
b) Food? Name them.
c) Musical instruments? Name them.
d) Clothing? Name them.

Q3 Me and My Pa | Level 1

a) Whose father was a car salesman?
b) Name the milkman's son.
c) The fathers of two of the personalities worked in associated fields of endeavor. Can you name those with connected professions and their daughters?

Q4 Before and After | Level 1

What are the six differences between this goldfish bowl and the one on page 11?

Q5 Family Tree | Level 1

a) How was David's paternal grandfather more affectionately known?
b) How old was David's father when David was born?
c) How much younger than her husband was Sadie?
d) What was the name of David's father?
e) What was the name of Cha-Cha's child?
f) What was Sadie's father's name?

Here's a gentle joke on the general theme of memory puzzles.

A rather slow-witted couple has dinner at another couple's house. After the meal, the wives leave the table and go into the kitchen. The two gentlemen are chatting and one says, "Last night we went out to a new restaurant, and it was really great. I recommend it highly."

"What was the name of the restaurant?"

The man knits his brow and finally says, "You can help me out. What's the name of that red flower you give to someone you love?"

"A carnation?"

"No, no. The other one."

"The poppy?"

"No! You know, it's red, it has thorns."

"Ah! You mean a rose?"

"Yes, yes, that's it. Thank you!" The man turns toward the kitchen and yells, "Rose, what's the name of that restaurant we went to last night?"

Q6 Jimmy O'Brien... | Level 1

a) How many eyes did the creature possess?
b) How many fingers did the creature have, altogether?
c) What school does Jimmy O'Brien's sister go to?
d) Why are Knoblings ludicrous?
e) What's the way to Herion from Meera's house?

7 Colorful Words | Level 1

Colors are often difficult to remember. Many men are color-blind, but that's no excuse for dodging this puzzle, because we've also spelled out the names of the special set of colors below. Examine them for about twenty seconds, then turn to page 16.

then turn to page 16.

HINT

People often use mnemonics to remember lists of things.
A mnemonic is a pattern of letters that helps you to remember things. For example, HOMES is a mnemonic that is useful as an aid to remembering a set of spectacular geographic features in the American landscape. Can you guess what?

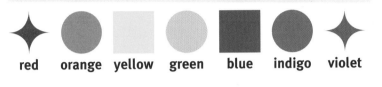

red   orange   yellow   green   blue   indigo   violet

8 Who Am I? | Level 1

It is interesting to consider what facts our brains latch on to, and which they choose to ignore.
Read through the list of clues to discover the identity of a famous person who is often in the public eye. How quickly do you identify the celebrity? What key fact switches on the answer? Or is it simply the combination of a series of half-remembered facts that leads you to the answer?

- She was born in 1958 in Bay City, Michigan.
- Her mother died when she was five years old.
- Her first single released was "Everybody."
- Her name when she was born was Louise Ciccone.
- Her albums have included *Bedtime Stories* (1994) and *Ray of Light* (1998).
- Her first marriage was to Sean Penn in 1985.
- She is married to the English film director Guy Ritchie.
- Her first work of fiction, *The English Roses*, was published in August 2003.
- Her children are called Rocco and Lourdes.
- She played the lead role in *Evita*.

9 Classic Cinema | Level 1

How quickly can you assimilate key details? Study Classic Cinema's Film Season listing, then turn to page 16.

then turn to page 16.

date	film	showing at	
10th	*Gone with the Wind*	2:30	5:50
10th	*Breakfast at Tiffany's*		1:05
11th	*Some Like It Hot*		3:05
11th	*Brief Encounter*		2:40
19th	*The Sound of Music*	4:15	
25th	*Psycho*	3:50	8:05
25th	*Brief Encounter*		2:30
30th	*The Birds*	8:00	

10 Spot the Differences | Level 1

It isn't always easy to remember what things look like, even when they're right in front of you.
Examine each of these pictures closely. There are six differences between them. Can you spot them all?

11 Numeracy | Level 1

Have a look at the sequence of numbers below, then turn to page 16.

54737539492

HINT
To help you remember this series of numbers, it may be useful to break up the number into blocks (for example, 5473 7539 492).

12 Titanic Tale | Level 1

Good stories are often exercises in remembering, and the narrative form makes it easy to register important details. Consider the story below, then turn to page 16.

Did You Know?
The British world memory champion has demonstrated, in competition, that he is able to memorize a sequence of 1,140 numbers in the correct order.

Brock Lovett, a treasure hunter, is hunting a famous diamond that went down with the ill-fated ship, *Titanic*. The stunning diamond once belonged to Louis XVI. What Lovett actually discovers, however, is a sketch of a young woman wearing the diamond on a necklace. Before long, the sketch appears in the media and an old lady called Rose Dawson comes forward, claiming to be the woman in the drawing. She doesn't know what happened to the jewel, but much to the fascination of Brock and his companions, she tells her own story of the fateful trip.

At the time she was a rich and miserable 17-year-old girl sailing to the US with her fiancé, Cal Hockley. She planned to commit suicide, but was talked out of it by a third-class passenger called Jack Dawson, who had won his ticket for *Titanic* in a pub.

The two were passionately in love when the "unsinkable" ship hit an iceberg. Rose jumped out of her lifeboat and vowed to stay with Jack. They were together in the freezing water when the ship sank. Jack perished, but Rose was rescued. In his memory, she gave her name as Dawson and set out to start a new life.

13   Things for Henry VIII To Do | Level 1

It's common to make lists to help us remember the tasks that have to be done, the places to be visited, the things that must be bought. Study the important fragment of parchment below, which affords a fascinating insight into courtly life in Tudor England, then turn to page 16.

April 15, 1534

buy a descant recorder
make an appointment for cut and color
* with royal hairstylist*
make appointment for varicose
* vein removal (ouch!)*
behead court jester
order a crate of ale
ask wife if we can have wild boar for tea
buy a new quill
if wife says no to boar, consider either goose
* or a new wife*
study report from the Vatican (no, really!)
place ad for new court jester
order slimming pills

14   The Island of Freeway | Level 1

If you have ever passed a signpost, then can't remember exactly what it said, you'll appreciate this challenge. Look at the sign from the imaginary island of Freeway for ten seconds, then turn to page 16.

Q7 Colorful Words | Level 1

Remember the colors on page 13? If you have identified why this is a special set of colors, you'll find the following questions easy.

a) What color comes first?
b) What color comes after green?
c) What color is before yellow?
d) In what naturally occurring feature would you find this set of colors, in this order?

Q9 Classic Cinema | Level 1

a) On what date is *Psycho* being screened?
b) How many opportunities are there to see *The Sound of Music*?
c) At what time is *The Birds* being shown?
d) If you want to see *Brief Encounter* and *Some Like it Hot*, on which date would you have to see *Brief Encounter*?
e) If you want to see *Breakfast at Tiffany's* and *Gone with the Wind*, which film must you see first?

Q11 Numeracy | Level 1

a) What is the last digit?
b) Can you write out the sequence in reverse order?
c) Look at these numbers: 5473739492. Which digit is missing from the original sequence?

Q12 Titanic Tale | Level 1

a) What was the name of the treasure hunter?
b) Who was Rose's fiancé?
c) How old was Rose when *Titanic* went down?
d) What did Rose say had happened to the missing diamond?
e) How did young Dawson obtain his ticket?

Q13 Things for Henry VIII To Do | Level 1

a) What was the date of Henry VIII's list of things to do?
b) What did Henry VIII want for tea?
c) From the list, it appears Henry VIII wasn't only careless with wives. Who else suffered?
d) What kind of musical instrument was he keen to obtain?
e) From which health problems did Henry VIII apparently suffer?

Q14 The Island of Freeway | Level 1

a) Look at the signs on the right. If you are going to Guava, which lane do you need to be in?
b) Which route should you take to get to Mango?
c) How far is it to Banyan?

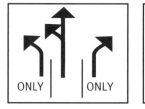

15 Picture Sets　　Level 1

If a disparate collection of items is arranged in a recognizable order, they are easier to remember. Certain ordering systems are so natural that we understand them in an almost intuitive way. Consider the two sets below, then turn to page 20.

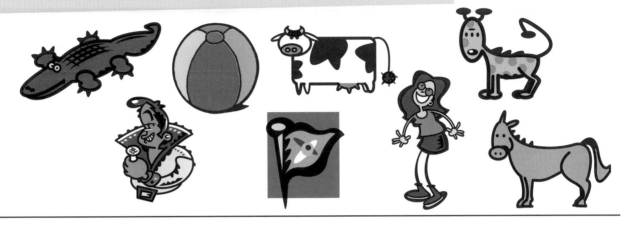

16 Who am I?　　Level 1

Historical personages tend to be remembered for public rather than for personal reasons.
Bearing this in mind, how quickly can you identify the person described opposite?

- He was born on February 12, 1809, in Kentucky.
- His father was a carpenter and a farmer.
- His mother, Nancy, died in 1818 from "milk sickness."
- His children were Robert, Edward, William and Thomas.
- His wife, from 1842, was Mary Todd.
- He was nearly six feet four inches tall.
- He made the so-called "House Divided" speech on June 16, 1858.
- In November 1860, he was elected the sixteenth President of the United States.
- He was President throughout the Civil War.
- He was the first President in American history to be assassinated.

17 Conversations　　Level 1

Read this conversation between two men shopping, then answer the questions on page 20.

"I'm so pleased with my new jeans," said Paul as they left the Denim store.

"Yeah, I'm glad you chose the dark blue rather than the black," said Chris. "They'll go better with that sweater you bought on Broad Street."

"OK," said Paul. "But what about you? You've only got that lousy T-shirt from the department store!"

"That happens to be the height of cool!" exclaimed Chris. "Ooh, let's go in here," he added as they passed a jeweler's. "I've needed a new watch for ages. And you can get that present you wanted for Claudia."

Ten minutes later:

"I still think you should have gone for gold!" said Paul as Chris strapped his new silver watch on his wrist. "Gold looks better for longer."

"Rubbish!" said Chris. "What do you know anyway? Let's see what you got for Claudia."

Paul carefully brought out the diamond-studded necklace and matching earrings he had bought for his wife. "Nice," admitted Chris. "So you've proved your taste is better than mine. Where shall we go now?"

"The café," said Paul. "I'm exhausted after all this spending!"

18 Symbol Order | Level 1

Abstract shapes are not, individually, hard to remember, but as a group, they can prove problematic. Study the set below, then turn to page 20.

19 Whodunit? | Level 1

Many of the goings-on in a Whodunit story can seem trivial. To get to the bottom of any problem, though, you need to have a good eye for detail. Read the following passage, then turn to page 20.

"I don't believe it. Someone's stolen my lunch!" exclaimed Elliot, with his head in the fridge. "It was the best one for ages—pasta salad, blueberries and a chocolate bar!"

"Wasn't me, mate," said Nigel as he tucked into a sandwich. "Sonia had a chocolate bar, though, and she always claims to be on a diet."

"A-ha!" said Elliot, and he called across the room, "Sonia, did you steal my lunch?"

"No! I've just come off a really tough diet. I only want to eat unhealthy stuff!"

Deciding not to question her reasoning, Elliot continued his investigation. "Thomas, have you seen my lunch?"

"No, sorry," replied Thomas. "I haven't had lunch either. I forgot mine. Milo gave me a taste of his pasta salad. That was very good."

"Hmm, thanks," said Elliot. Sure enough, on Milo's desk lay the remains of Elliot's lunch, along with a plastic tray and two balled-up bags. "Hey, that was my lunch!" he cried out, as Milo entered the room.

"Oh, was it?" said Milo. " I must have mistaken it for mine! Sorry about that. You can help yourself to my lunch if you like."

Elliot found Milo's lunch at the back of the fridge— a bruised apple and a stale cheese sandwich in a blue box.

20 Duck Shoot | Level 1

Look closely at this picture of a sideshow duck shoot, then turn to page 20.

Keep It In Mind

Puzzles 21–41

Level 2

Level 2—now that you are getting a bit more confident, we'll crank up the level of difficulty!

21 Kim's Game   Level 2

Examine these objects for no longer than thirty seconds, then turn to page 20. Look to find some easy way of classifying this information in subgroups. This will give you easier access to the information you need in order to answer the questions.

22 Word Links   Level 2

These words can be paired to make new words.
This should make it easier to remember them.
Find the pairs, then turn to page 20.

CASE	HOUSE	BOOK	STORM	TREE
FOOT	NAP	SAND	BALL	KIN

Q15 Picture Sets | Level 1

a) Which item is missing from the first row of four items: DOG, ALLIGATOR, COW.

b) Which item is missing from the second row of four items: GIRL, ELVIS, FLAG.

c) Write both rows of items in the original order.

Q17 Conversations | Level 1

a) What color are Paul's jeans?

b) Where did he get his jeans?

c) Who is Claudia?

d) What does Chris buy at the jeweler's?

Q18 Symbol Order | Level 1

a) Two of the following symbols were not part of the original set. Which two?

✖ ★ ◗ ✳ ▼ ●

b) See below. Which two symbols are in different positions from the original pattern?

✖ ◗ ▲ ◆ ▼ ● ■

Q19 Whodunit? | Level 1

a) What did Elliot's lunch consist of?

b) Who was eating a sandwich?

c) How did Sonia attempt to exonerate herself?

d) Why isn't the culprit's excuse very credible?

Q20 Duck Shoot | Level 1

a) Which duck has been shot the least times?

b) What is the color of the second duck from the left?

c) How many different colors of beak are there on the ducks?

d) What is the color of the blue duck's beak?

Q21 Kim's Game | Level 2

a) How many objects are not living creatures?

b) How many of the pictured mammals can you name?

c) Three of the nonliving items are devices that are used to convey information of one sort or another. Name them.

d) How many of the animals pictured have fewer than four legs?

e) Most of the creatures are kept as pets or are domestic creatures. One is not. Which one?

Q22 Word Links | Level 2

These questions relate to the unpaired words. If you managed to make the connections, you should find these questions straightforward.

a) Which word can also be paired with green, dog, and full?

b) Which word can also be paired with note, suit, and stair?

c) Which word is also part of a 70s pop group and a two-piece swimsuit?

d) Which word can be found in the middle of New York's main financial thoroughfare?

23 Pelmanism — Level 2

The ability to remember the exact location of items is a special skill.
Look carefully at the pairs of color blocks below, then turn to page 24.

24 Band Practice — Level 2

You have received the following memo from Miss Noted, the music teacher. You only have time to read it once.
Turn to page 24 to enter a dialogue with Miss Noted.

HINT

As you can only read the note once, read it slowly. Think about each word. This will force you to concentrate. Concentration is the key to memory training.

Photocopy music for 2 trumpets and 1 flute
Ask Janice if she'll play the piano part.
If not, call extension 3756, ask for Mr. Atkinson
LV now clarinet leader (GF has pulled out)
Find clothes for TB, WS and CS for concert
Photocopy letters re: Fun Day on June 7, then distribute
New reed for OC—give to Mr. Kilmarnock by Tuesday
Renew library copies of Gershwin and Joplin
Fax thoughts on arrangement to JB, 432 5715
Number pages on master score

Consider the pictures below, of dastardly crooks going about their criminal business, and pay particular attention to their clothing. Then turn to page 24.

26 Monument | Level 2

Here is another chance to find out how much you know about something. How many facts do you need to identify the monument? When you have made a positive identification, turn to page 24.

- This monument is 305 feet 1 inch or 92.99 meters high.
- It was designed by the sculptor Frederic Auguste Bartholdi.
- It was transported to its current location on board a frigate called *Isere*.
- In 1984 it was designated a World Heritage Site by the United Nations.
- It was a gift from France.
- It was dedicated on October 28 1886, and became a National Monument on October 15 1924.
- There are 354 steps inside it.
- Its location was formerly known as Bedloe's Island.
- It overlooks New York Harbor.

Take a look at the shopping list below, compiled by Shakespeare. Try to memorize the items on the list. Then turn to page 24.

Quill repair kit
Ink
Paper
Tights
Apples
Theatre tickets
Fake blood
Weekly entertainment
review
Dagger

HINT
Make a visual association between each item and a picture. For example, to remember the quill repair kit, think of a feather snapped in two.

Did You Know?
Your memory can store about ten thousand images. You can use this database of pictures to form any number of connections with ideas or chains of association.

28 Name Game | Level 2

Have you got a good memory for names and faces? Have a look at this distinctive group of people with deliberately ordinary names, then turn to page 24.

HINT
Try to make a connection between one aspect of each character and each name. For example, Peter Davis has a tie with dots—you could nickname him Peter "Dotty" Davis to help you remember him!

Peter Davis **Steve Jones** **Sarah Bland** **John Smith** **Julie Kyoto** **David Brains**

Q23 Pelmanism | Level 2

One from each pair of colors has been removed. Can you remember the exact location of each of the missing colors?

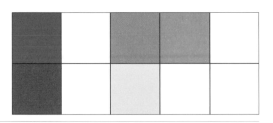

Q24 Band Practice | Level 2

Miss Noted calls you to ask about the memo she sent around. Apparently, she has lost it, and she wants you to remind her about a few things. Trouble is, you've lost it, too. Do your best to answer her questions.

a) Janice isn't willing to play the piano part, so I've got to call Mr. Atkinson. Can you give me his extension?

b) I've got to do something to the master score, but I can't remember what. Can you remind me?

c) I know I've got to give something to

Mr. Kilmarnock, but I can't remember what or when. Can you help me out?

d) I'm trying to fax my thoughts on the arrangement to JB, but the pages won't go through. The number I'm calling is 432 5175. Is that right?

e) Can you tell me the date of the Fun Day?

Q25 Crime Spree | Level 2

Can you spot the four criminals in the scene below?

Q26 Monument | Level 2

You may have identified the Statue of Liberty, but can you remember the key points?

a) How tall is it, in feet and inches?

b) Which nation donated the monument?

c) How many steps are there inside the monument?

d) What was the name of the frigate that transported the monument to its current location?

e) What was the former name of its location?

f) Can you remember the full name of the sculptor?

Q27 Shopping List | Level 2

There were nine items on Shakespeare's shopping list. How many can you remember?

Q28 Name Game | Level 2

Write the name of each person below the picture.

29 Family Tree | Level 2

If you tackled the first level puzzles successfully, you'll know just how to examine the family tree. Then turn to page 30. The Norton family has just bought a new dog, Genie. This tree shows the three previous generations of her family and highlights (in a bolder font) the dogs that "suffered" from a fairly benign inherited disorder that left them a little hard of hearing.

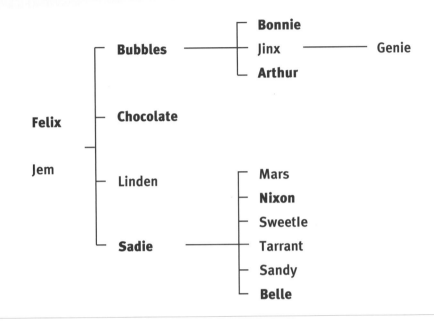

30 Spot the Differences | Level 2

How good are you at registering small details? Can you spot six differences between these two rush hour pictures?

31 Quick Dial Pyramid | Level 2

Even people who are not used to memorizing numbers should attempt this game. The object is to learn the eleven-digit number. It seems challenging, but with the aid of a simple visual trick, it should become possible. Start at the top of the pyramid and work your way down. Don't take more than a minute. Then turn to page 30 and see if you can complete the pyramid grid.

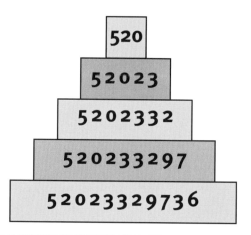

520
52023
5202332
520233297
52023329736

---

32 Apartment | Level 2

Imagine you are a real estate agent desperate to clinch a sale. You're out of the office when a viewer calls to ask a few questions about an apartment she has just visited. You have never been there, but you've seen the plan pictured opposite. Look at the plan for two minutes, then put yourself in the salesman's hot seat on page 30.

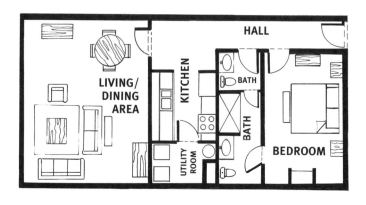

---

33 Chicago | Level 2

Here's a story that might be familiar. Read the details carefully, then turn to page 30.

Roxie Hart spends her nights in the jazz clubs of 1920s Chicago, hoping for a big break and a lifestyle to match that of her idol, Velma Kelly.

Roxie has an affair with Fred Cassely. When she finds out that Cassely lied about kick-starting her showbiz career, she kills him in a fury and is sent to jail. There she meets the aloof Velma, in jail pending trial for murdering her philandering husband and her sister, after discovering their affair.

"Mama" Morton, the matron of the prison, offers Roxie the chance to be represented in court by smooth-talking lawyer Billy Flynn. When Flynn receives $3000 from Amos, Roxie's loyal husband, he creates an image of an innocent, vulnerable Roxie. She shoots to fame, in sharp contrast with Velma, whom the media have suddenly forgotten.

Velma appeals to Roxie for help, but Roxie is not about to share her new-found fame. Roxie's own celebrity status suddenly seems shaky, however, when the wealthy Kitty is brought to the jail on multiple murder charges and becomes the papers' new darling. Roxie manages to turn their attention back on herself with a wild claim that she is pregnant.

Eventually, after a lot of manipulation, both women get off the hook. The downside is that the media have lost interest in them. Roxie and Velma realize that they can go further if they work together. A new act is born!

34 Handbag Haul | Level 2

A close examination of Marilyn Monroe's handbag revealed a number of colorful objects. Consider these items carefully, then turn to page 30.

Gloves, baby pink
Mascara, black
Hair dye, blonde
Hairbrush, black
Address book, pink
Diamond tiara
Gold watch
Mirror, green-rimmed
Sunglasses, pink-rimmed
Tights, natural
Scarf, green
Purse, black
Lipstick, scarlet

HINT
Use the colors to group the items in your mind.

35 Negative Memory | Level 2

It is difficult to remember a large group of objects, but if you are shown a single separate object, it's often quite easy to say whether or not that item was part of the original set. At least, this is our premise. You get to test it. Look at the images below, then turn to page 30.

Study the two sequences for two minutes, then turn to page 30 and answer the questions.

A

B

---

37 Exchange Student | Level 2

This is the schedule for an exchange student on his first visit to London. Look at it and answer the questions that follow on page 30 without referring back.

Monday	Tuesday	Wednesday	Thursday	Friday
Arrive 10:30am, Heathrow Airport	Madame Tussaud's	Big Ben	Shopping in Oxford Street and Bond Street	British Museum
Meet host family	London Eye	Westminster Abbey	Covent Garden	Concert in Royal Albert Hall
Picnic in Hyde Park	Dinner and West End show	Lunch in St. James' Park	Buckingham Palace	**Saturday**
Dinner in Chinatown		Houses of Parliament tour	Regent's Park open-air theatre	Tate Modern Art Gallery
		IMAX cinema		Football match

---

38 Word Patterns | Level 2

Consider both the pattern and the individual meanings of the familiar fairy tale characters in the box. On page 30, you will be asked to recreate this arrangement exactly.

HINT
To enable you to remember the words, create some kind of narrative (it can be anything at all, it doesn't need to make sense) that links all the words.

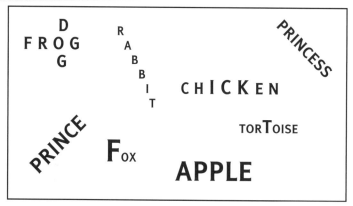

D
FROG
G

R
A
B
B
I
T

PRINCESS

CHICKEN

torTOISE

PRINCE

Fox

APPLE

39 Battleship | Level 2

The principle of Battleship is very simple. You and an opponent secretly position equal-sized fleets of ships on separate grids, then take turns firing at each other's ships by means of grid references. If a player gives a grid reference that contains part of the opponent's ship, a hit is scored and that part of the ship is considered sunk. The first player to sink every part of an opponent's fleet wins.

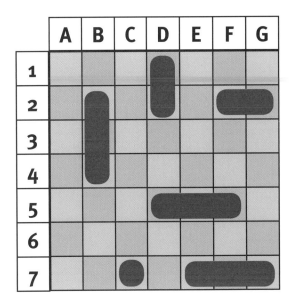

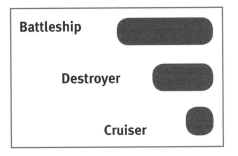

Battleship

Destroyer

Cruiser

Study this typical Battleship formation, then turn to page 32.

40 Identity Parade | Level 2

Look closely at the faces below, then turn to page 32. You'll be shown a similar lineup, but only one face will be identical. Your task is to decide which one, so look closely.

41 The Bemused Bard | Level 2

The sources for certain Shakespeare plays are not as authoritative as we might wish. The copies prepared by prompters, for example, or those scribbled by Thespian pirates during performances, are riddled with errors. Piecing together the correct text is a job for experts. Consider these lines, then look at the version on page 32.

Friends, Romans, countrymen, lend me your ears;
I come to bury Caesar, not to praise him.
The evil that men do lives after them;
The good is oft interred with their bones;
So let it be with Caesar. The noble Brutus
Hath told you Caesar was ambitious:
If it were so, it was a grievous fault,
And grievously hath Caesar answer'd it.

Q29 Family Tree
Level 2

a) Which second generation dogs were hard of hearing?
b) Which two second generation dogs were parents?
c) Which two of Sadie's puppies inherited the problem?

Q31 Quick Dial Pyramid
Level 2

Can you add the numbers at the correct levels to complete the pyramid?

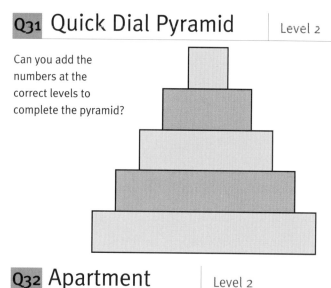

Q32 Apartment
Level 2

The buyer asks the following questions about the apartment. Can you answer correctly?

a) Which room leads off from the kitchen?
b) There are two doors leading off from the hallway into different rooms. Which rooms?
c) The door to which room is visible directly ahead when entering the hallway?
d) In terms of other rooms, what length are the two bathrooms combined?

Q33 Chicago
Level 2

a) Where does Roxie Hart spend her nights?
b) With whom does Roxie have an affair?
c) Why is Velma in jail?
d) What is the name of Roxie's high-flying lawyer and why does he represent her?
e) Who threatens Roxie's time in the limelight?

Q34 Handbag Haul
Level 2

a) What color were the tights?
b) How many objects were pink?
c) What color was the lipstick?
d) How many items were black?

Q35 Negative Memory
Level 2

What objects are missing from the original group and what items have replaced them?

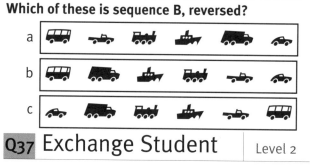

Q36 Match the Sequence
Level 2

Which of these is sequence A?

a
b
c

Which of these is sequence B, reversed?

a
b
c

Q37 Exchange Student
Level 2

a) On which day does he visit the British Museum?
b) Where does he go on Saturday after the Tate?
c) When and where does he go shopping?
d) What airport does he fly in to?
e) On what day does he take in a West End show?

Q38 Word Patterns
Level 2

Write the words in the box as they were in the puzzle.

Keep It In Mind

Level 3

Puzzles 42–60

At Level 3, your memory should already be more finely tuned than it was at the start of this section.

42 Sequence Challenge | Level 3

Study the pictures, then turn to page 32.

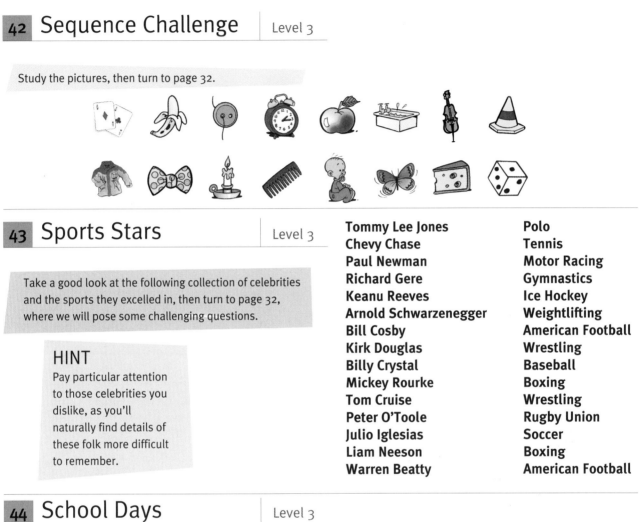

43 Sports Stars | Level 3

Take a good look at the following collection of celebrities and the sports they excelled in, then turn to page 32, where we will pose some challenging questions.

HINT
Pay particular attention to those celebrities you dislike, as you'll naturally find details of these folk more difficult to remember.

Tommy Lee Jones	Polo
Chevy Chase	Tennis
Paul Newman	Motor Racing
Richard Gere	Gymnastics
Keanu Reeves	Ice Hockey
Arnold Schwarzenegger	Weightlifting
Bill Cosby	American Football
Kirk Douglas	Wrestling
Billy Crystal	Baseball
Mickey Rourke	Boxing
Tom Cruise	Wrestling
Peter O'Toole	Rugby Union
Julio Iglesias	Soccer
Liam Neeson	Boxing
Warren Beatty	American Football

44 School Days | Level 3

Imagine you've been sent back to high school. It's the first week and you want to make a good impression on your new teachers. Turning up at their classes on time is a good start. Study the time-table for a few seconds, then turn to page 32.

	Monday	Tuesday	Wednesday	Thursday	Friday
9:00	French	Physics	Geography	Geography	History
9:45	Spanish	Chemistry	Math	Drama	Music
10:30	**BREAK**	**BREAK**	**BREAK**	**BREAK**	**BREAK**
11:00	History	Biology	Math	Drama	Chemistry
11:45	History	Math	Spanish	Spanish	Physics
12:30	**Volunteer work**	**BREAK**	**BREAK**	**BREAK**	**Piano lesson**
2:00	Physics	Music	French	French	Biology
2:45	Geography	Music	Chemistry	Biology	Drama

Q39 Battleship | Level 2

These questions employ the rules of Battleship.
a) Is C7 a hit or a miss?
b) Can you mark the position of the Battleships on the grid opposite?
c) D2 is a direct hit on a Destroyer. In which square is the final part of the ship, D1 or E2?
d) If you think you can mark the exact positions of any other ships on the grid at right, do it now.

	A	B	C	D	E	F	G
1							
2							
3							
4							
5							
6							
7							

Q40 Identity Parade | Level 2

Which of the faces below is identical to a face on page 29?

Q41 The Bemused Bard | Level 2

Consider this unreliable version of the text. Can you correct all the faults, without looking back at the original?

Friends, Romans, countrymen, lend me your fears;
I come to bury Caesar, not to raise him.
The evil that men do lives after them;
The food is oft interred with their bones;
So be it with Caesar. The novel Brutus
Hath told you Caesar was ambidextrous:
If it were so, it was a grave fault,
And gravely hath Caesar answer'd it.

Q42 Sequence Challenge | Level 3

a) Did the cello have a bow next to it?
b) What row was the baby in?
c) What was beneath the cello?
d) What column was the button in?
e) What was above the butterfly?

Q43 Sports Stars | Level 3

a) Which two celebrities excelled at boxing?
b) Which two celebrities excelled at American Football?
c) Who needs a car to indulge his enthusiasm?
d) What was Richard Gere's special sport?
e) Kirk Douglas and Tom Cruise have a pastime in common. What is it?

Q44 School Days | Level 3

You've lost the timetable you've just been given. Not a good start! How much can you remember?

a) On Tuesday morning, you have Biology after the morning break. But then what?
b) On which day is your piano lesson?
c) You've got History on two days every week. Which two?
d) Which day ends with double Music?
e) Only two subjects span a break. Which two?
f) Where should you be at 11:45 on Thursday?

45 House Numbers | Level 3

When patterns don't follow the expected sequence, it's more difficult to remember the details. Take this small, irregularly numbered block of houses. These are occupied by the following families:

7 Smith
12 Jones
19 Davies
33 Maddox
43 Calver
76 Cox

HINT
The irregular numbers will make it more difficult to get a spatial imprint of who lives where, and you must overcome this deliberate confusion to get a clear visual impression of the occupants.

Now turn to page 36.

46 Party People | Level 3

You've been schmoozing at a party and you picked up a number of useful contacts. You made some notes about each of them on scraps of paper. Here are the notes you made. Turn to page 36.

Jennifer Ross
Big hair
Psychologist

David Major
Age 52
Sales Manager
Sharp suit

Claire Bull
Flowery!
Receptionist

Frank Gardiner
Unshaven
Engineer
Collects stamps!

Bob Langley
20
Student
Unwashed

Sarah Waters
Pink glasses
Civil servant

47 Table Service | Level 3

You have just begun work in a restaurant, as a waiter. When you come to take your first order, your pen doesn't work. Rather than inconvenience the diners, you decide to try to remember their orders. To make things easier for yourself, you think of each diner at the table as a number. This is how you remember the order, when you're standing at the table. Turn to page 36.

- 1: Soup, then spaghetti carbonara
- 2: Shrimp cocktail, ravioli alla olio
- 3: Bruschetta, pizza 4 cheeses
- 4: Same as 1
- 5: Artichoke, chicken rosemary, no tomatoes
- 6: Stuffed clams, lasagne, no meat
- 7: Soup, ravioli tomato sauce
- 8: Bruschetta, filet mignon, medium

Look at the arrangement of shapes, then turn to page 36.

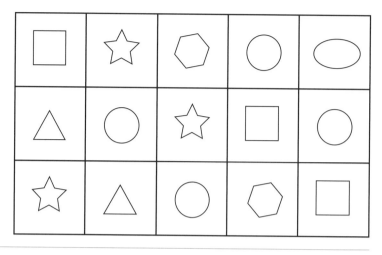

Each of the words at right is half of a pair. Find the pairs, then turn to page 36.

CALL
CLOCK
CURTAIN
HAIR
HOLE
HORN
MAN
PAL

PEN
PIECE
POLE
POSITION
ROPE
SHOE
TIGHT
TOWER

HINT
This puzzle shows the importance of making associations. To remember all eighteen words without any kind of a scheme would be tricky. Once you have identified the pairs, this puzzle should be simple!

Read this conversation through twice, then see if you can answer the questions that follow on page 36, without looking back at the text.

"So, how are you all getting home this evening?" asked the coach after the hockey practice.

"My Mom's picking me up in her new car!" boasted Kitty.

"At least I have my own," retorted Pete as he rummaged through his pockets for his keys.

"All right you two, that's enough," the coach said as Kitty opened her mouth to answer. "What about you three in the corner?"

"Oh, we're getting the train, as usual," chorused Sophie, Rosie and Millie.

"So will I, if the bus doesn't come soon," chipped in Alex. "Are you coming too, Joe?"

"No, forgot the fare," he mumbled. "Have to walk, worse luck."

"Well, I see James is riding back," said the coach, looking at the fast-disappearing figure on his motorbike. "That just leaves you, Simon. How are you getting home?"

"I'll just hop into a cab," Simon replied. "Thanks, coach!"

"Yeah, bye! See you next week!" all the players called as they set off home.

51 Six Blind Mice | Level 3

Give yourself a breather with this simple test that challenges your ability to remember visual details. Identify the odd one out.

52 Who Am I? | Level 3

Study the clues one at a time. You will almost certainly know this person, but which fact jogs your memory? Or do you guess the identify of the person by association; that is, by making a link between certain details that lead you to the right answer? At what point do you recognize the person referred to?

- This man was born in a village called Qunu on 18th July 1918.
- He has a daughter called Zinzi.
- He joined the African National Congress in 1942.
- He was nicknamed "The Black Pimpernel" for his skill at evading the police.
- He was commander-in-chief of the organization Umkhonto we Sizwe, formed in 1961.
- With Oliver Tambo, he set up the first black legal firm in South Africa.
- He started a life imprisonment sentence at Robben Island Prison.
- He was elected President of the ANC in 1991.
- He was the first democratically elected State President of South Africa from May 1994 to June 1999.

53 Funny Fakes | Level 3

Van Ick, the master painter, has produced twelve "masterpieces" for his exhibition at a new gallery. Study the paintings carefully, then turn to page 36.

Q45 House Numbers | Level 3

This puzzle involves not only the ability to recall numbers and names, but also a good spatial memory.

a) Who lives at number 33?
b) Who lives next door to (due west of) the Smith family?
c) Is the house numbered 12 south or north of 19?
d) Who occupies the house that lies due south of 76?
e) Does the Calver family (at 43) live south or north of the Jones family?

Q46 Party People | Level 3

When you get home, you can't find your notes! But you can remember most of the details! Here are the notes you've rewritten. Is there anything missing? Or wrong? If so, can you complete or correct the notes?

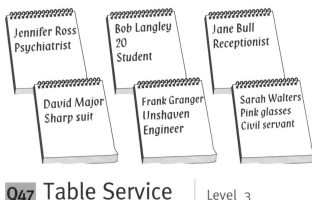

Jennifer Ross
Psychiatrist

Bob Langley
20
Student

Jane Bull
Receptionist

David Major
Sharp suit

Frank Granger
Unshaven
Engineer

Sarah Walters
Pink glasses
Civil servant

Q47 Table Service | Level 3

a) How many people ordered soup?
b) Who ordered clams?
c) How did the customer want her filet mignon?
d) How many bruschetta?
e) What was special about 5's order?
f) How many spaghetti carbonara?

Q48 Shape Up | Level 3

Can you recreate the full sequence of shapes?

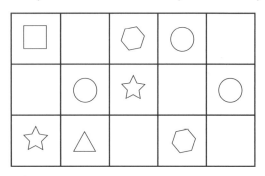

Q49 Pairs | Level 3

Which two words from the list can be combined to make the following:
a) A distant friend
b) A circus entertainer's wire
c) A tall structure for a chronometer
d) The first place on a racetrack
e) A wig
f) A stagey shout
g) A fitting device
h) Maintenance opening in the street

Q50 Conversations | Level 3

a) What event are people going home from?
b) Which three players will be traveling by car?
c) How is Rosie getting home?
d) Under what circumstances will Alex get the train home?
e) Why does Joe have to walk home?
f) How is Simon getting home?
g) When will the players and coach next get together?

Q53 Funny Fakes | Level 3

On the way to the gallery, a number of Van Ick's paintings were stolen and replaced with fakes. These twelve people all believe they have purchased a genuine Van Ick, but only seven of them have. Can you spot the five fakes?

Q54 Family Tree | Level 3

a) When was Frances Jenings' daughter born?
b) Who were Ann Hill Carter's parents?
c) How many men called Henry Lee are there in the tree?
d) When was Robert Edward Lee born?
e) What were the names of Charles Carter's parents?
f) When was the eldest Henry Lee born?

Q55 Spot the Differences | Level 3

How many differences can you spot between this picture and the one you studied on page 38?

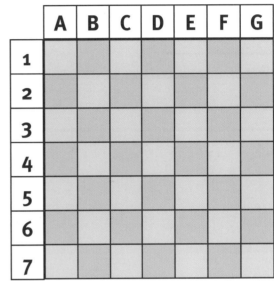

Q56 Being Earnest | Level 3

Let's see how closely you followed this outrageous plot.
a) Where does Cecily live?
b) What excuse does Jack give for going to London so frequently?
c) What relation to Algernon is Gwendolen?
d) What is the name of Gwendolen's mother?
e) Where was Jack found as a baby?
f) Why does Algernon impersonate the imaginary Ernest?
g) Why are Gwendolen and Cecily disappointed when they learn their fiancés' real names?
h) What do we ultimately learn is the relationship between Algernon and Jack?

Q57 Match the Sequence | Level 3

a) What row was the pencil in?
b) Was the mug red with a blue stripe or blue with a red stripe?
c) What column was the pipe in?
d) What was to the left of the present?
e) What item was above the purse?
f) Was the lipstick lid on or off?
g) How many dots did the ladybird have on its wings?
h) Did the present have a label on it?
i) What fruits were in the group?
j) What item was below the racket?

Q58 Battleship | Level 3

a) Is D4 a hit or a miss?
b) Can you mark the position of the Battleship on the grid below?
c) A3 is a direct hit on a Destroyer. In which square is the final part of the ship?
d) If you think can mark the exact positions of any other ships on the grid below, do it now.

	A	B	C	D	E	F	G
1							
2							
3							
4							
5							
6							
7							

Q59 Picture Strip | Level 3

Which of these sequences is the reverse of the sequence on page 39?

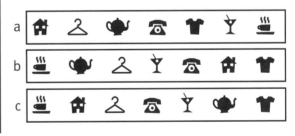

Q60 Barman! | Level 3

a) How many bottles of beer altogether?
b) How many dry white wines were ordered?
c) How should the gin and tonic be served?
d) If each drink cost $5, how much would the order come to?

54 Family Tree | Level 3

Study the family tree of the famous Civil War military leader Robert E. Lee for three minutes. Can you answer the questions on page 37 without referring back to the tree?

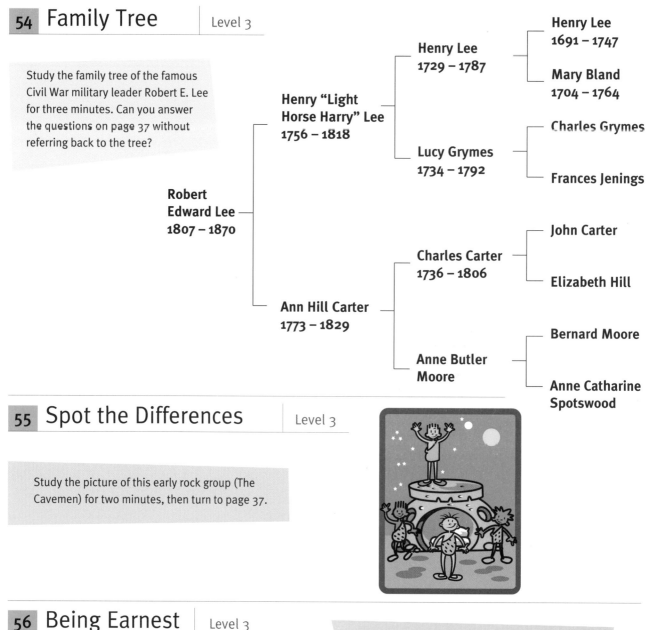

Robert Edward Lee
1807 – 1870

Henry "Light Horse Harry" Lee
1756 – 1818

Henry Lee
1729 – 1787

Henry Lee
1691 – 1747

Mary Bland
1704 – 1764

Lucy Grymes
1734 – 1792

Charles Grymes

Frances Jenings

Ann Hill Carter
1773 – 1829

Charles Carter
1736 – 1806

John Carter

Elizabeth Hill

Anne Butler Moore

Bernard Moore

Anne Catharine Spotswood

55 Spot the Differences | Level 3

Study the picture of this early rock group (The Cavemen) for two minutes, then turn to page 37.

56 Being Earnest | Level 3

Study this unlikely plot, then turn to page 37.

Jack Worthing is a fashionable young man who lives in the country with his ward Cecily Cardew. He has invented a rakish brother named Ernest, whose exploits give Jack an excuse to travel to London periodically. On these visits he spends time with his love, Gwendolen Fairfax, the cousin of his friend Algernon Moncrieff. Gwendolen, who thinks Jack's name is Ernest, returns his love and they get engaged. Her mother, Lady Bracknell, objects to their marriage, because as a baby, Jack was found in a handbag at Victoria station.

Now that he is engaged, Jack decides to dispose of his invented brother Ernest, and goes to the country to break the news of his "death" to Cecily. Meanwhile, Algernon has been impersonating Jack's imaginary brother in order to woo Cecily, who has always been in love with the idea of Ernest. The two, having now met, also get engaged. But there is some confusion on Gwendolen's visit to the country, as both girls think they are engaged to Ernest and out of jealousy become sworn enemies.

On Jack and Algernon's arrival, their true names are revealed —much to the disappointment of Cecily and Gwendolen, who had each dreamed of marrying someone called Ernest. It is also revealed that Jack is in fact Lady Bracknell's nephew, that his name before he was found was Ernest, and that Algernon is actually his brother. Both couples end up happily united.

57 Match the Sequence | Level 3

Study the pictures for about 30 seconds, then turn to page 37.

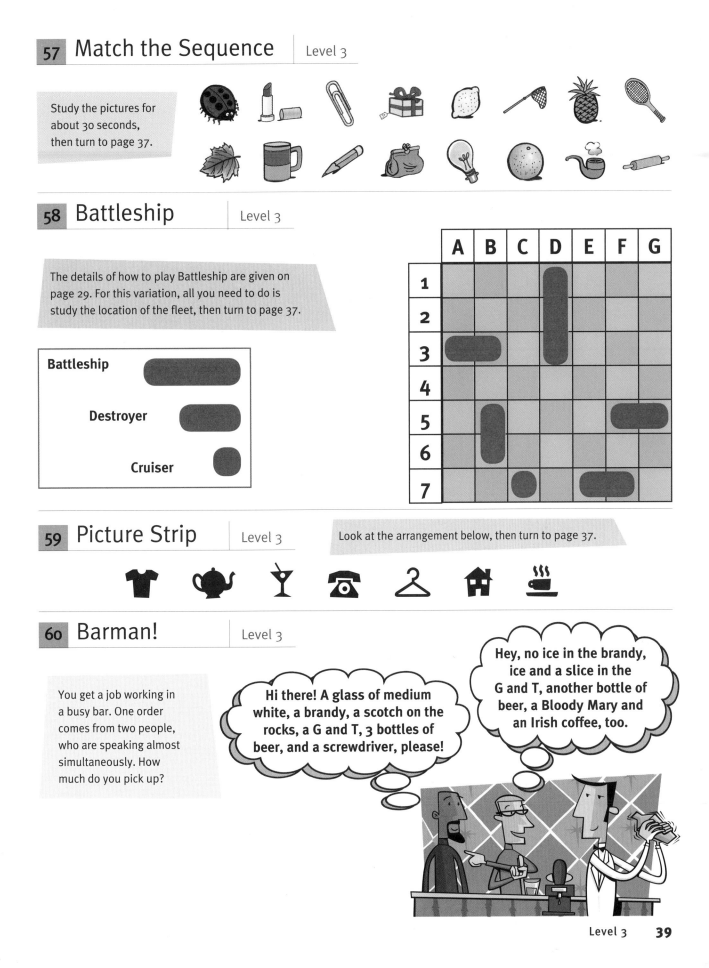

58 Battleship | Level 3

The details of how to play Battleship are given on page 29. For this variation, all you need to do is study the location of the fleet, then turn to page 37.

Battleship

Destroyer

Cruiser

	A	B	C	D	E	F	G
1							
2							
3							
4							
5							
6							
7							

59 Picture Strip | Level 3

Look at the arrangement below, then turn to page 37.

60 Barman! | Level 3

You get a job working in a busy bar. One order comes from two people, who are speaking almost simultaneously. How much do you pick up?

Hi there! A glass of medium white, a brandy, a scotch on the rocks, a G and T, 3 bottles of beer, and a screwdriver, please!

Hey, no ice in the brandy, ice and a slice in the G and T, another bottle of beer, a Bloody Mary and an Irish coffee, too.

61 Match the Sequence | Level 4

There are no striking visual differences to latch onto between these pictures, so you'll need to work hard to memorize the sequence. When you think you've got it, turn to page 42.

62 Virtual Tour | Level 4

Read this passage just once, then turn to page 42 to see how much you can remember about the property being described.

You are standing in front of a white, detached house with a green door. There are three steps leading up to a covered porch, which has two green plant pots and the figure of a gnome sitting in a rocking chair. Opening the door you are immediately in the hallway. On the wall to your left are hooks for coats and a shelf with keys, a potted plant and a notebook and pen on it. In front of you are stairs to the next floor, and the hall continues to the right of the stairs. The first door you come to in the hallway is on your right, and leads into a living room. There are a couple of sofas and an armchair clustered around a television near the window at the front of the house, and behind them a circular dining table with four chairs around it. At the far end of the room there is a door leading into a small study containing a computer and a black piano. On the back wall of this room there is a glass patio door leading outside, and a sliding door in the wall on the left leads into the cream-colored kitchen.

At the top of the stairs is the main bathroom. The smallest bedroom is directly opposite it at the front of the house; it is decorated in blue and has one small window. The guest room is next door. It contains a double bed, windows on two walls and another computer. The main bedroom is between the guest room and bathroom, and contains a bathroom with a shower, toilet and basin. The bedroom has yellow walls, white furnishings and two windows.

HINT
Try to visualize your tour around this property and to see it in as much detail as you can, without adding your own details to the information you are given. Imagining your reaction as a potential buyer to what you are seeing will improve your ability to recall it.

63 Number Crunching | Level 4

Even in these days of electronic address books, memorizing numbers of ten digits is something we do regularly. Remembering the numbers exactly as they appear here is harder. Study these four sequences carefully for three minutes, then turn to the questions on page 42.

A. 4 2 2 TWO 7 FIVE THREE 6 6 FOUR

B. SIX TWO 2 SEVEN 7 7 ONE 8 6 THREE

C. 7 NINE ONE 3 FOUR 2 8 SEVEN 6 4 6

D. FOUR 9 5 6 4 TWO FOUR 3 9 ONE

64 Before and After | Level 4

Give yourself a minute to study this picture, then turn to page 42.

HINT
You will have had some practice at these puzzles by now, and will realize that staring hard at them is not usually enough to retain the information you see. It will help if you work with the images in your mind – count objects of a certain color, compare the expressions or clothes of the two characters, imagine what you would see if the girl and boy were removed and so on.

65 Memory Maze | Level 4

You and a group of friends are on a tour of a stately home, and decide to try the maze. Take your time to study the maze and how you would negotiate it, then turn to page 42.

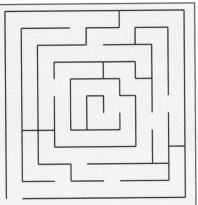

66 Whodunit? | Level 4

Read this murder mystery through twice, then turn to page 42.

"Right," said Miss Know-It-All, slowly surveying the people who had been in Haversham Hall on the night of Major Bartlett's murder. "I'm going to ask you all where you were, and what you were doing at 8:15pm last Friday, the 7th of September. Dr. Paterson, would you start, please?"

"I thought we'd been over all this," the doctor grumbled, irritably tapping an unlit cigarette against a silver case. "I was in the billiards room with George. We'd finished our game and were in the chairs by the fire drinking brandy. Isn't that right, George?"

"Absolutely," said George, whose bright yellow jacket displayed a startling lack of both taste and propriety in the circumstances. "We heard all the commotion at about 9, when Sam was found, and went to see what was going on."

"What about you, Madame Richaux?" said Miss Know-It-All. "Did you say you were still in the dining room?"

"Only until about 8 o'clock. Then I went out for a walk in the rose garden, where I bumped into Mr. Harper." She looked down at her skirt, and brushed an invisible speck from it. "We came inside again when it got too cold. I found the Major when I popped upstairs to get my diary."

"I went to find June to see if there had been any post that morning," added Clive Harper. "I was expecting a letter from my mother and it hadn't arrived."

"Did you find your wife?" asked the detective.

"No, he didn't," interrupted June. "I was upstairs having a bath after dinner, and didn't come out until I heard Madame's cries for help."

"I was in the dining room with Madame Richaux until she left," said Sylvia quickly, prompted by a questioning look from Miss Know-It-All. "Then I joined Martin and Rose in the reading room and, like the others, didn't move until Sam was found." Martin and Rose Lockgear nodded in agreement.

"Thank you," said Miss Know-It-All. "That's all I need to know… for now." She could almost hear the sighs of relief as she closed the door behind her.

Q61 Match the Sequence | Level 4

Does either of these two sequences match that on page 40?

Q62 Virtual Tour | Level 4

a) How many bedrooms does the house have?
b) Where is the smallest of them located?
c) What colors did you notice before entering the house?
d) How many potted plants did you see on your tour?
e) How many rooms do you know have two windows?
f) How many seats of various sorts are to be found in the first room you visited?
g) What color is the decor of the smallest bedroom?
h) How many ways into the study are mentioned?

Q63 Number Crunching | Level 4

a) How many of the sets end with a digit rather than a word?
b) What is the total made by adding the final numbers (word or digit) from the four sets?
c) Does four appear more times throughout the sets as a digit or word?
d) Does any number appear as a digit, but not as a word?
e) What is wrong with this version of set B:
   SIX TWO 2 7 SEVEN 7 ONE 8 6 THREE?

Q64 Before and After | Level 4

Can you spot the five differences between this picture and the version you studied on page 41?

Q65 Memory Maze | Level 4

You have found your way in and out of the maze on page 41, but have just noticed that one of your companions is missing. He calls you on his cell phone from the center. Using the instructions of left, right, and straight, can you talk him out?

Q66 Whodunit | Level 4

Miss Know-It-All considered the information she had been given. Of course, more than one of the party might have been responsible for the Major's death, but for now, her suspicions rested firmly on the one guest whose alibi could not be supported by the others.

Now see if you can answer the following questions about the passage on page 41.
a) What was the full name of the victim?
b) What is Mr. Harper's first name, and which two members of his family are also mentioned?
c) What was the profession of the man with the cigarette, and in which room did he claim to be at the time of the murder?
d) What is the surname of Rose?
e) Which two rooms were mentioned in Sylvia's alibi?
f) Why did June and Madame Richaux go upstairs on the night in question?
g) Which two guests have not been mentioned in the questions so far?
h) Who did Miss Know-It-All suspect?

67 Picture Perfect | Level 4

You have just two minutes to study these pictures before turning to page 47.

68 What's the Score? | Level 4

Look at this radio announcement for two minutes, then turn to page 47.

"Here are the results from the Spanish league. It's been a good day for the leading side, Salamanca, beating Barcelona 34 points to 20, however Valladolid lost their second position to an excellent side from Tarragona, defeated as they were 45 points to 38. Tensions ran high at the run-up to the Granada versus Malaga match and three people were arrested before it started, forcing the authorities to postpone it until Wednesday. Elsewhere, Murcia just scraped a victory at Sevilla by 2 points, and Valencia were dominant at Madrid, winning by 54 points to 19. Zaragoza continued their winning streak with a resounding defeat of Pamplona 51 to 4, and Cordoba stay at the bottom of the table despite a win of 23 points to 17 at Vitoria. Burgos and Santiago could only manage a 15-all draw while Cadiz defeated Lorca 32 to 20. You can hear all these results again at 6:30 this evening."

69 Presidential Selection | Level 4

This crossword-style diagram contains the surnames of US presidents. Study the arrangement for three minutes, then try to recreate it on page 47.

HINT

If you can remember the order of names Across and Down, then the intersecting letters will help you to reconstruct the diagram.

70 Non-word Search | Level 4

The brain is adept at finding sequences of characters in which it recognizes patterns, but finds it far harder with sequences that display no familiar logic. Study these collections of letters for two minutes, then turn to page 48.

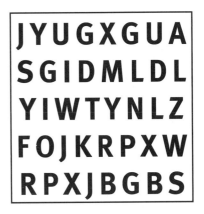

71 Domino Doubles | Level 4

Here's a tricky variation on the popular pairs puzzle. Spend up to three minutes studying this grid of dominoes, taking note of the pairs, then turn to page 48.

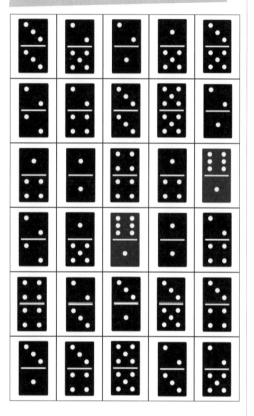

72 Present and Correct? | Level 4

Read this passage twice, then turn to page 48 to see how Bob does with his shopping.

"Christmas this year is going to be easy," said Bob. "I've asked everyone what they want and I'm sure I can get everything I need in one trip. My father wants a dozen Maxfli A3 golf balls and my mother wants a warm, brushed cotton nightie, size 14, preferably blue. There's Frommer's guide to New Zealand for Uncle Jim's trip next year and a Parker Sonnet ballpen for Barbara. Grandpa wants his usual bottle of Jim Beam, and my grandma says she doesn't really want anything at all, but if I insist on getting her something, she'd like a set of those nice Crabtree & Evelyn Tea Rose Glycerine soaps.

My big sister wants an Anne Tyler novel—I can't remember the name, but it's the most recent one, and her husband wants a set of stainless steel barbecue tools. Their two girls want something pink for their bedroom. My little sister wants a Nike hooded top, medium in dark obsidian (whatever color that may be) and her husband just needs the DVD of *Goldeneye* to complete his Bond films collection. My wife's brother John wants Lance Armstrong's autobiography, It's Not About the Bike. His daughter wants to be surprised (there's always one), his son wants a Wilson Supreme basketball and his wife Hannah has asked for dangly silver earrings.

Then there's my wife's parents. Her father's a bit of a wine buff, and wants a bottle of Buckeye Vineyard Cabernet Sauvignon 1996, and her mother would like a 3.4 fl. oz. bottle of Estée Lauder Pleasures Eau de Parfum Spray. Her sister wants two weeks in the sun, away from the kids, but will settle for Lancôme's Aroma Fit Vitamin-enriched Massage Oil. Her husband, gadget man, is getting an almost-indestructible LED flashlight and their three children, Ben, Greg and Lottie, want The Twist and Slam Hulk Action Figure, Tomb Raider: The Angel of Darkness and anything Barbie, respectively.

Finally there's my wife's present, not that she deserves one, having left me with all the shopping! Hers is the Krups Novo 3000 Espresso/Cappuccino Maker I'm going to have to work overtime to pay for."

73 Negative Memory | Level 4

You've already had some practice at this type of challenge, so let's increase the time pressure. Study these images for a minute only, then turn to page 48.

74 Burger Bar

It's your first day as a trainee at MegaBurgers, and the computerized ordering system has gone down. Your colleagues are even more flustered than you. Glance at the last four orders you've taken, then see if you can answer their questions on page 48.

Order 1
10:24
1 MegaBurger meal with MegaLemon
1 MegaBurger meal with MegaCola
6 Turkey Niblits with BBQ sauce
1 TurkeyBurger no tomato
1 standard Fries
1 Coffee

Order 2
10:25
1 Double MegaBurger with fries
1 MegaBurger with cheese
2 Onion rings
2 MegaFries
1 Dipping Donut with strawberry sauce

Order 3
10:27
1 CheeryMeal with ChickStrips and MegaOrange
1 CheeryMeal with FishSticks and MegaCola
9 Turkey Niblits with Salsa sauce
1 MegaBurger with cheese, no onion
2 MegaColas

Order 4
10:27
1 MegaBurger no pickle
1 MegaBurger meal with MegaCola
1 CheeryMeal with Turkey Niblits and MegaLemon
1 standard Fries
1 Dipping Donut with chocolate sauce

75 Family Tree

Take your time to study this diagram of the Kennedy family tree, then turn to page 49.

John Fitzgerald Kennedy 1917 – 1963

Joseph Patrick Kennedy 1888 – 1969

Patrick Joseph Kennedy 1858 – 1929

Patrick Kennedy 1823 – 1858

Bridget Murphy 1821 – 1888

Mary Augusta Hickey 1857 – 1923

James Hickey 1837 – 1900

Margaret M. "Martha" Field 1836 – 1911

Rose Elizabeth Fitzgerald 1890 – 1995

John Francis Fitzgerald 1863 – 1950

Thomas Fitzgerald 1835 – 1885

Rosanna "Rosey" Cox 1835 – 1879

Mary Josephine Hannon 1865 – 1964

Michael Hannon 1832 – 1900

Mary Ann Fitzgerald 1835 – 1904

76 Take Your Cue Level 4

Study the picture carefully, then turn to page 49.

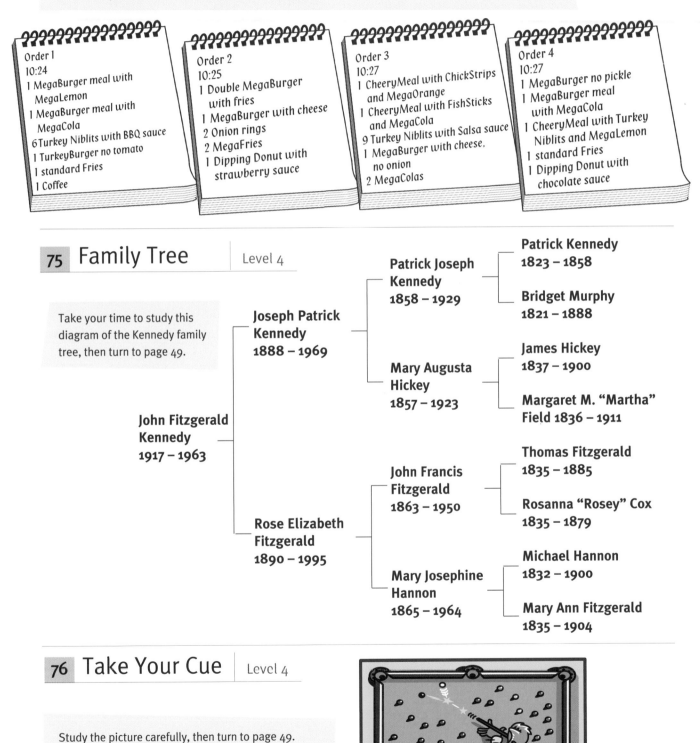

Level 4 **45**

77 Dinner Party | Level 4

Here's the seating plan at Bruce and Diane's dinner party, to which five other couples have been invited: Jane and Richard, Larry and Sharon, Adam and Sarah, Sandra and Dean, and Paul and Jennifer. As you can see, the hosts have made sure that no partners sit next to each other. Study the diagram for two minutes, then turn to page 49.

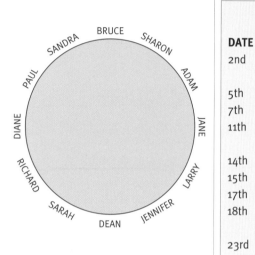

78 What's On | Level 4

In an attempt to impress your prospective employers in the Conference and Banqueting section of the Welcome Hotel, you have taken a quick look at their timetable of functions for March. Study it for two minutes and then answer the questions on page 49.

Welcome Hotel, England

DATE	GROUP NAME AND FUNCTION	CONTACT	NO. EXPECTED
2nd	Robinson's Plastics – AGM	Peter Smith	15
	Mrs. Alison Parker – Birthday	Mr. Douglas Parker	50
5th	The Roman Society – Seminar	Ronald Syme	22
7th	Black/Jones – Wedding Reception	Anna Jones	150
11th	Albany Bird Watchers – Seminar	Chester Peterson	30
	Tom Belton – Birthday	Chris Campbell	10
14th	Simon-Peters – Wedding Reception	Mrs. Julia Anderson	220
15th	CTC Electronics – Conference	Roger Hargraves	55
17th	Eye See Opticians – Conference	Sarah Hutchinson	20
18th	Animated Graphics – Seminar	Bill Apple	40
	Riverside Chess Club – Meeting	Charles Franks	14
23rd	Pinkerton Publishing – AGM	Michael Pinkerton	10
27th	Origami Association – Annual Party	Bob Lee	35

79 Bedroom Booby Trap | Level 4

Following instructions and their accompanying diagrams is an activity that divides people into two camps. There are those who read every word, then wonder why nothing tallies with what they see, and those who read nothing, work out their own instructions, and end up with a leftover piece. The former approach, however painful for you, is recommended for this timed challenge.

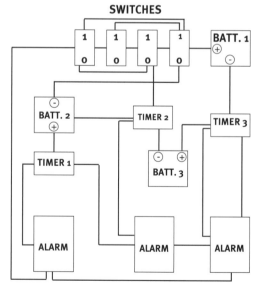

Anne Ode and her sister Kath have a keen sense of rivalry, and an irresistible urge to raid each other's wardrobes. Anne has set up an elaborate electronic alarm system in her bedroom, which is primed to go off three minutes after the door is opened, but Kath has managed to sneak a look at the instructions for disabling it. Study the diagram and instructions for no longer than three minutes, then turn to page 49.

Instructions for disabling an alarm with three timers and switches

The steps must be taken in the following order:

1. Turn off switch connected to timer 2.
2. Cut wire between battery 2 and switch.
3. Cut wire between battery 1 and timer 3.
4. Cut wire between timer 2 and alarms.
5. Disconnect wire running from anode (positive electrode) of battery 3 to timer 3.
6. Cut wire between switches and alarm attached to timer 1.

80 Card Sharp | Level 4

Memorizing the order in which the cards of a pack are turned over is a favorite party-piece of memory experts, who can commit an entire pack to memory in less than a minute. You're not expected to match that here. Instead, take as much time as you like to work through this sequence, but don't look back—once you've looked at each card, move on. When you've gone through the sequence, turn to page 49.

10♦ 6♦ 9⑨ A♣ 6③ A⑨ 5♣ 5♦ 8♣ 6⑨ J♣ 10③ 2♦ K♣ 8♦ 10⑨ 8⑨ A③ 3♣ Q♣ J③ 4③ 7♣

8③ 7③ K♦ 5⑨ J♦ 2⑨ 3⑨ 4♣ Q♦ 6♣ 7⑨ 9♦ Q⑨ 4♦ 5③ 2♣ K⑨ 9③ 3♦ 4⑨ 3③ 9♣ A♦ K③

Q67 Picture Perfect | Level 4

How well do you remember the pictures from page 43?
a) In which row is the guitar?
b) Which is higher—the hat or the hut?
c) Which object is two below the glasses?
d) Is the iron to the left or the right of the handcuffs?
e) Are any of the pictures of living things?
f) If the ice cream and jug swapped places, which would be closer to the guitar?
g) What color forms the top-right triangle of the kite?
h) What is the design on the jug?

Q68 What's the Score? | Level 4

How accurately can you remember the radio report from page 43?
a) Which teams are top and bottom of the table?
b) Who suffered the heaviest defeat of the day?
c) Which team played Santiago?
d) How many points did Barcelona manage?
e) Who won by only 2 points?
f) How many points did Vitoria get, and did they win or lose?
g) Which team lost by 7 points?
h) At what time will the scores be repeated?

Q69 Presidential Selection | Level 4

See how quickly you can recreate the diagram from page 43 in this blank grid.

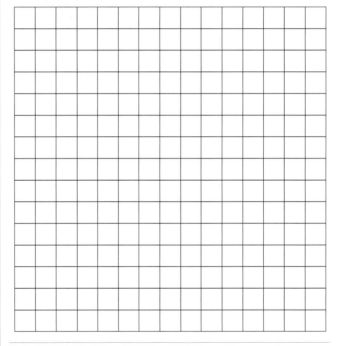

Q70 Non-word Search | Level 4

How quickly can you find the five sets of characters from page 43 in this grid? The sets appear in straight lines in the grid, reading horizontally, vertically or diagonally, either backward or forward.

W	E	H	W	E	M	Z	M	W	K	A	L
X	Z	L	N	Y	T	W	I	Y	X	M	D
P	V	F	D	B	F	O	J	N	N	G	L
Y	X	O	C	L	W	C	S	H	L	B	O
U	P	J	V	S	U	B	X	N	Z	C	I
G	E	K	A	U	G	X	G	U	Y	J	H
O	N	R	H	B	A	I	C	B	D	R	K
V	Q	P	J	K	M	Q	D	C	Y	Q	E
F	L	X	D	I	G	J	G	M	T	Z	B
U	P	W	F	O	P	E	R	J	L	F	K
R	Q	S	G	X	G	U	S	A	B	D	Z
R	V	Q	T	N	Y	E	N	M	I	A	L

Q71 Domino Doubles | Level 4

Can you remember where all the partners of these dominoes are?

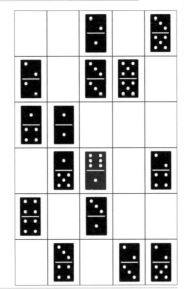

Q72 Present and Correct? | Level 4

Catch up with Bob, after the shopping trip he planned on page 44...

"Well that's that done," said Bob. "Let's just check what I've got. There's the Lance Armstrong autobiography for John, the latest Annie Proulx for my big sister and Fodor's guide to New Zealand for Uncle Jim. I've got my mother's size 14 blue nightie, and a medium-sized Nike top in that ridiculous color for my little sister. Her husband's got the DVD of *Goldfinger*, and *Tomb Raider: The Angel of Darkness* for Greg was in the same shop.

I very nearly forgot Greg's father's stainless steel barbecue tools, but spotted them while I was looking for the Krups Novo 3000 Espresso/Cappuccino Maker. My big sister's daughters get a pink umbrella and coat set each, there's the Hulk Action Figure for Ben, and Lottie should be happy with her Barbie duvet cover. John's daughter is getting a watercolors set, and I got her basketball-mad brother's Wilson Supreme at the same time as the Maxfli M3 Tour golf balls for Dad. The Buckeye Vineyard Cabernet Sauvignon for my father-in-law proved a bit trickier than Grandpa's Jack Daniel's, but I eventually found both.

The Aroma Fit Massage Oil for my wife's sister and Estée Lauder Beyond Paradise Eau de Parfum Spray for my mother-in-law were so expensive that the assistant took pity, and gave me money off Grandma's Crabtree & Evelyn Rosewater Glycerine soaps. I couldn't get the LED flashlight for my sister's husband, but still have time to order it on the the Internet. And finally, the Parker Sonnet pen for Aunt Barbara. I had no idea it was going to be that pricey—I must remember not to ask what she wants next year, especially if I get socks again in return. That just leaves my wife to wrap this lot up."
Despite being rather pleased with himself, a number of Bob's relatives are going to be disappointed. See how many of his shopping mistakes you can spot.

Q73 Negative Memory | Level 4

Which objects from the picture on page 44 are missing here, and what items have replaced them?

Q74 Burger Bar | Level 4

You've shouted the orders from page 45 to your colleagues once, but now come the inevitable questions...
a) Is the Order 4 Megaburger meal with MegaCola or MegaLemon?
b) Which came in first, the MegaBurger with cheese or the MegaBurger with cheese and no onion?
c) Was the 9 Turkey Niblits with the Barbie or Salsa sauce?
d) What time was the coffee ordered?
e) What drink was ordered with the Turkey Niblits CheeryMeal?
f) Did anyone order a MegaBurger with cheese, but no pickle?

Q75 Family Tree | Level 4

See how many of these questions you can answer, based on your studies of the family tree on page 45.
a) What was the affectionate name for Thomas Fitzgerald's wife?
b) What were the names of Rose Elizabeth Fitzgerald's parents?
c) What were Michael Hannon's dates?
d) What was the name of Margaret M. Field's daughter?
e) Who was born in the same year that Bridget Murphy died?
f) Which of John Fitzgerald Kennedy's grandparents lived the longest?
g) When was John Francis Fitzgerald's father born?
h) Which two of John Fitzgerald Kennedy's great-grandparents died in the same year?

Q76 Take Your Cue | Level 4

Which of these four pictures exactly matches the version you saw on page 46?

Q77 Dinner Party | Level 4

After the first course of the dinner described on page 46, the hosts felt that conversation was dwindling, so they got the guests to move around, some clockwise, some counterclockwise. Using the following information, can you place the guests in their new seats?

No one stayed in the same seat and, again, no partners ended up sitting next to each other. Bruce and Adam moved clockwise eight places. Richard moved around six places. Jane, Sharon, Larry and Sarah moved around four places. Diane, Dean and Sandra moved around two places. Which female guest, who was quite happy with the first arrangement, made sure that she ended up with the same neighbors as before?

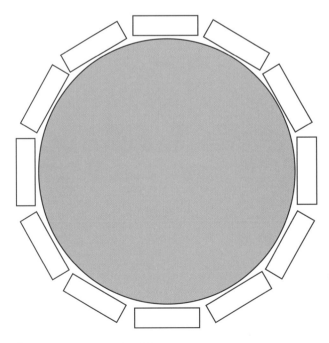

Q78 What's On | Level 4

Having taken a look at the timetable on page 49, how many of these answers could you impress your selection panel with?
a) What is the surname of the man Anna Jones is marrying on the 7th?
b) Which of the AGMs is likely to be better attended?
c) For which function is Sarah Hutchinson the contact?
d) Whose birthday is the smallest affair?
e) What is being held on the 15th?
f) How many seminars are lined up?

Q79 Bedroom Booby Trap | Level 4

You have three minutes to disable the alarm by putting these steps in the correct order.

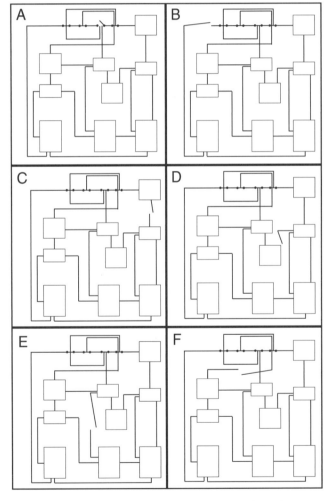

Q80 Card Sharp | Level 4

The sequence you studied on page 47 was five cards short of a full deck. What were the missing cards?

Improve Your Word Power

What's In a word? It seems that we humans have always been keen to find out, because word puzzles have been popular for thousands of years, as the historic word square below goes to prove. Perhaps the most famous type of word puzzle, the crossword, is loved by so many people that the majority of daily newspapers now feature a puzzle of this type. In fact, it's not unheard of for readers to base their choice of newspaper on the crossword alone!

WORD PUZZLE HISTORY

The first crossword-type puzzles were created in England in the 19th century, and are believed to have evolved from the first Word Square (pictured at right), which was discovered in Pompeii. As you can see, the Word Square reads exactly the same across and down.

CREATE YOUR OWN

In the grid underneath this square, we'd like you to create your own 4x4 Word Square by answering the clues we've given you (which are in no particular order), then fitting those four-letter answers into the grid, so that they read the same across and down.

THE VERY FIRST WORD SQUARE

R	O	T	A	S
O	P	E	R	A
T	E	N	E	T
A	R	E	P	O
S	A	T	O	R

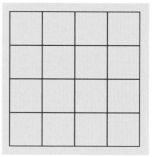

Connection or common interest
Woodwind instrument
Midday
Depression in a surface

Word Squares of many shapes and sizes can be found these days, but so far nobody—not even a computer—has managed to create a ten-letter word square. Now there's a challenge!

WHY WORDSEARCHES?

To some people, the wordsearch may seem a strange puzzle to include here. The object of this puzzle is very simple: you must seek out particular words within a random jumble of letters—and the words might be reading in any direction. This may not seem much of a challenge in comparison to some of the other puzzles in this section. But solve a few wordsearches and you'll soon notice how much quicker you become at spotting the relevant words. Your brain is learning to focus quickly on what is relevant, filtering the important information from the background noise. This is a vital skill, and one which is likely to prove useful in solving many of the other word puzzles in this book.

CRYPTIC CHALLENGE

In the final two levels of this section, you'll be faced with a version of the crossword that many of us find the most challenging, but which can also be the most rewarding: the cryptic. If you're unfamiliar with this puzzle, you'll find that it forces you to think in a totally new way, but your brain will soon get the hang of it. Here are a few tips to help you out:

ANAGRAMS: Many clues contain an anagram of the actual answer somewhere in their wording. For example: **Dutiful person in taverns, drunk (7)** (SERVANT). The words taverns is actually an anagram of the answer SERVANT. Dutiful person defines that answer. In all cryptic clues, look out for words which suggest that there is an anagram that must be rearranged. In this example, that word is drunk. Other words implying an anagram may include badly, unfortunately, strangely, wrongly, and so on.

PARTS OF WORDS: The answers to many cryptic clues are made up of smaller words which are all put together to give you the final answer. For example: **US city in vogue in the past (7)** (CHICAGO). The words in vogue give you the word CHIC and in the past gives you AGO. Put those words together and you have CHICAGO, that is obviously the answer to the first two words of the clue, US city.

DOUBLE MEANINGS: Sometimes a cryptic clue leads to a word that has two different meanings, and the clue gives a definition for both, eg: **Refuse to come down (6)** (DECLINE). The answer DECLINE can mean both Refuse and come down.

To start you off, here's a cryptic definition for you to work out. The solution is at the bottom of this page, but think hard about it before you take a look.

Where hands move constantly? (5,3,5)

CRACK THE CODE

Another fiendish type of puzzle you'll find in this section is the Codeword, in which we've replaced every letter of the alphabet with a number between 1 and 26. Your job is to complete it like a normal crossword by replacing each number with its correct letter. There are no other clues! This may sound tricky, but you'll be able to work out many words through a logical process of looking at where other numbers appear in the grid, and how often they are used. Bear in mind that vowels are likely to appear most often. Apart from that small clue, we'll leave the deciphering up to you!

WORDS OF WISDOM

Not all of the puzzles in this section involve grids; there are also a number of anagram puzzles, quizzes and riddles. You will face different challenges as you make your way through this section of the book with one thing in common—they're guaranteed to test your word power to the limit. Make a start by unraveling each word of this sentence to discover a relevant quotation from educator John Dewey.

HTOHUGT SI SPOBIMELIS

UTWTIHO SDWRO.

CRYPTIC CLUE SOLUTION: Round the clock.

Improve Your Word Power | Level 1

Welcome to Level 1. You should find these puzzles pretty easygoing, so get a pencil and dig in.

Puzzles 1–20

1 Anagram Initials | Level 1

When you've solved the six anagrams, the initial letters in the shaded column will spell out an animal.

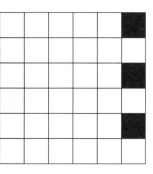

CHABE

RHACRE

ODPOR

EVIREG

NOBYE

SUCRIT

2 Quick Cross | Level 1

See how quickly you can complete this simple crossword.

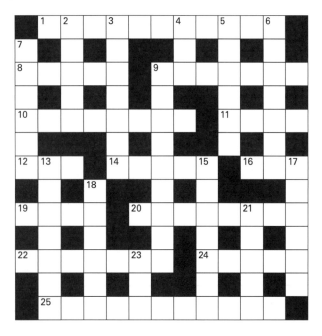

ACROSS

1. Emergency engine's shelter (4, 7)
8. Dim (5)
9. Pours off (wine) (7)
10. Puts on hold (8)
11. Artistically engrave (4)
12. Remiss (3)
14. Do really well (5)
16. Cleopatra's fateful serpent (3)
19. Highly excited (4)
20. Direction indicator (8)
22. 1988 Dustin Hoffman film (4,3)
24. Public (5)
25. Spouse's female relative (6-2-3)

DOWN

2. Small dots of land (5)
3. Drastic (7)
4. Traditional pub drink (3)
5. Effigies (6)
6. Discerns (7)
7. Seafood item (6)
9. Logical conclusion (9)
13. Large hounds (7)
15. US president 1861–65 (7)
17. Root vegetable (6)
18. Representatives (6)
21. Musical play (5)
23. Consumed (3)

3 Odd One Out

Level 1

In each case, which is the odd word out, and why?

1. **CRIMSON, TURQUOISE, VERMILION, CERISE**
2. **UPPER, SOLE, STEP, WELT**
3. **CLARINET, TUBA, FLUTE, OBOE**
4. **SUN, STAR, CLOCK, WHEEL**
5. **PINE, ASH, AZALEA, BEECH**
6. **TOMATO, LEMON, POTATO, ORANGE**

4 Arroword

Level 1

These are probably the most popular word puzzles in the world. They are essentially crosswords with clues embedded in the grid. Simply follow the arrows and write in your answers.

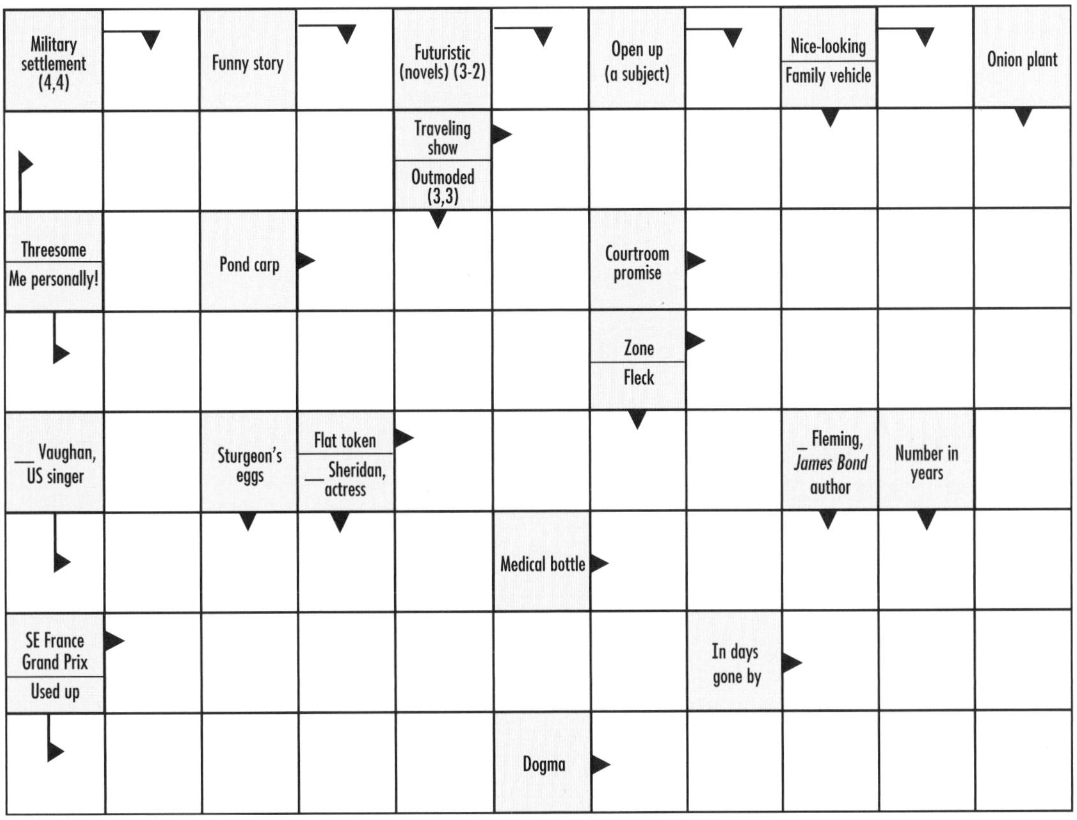

Military settlement (4,4)
Funny story
Futuristic (novels) (3-2)
Open up (a subject)
Nice-looking
Family vehicle
Onion plant
Traveling show
Outmoded (3,3)
Threesome
Me personally!
Pond carp
Courtroom promise
Zone
Fleck
__ Vaughan, US singer
Sturgeon's eggs
Flat token
__ Sheridan, actress
__ Fleming, James Bond author
Number in years
Medical bottle
SE France Grand Prix
Used up
In days gone by
Dogma

Answers on page 224

A straightforward crossword—give yourself
a time limit of 20 minutes to solve it.

ACROSS

3. Attain (7)
7. Slowly build up (5)
8. High tennis shot (3)
10. Chimer (4)
11. Passes on knowledge to (8)
13. Painful experience (6)
14. Dried, sweet grape (6)
16. Muddy pool (6)
18. Pungent condiment (6)
22. Obviously! (2, 6)
24. Region (4)
26. Golf-ball's position (3)
27. Lariat (5)
28. Speaker's platform (7)

DOWN

1. Gigantic tropical grass (6)
2. Went by ship (6)
3. Donkey (3)
4. Cowlings (5)
5. ___ Clapton, musician (4)
6. Exalts (6)
9. Sink (5)
12. ___ Newman, actor (4)
15. Winning serves (4)
16. Search for prey (5)
17. Ship unloader (6)
19. Most innocent (6)
20. Excuse (6)
21. ___ Hammerstein II, US songwriter (5)
23. Giant tea-brewing vessels (4)
25. Deciduous tree (3)

6 Match the Meaning | Level 1

In each case, which of the four
words is the synonym?

A SYNONYM is a word that means
exactly the same thing as another
word in the same language.

1. MACABRE — A. Sordid B. Cruel C. Unbalanced D. Ghoulish

2. DESPOT — A. Crook B. Maniac C. Tyrant D. Governor

3. WAIVE — A. Relinquish B. Delete C. Overcome D. Expose

4. INSIGNIA — A. Pride B. Regalia C. Stain D. Signature

5. INSIDIOUS — A. Unlikely B. Dangerous C. Uncomfortable D. Deceptive

6. DECRY — A. Comfort B. Embarrass C. Criticize D. Praise

Can you find all the names of the books in the grid to the right? They may be reading diagonally, horizontally or vertically.

```
S U C I T I V E L E N E
M R U T J O M H U U T H
L A G A H A O V E R B Z
A G D C T Z U D O B O R
S E U T S E M A J P E O
P N H S N J J R R H N A
J E K U L E O O T Z J N
W S T H G M V S B O E A
O I R E A E E H D U H
E S E R R N S N T U A E
H L K B E X O D U S A Z
T V S E G D U J R O E R
U E G D U J I S S I K B
N O I T A L E V E R U A
```

ACTS
ESTHER
EXODUS
EZRA
GENESIS
JAMES
JOB
JOHN
JONAH
JOSHUA

JUDGES
LEVITICUS
LUKE
MARK
MATTHEW
PETER
PROVERBS
PSALMS
REVELATION
RUTH

HINT
If there are uncommon letters in a word, look for those letters in the grid to locate the word.

The countries at left have each had their vowels removed. Can you name them all?

1. FRNC
2. CND
3. JPN
4. THP
5. LBN
6. CRT
7. TLY
8. STRLA
9. JMC
10. CLND

(handwritten notes)
vowel they must up

1. France
2. Canada
3. Japan
4.
5.
6.
7. Italy
8. Astrlua
9. Jamaca

This long, thin crossword may require some long, hard thought! How quickly can you complete the grid?

ACROSS
1. Genuine (7)
7. Brick-carrying trough (3)
9. Crease-resistant polyester fabric used in UK (9)
10. Ponder, consider (4)
13. Ill-mannered person (4)
14. Fluorescent-light gas (4)
15. Ready to pick (4)
17. Hairless (4)
18. Corrosive liquid (4)
19. Tree affected by 'Dutch' disease (3)
20. Uses needle and thread (4)
22. Small and cramped (4)
23. Module (4)
24. Burning fever (4)
26. Deities (4)
27. Extremities (4)
30. Silent (9)
32. Break in continuity (3)
33. Satiated (7)

DOWN
2. Frozen water spike (6)
3. Headland (4)
4. Oratory (8)
5. Vast age (3)
6. Dirty froth or foam (4)
8. Ordered (7)
11. Not consumed (7)
12. Making the most noise (7)
15. Run riot (7)
16. Preserved in vinegar (7)
20. Heaving tumultuously (7)
21. Passage from the back of the nose to the lungs (8)
25. Disquiet (6)
28. Waist scarf (4)
29. Relate (4)
31. Rowing blade (3)

---

1. HAPPINESS
A. Silence
B. Annoyance
C. Misery
D. Secrecy

2. CAUTIOUS
A. Foolhardy
B. Raucous
C. Comprehensive
D. Overwhelming

3. ESSENTIAL
A. Convenient
B. Disallowed
C. Ascetic
D. Superfluous

4. ACTIVITY
A. Inertia
B. Liveliness
C. Slumber
D. Laziness

5. POWER
A. Strength
B. Slowness
C. Stupidity
D. Impotence

6. ELEGANCE
A. Ugliness
B. Clumsiness
C. Sadness
D. Frailty

10 Total Opposites | Level 1

In each case, which of the four words is the antonym?

AN ANTONYM is a word opposite in meaning to another.

Something Fishy | Level 1

Fancy a bite? Then try catching all of the fish floating in this grid.

BASS
CARP
CRAB
CRAYFISH
ELVER
FLOUNDER
HADDOCK
HAKE
HALIBUT
HERRING
LOBSTER
MINNOW
PILCHARD

PIRANHA
PRAWN
SALMON
SARDINE
SCAMPI
SHRIMP
SKATE
SQUID
TROUT
TURBOT
WHITLING
WRASSE

```
W  R  A  S  S  E  N  M  A
S  I  R  E  I  E  P  R  H
Q  L  V  E  R  I  T  D  C
U  F  Y  A  R  E  V  L  E
I  P  M  A  C  S  N  I  P
D  N  N  P  R  W  D  P  I
I  H  M  B  A  S  S  M  L
A  A  A  R  Y  A  E  I  C
L  I  P  R  F  N  K  R  H
T  T  U  B  I  L  A  H  A
I  U  R  D  S  B  K  S  R
R  E  R  P  H  S  T  V  D
R  A  R  B  W  U  T  L  F
S  A  L  M  O  N  E  E  Y
C  L  K  R  N  T  P  R  A
N  E  T  E  N  V  I  E  R
L  M  L  T  I  C  L  W  C
H  A  A  S  M  A  H  S  L
E  M  L  B  K  I  H  T  R
R  P  M  O  T  A  R  E  S
R  A  O  L  D  I  T  R  S
I  H  I  D  H  A  K  E  A
N  N  O  I  C  R  A  D  E
G  C  O  I  B  U  B  N  H
K  B  B  H  I  T  L  U  E
S  I  N  K  E  Q  M  O  T
I  N  L  O  U  N  D  L  A
I  N  O  V  E  R  E  F  E
```

12 Bright Ideas | Level 1

When you've solved the five anagrams, the initial letters in the shaded column will spell out a shade of purple.

MICSTY
LOWLA
TIPFUL
NOVEM
THERAY

13 Starter Blocks Level 1

In each case, which three-letter prefix will make three longer words?

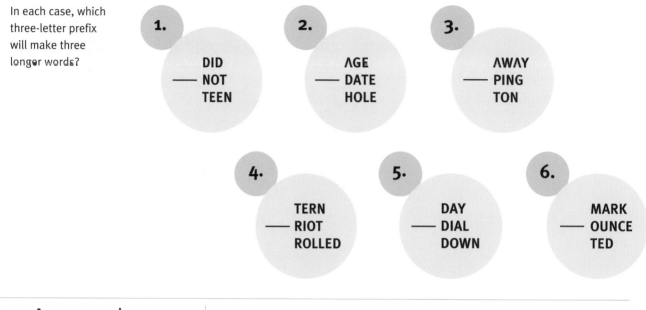

1.
— DID
— NOT
— TEEN

2.
— AGE
— DATE
— HOLE

3.
— AWAY
— PING
— TON

4.
— TERN
— RIOT
— ROLLED

5.
— DAY
— DIAL
— DOWN

6.
— MARK
— OUNCE
— TED

14 Arroword Level 1

Let the arrows direct your answers and this one should be a cinch!

Look after yourself (4,4) ▼		Stout cord ▼		Discussion group ▼		Russian wolfhound ▼		Light-haired ▼ Regret		Device on a door
⚑				Outer garment ▶ Tough paint				▼		▼
Stuffed tortilla Blissfully calm		Female swan ▶		▼		Destroy ▶				
⚑						Nil ▶ Awry				
Courtesy title		Morning dampness	Too ▶ Top card		▼			Peculiar	Take to court for money	
⚑		▼	▼		Small shop ▶			▼	▼	
Flow back Gemstone ▶							Expected ▶		
⚑				Fisherman's boot ▶					

THEWIN
CATMIP
BURMEL
CHANUL
DORICH
YETWAR

When you've solved the six anagrams, the initial letters in the shaded column will spell out a species of tree.

16 Word Ladders | Level 1

Fill in each step of each ladder with a word, changing one letter at a time as you climb down, so that you end up with the word at the bottom.

A.

BOOK
___
___
___
READ

B.

GIVE
___
___
___
TAKE

C.

NAIL
___
___
___
FILE

D.

CALM
___
___
___
RAGE

DID YOU KNOW?

Charles Dodgson, better known as Lewis Carroll, the author of *Alice In Wonderland*, is credited as the inventor of this puzzle.

17 The Missing Word | Level 1

In each case, which four-letter word can complete all the other words?

1. PLA____   DIS____ING   ____IGAN   ____AMOM

2. A____   DF____RY   EN____N   S____R

3. PL____NG   ____QUE   ____BODY   FR____C

4. MU____D   ____DOM   UP____T   JUMP____T

5. AB____EE   CON____   DI____ANGLE   ES____IAL

6. OR____   I____IZE   MIS____   ____ERSHIP

18 Pyramid | Level 1

Write the answers to the clues in the pyramid. Each answer contains the letters of the previous answer, plus one extra.

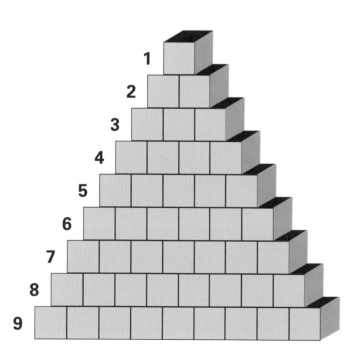

1. Indefinite article
2. Publicity film
3. Boy
4. Core of a pencil
5. Handed out cards
6. Unimportant fact
7. Regional way of speaking
8. Fragile
9. Explain

RUNDIG
MARUTEA
ARCIND
BLUEROT
SLOMBY

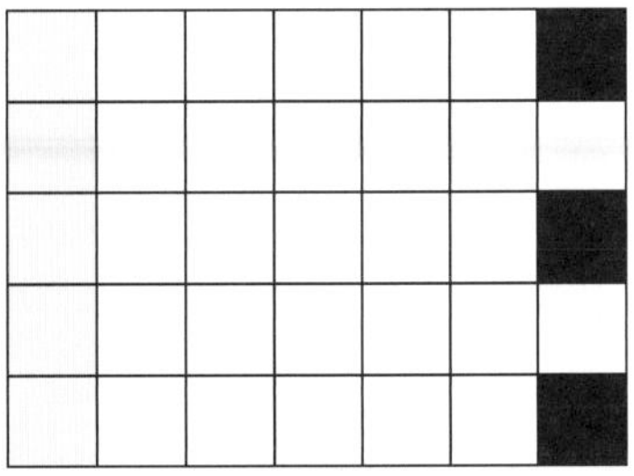

When you've solved the five anagrams, the initial letters in the shaded column will spell out an indoor game.

20 Straight Forward | Level 1

Another slender crossword to keep your brain working.

ACROSS
1. Musical percussion instrument (4)
4. Not gray (4)
7. Appellations (5)
8. Misplaced (4)
9. Regretted (4)
10. Complete, absolute (5)
12. Alpine flower, subject of a well-known song (9)
15. Piece of metal money (4)
17. Fever (4)
18. Unwell (3)
19. Cain's brother, in the Bible (4)
21. Optical glass (4)
24. Distinguished politicians (9)
28. Hanging part of the palate (5)
31. Scottish hill-slope (4)
32. Burden, responsibility (4)
33. Brownish-gray color (5)
34. Type of ice-skating jump (4)
35. Greek god of love (4)

DOWN
1. Erase (6)
2. Not certain (6)
3. Not glossy (4)
4. In this place (4)
5. Taking power by force (8)
6. Extinct bird of Mauritius (4)
11. Urban community (4)
13. Team of two (3)
14. Broods (5)
15. Cowboy's leather leggings (5)
16. Zero score (3)
17. The lot (3)
20. Move people from a place of danger (8)
22. Originally called (3)
23. Restaurant's bill of fare (4)
25. Less generous (6)
26. Sounds (6)
27. Former Swedish supergroup who sang "Waterloo" (4)
29. Calf meat (4)
30. Run with a long, bounding stride (4)

Improve Your Word Power | Level 2

Now you've reached level 2, where you'll have to work a bit harder, so get those brain cells in gear.

Puzzles 21–40

21 Who Said What? Level 2

Write the answers to the clues in the rows of the top grid, and the name of a famous person will appear in the shaded column of squares. Now transfer the cross-referenced letters from this grid to the lower grid to reveal something this person said.

1. Bee boxes • Woodwind instrument
2. Mixture
3. Heaps? • Common sense
4. Back scrubber • Novel
5. Refrain from • Metal container
6. Unzipped fruit? • Concealed
7. Result, outcome • Dress stitching
8. Correct • Shortly
9. Container
10. ___ truly, letter ending • Chair

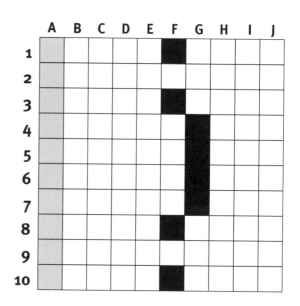

	A	B	C	D	E	F	G	H	I	J
1						■				
2										
3						■				
4							■			
5							■			
6							■			
7										
8						■				
9										
10						■				

8B	7F	'	5B	■	4D	8H	2E	■	7A	1C	4I	8A	10A		2I	6B	7J	9D	3A	2H	1F	10G
7C	4E	5C	9J	4A	7I	2B	8G		5F	8I	2G	9G	3G		4B	7B		5H	1G	9I	3H	9A
10J	7H	3C	2F		6E	3B	4J		6H	5I	3E		10I		9H	5D	2A	6C	9C	1D		
1H	5A	7E	6F	3I	2C	7D		9F	8D	6I	10E		3D	4C	1I	9A						
2J	10B	8J	1B	8C	4F	8E		1A	6D	3J		6A	9B	1J	5J		2D	9E	5E	4H	10H	6J

22 American Anagrams Level 2

1. IAN MOSTEN
2. ANDY MARL
3. KEN ARBAS
4. LENNY SPAVIAN
5. TOM VERN
6. DAN AVE
7. STAN HOWING

Each of these men's names is an anagram of the state in which they live. Can you locate them all?

23 Codeword · Level 2

In this crossword, there are no clues, but each number represents a letter, and we've given you three letters to start you off.

HINT
First, fill in every instance of the three given letters in the grid, then try to complete the rest of the puzzle, filling in the reference grid as you work out which letter each number represents.

Alphabet reference (cross off as solved): A B C D E F G H I J K L M — N O P Q R̶ S T̶ U V W X Y Z (given: A, R, T)

Grid (█ = shaded/blocked cell):

26	13	16	15	20	16	5	20	14	█	8	14	5	3	26
5	█	26	█	15	█	17	█	3	█	13	█	8	█	3
4	24	2	26	16	█	2	11	20	13	26	8	1	3	25
14	█	25	█	3	█	17	█	█	█	26(R)	█	█	█	13
13	23	25	2	8	13	█	25	5	26	5(A)	4	4	3	20
26	█	13	█	14	█	19	█	19	█	14(T)	█	9	█	13
█	11	26	22	█	19	15	19	6	9	13	█	22	13	8
19	█	█	█	█	16	█	9	█	█	█	█	█	█	8
13	11	13	█	9	2	16	17	13	26	█	3	10	22	█
20	█	19	█	5	█	9	█	26	█	24	█	3	█	6
8	18	15	5	14	14	13	26	█	6	13	11	5	3	9
11	█	█	█	14	█	█	█	12	█	14	█	16	█	3
13	26	5	16	3	21	5	14	13	█	8	25	15	26	14
5	█	14	█	21	█	26	█	5	█	5	█	21	█	1
26	13	13	10	13	█	7	3	9	2	19	13	14	26	13

Reference Grid

1	2	3	4	5 A	6	7	8	9	10	11	12	13
14 T	15	16	17	18	19	20	21	22	23	24	25	26 R

---

24 Pathfinder · Level 2

Starting from the bold letter P, move up, down or sideways (but not diagonally), one letter at a time, to find a continuous path through the names of 21 seas and oceans. (The words sea and ocean have been omitted from the names.) When you've finished, every letter in the grid will have been used. The trail begins with the world's largest ocean.

G	N	O	S	S	A	C	I	T	R	D	I	B	A	N	B	A
R	I	I	R	R	G	M	E	A	I	A	R	B	E	I	T	L
E	E	R	I	A	A	R	D	I	I	C	A	C	A	C	R	W
B	D	H	S	S	N	R	E	T	F	I	U	T	N	N	O	E
E	A	O	R	T	E	L	A	**P**	A	C	O	H	I	R	A	G
B	U	F	E	A	A	T	N	T	I	C	S	C	H	E	B	I
W	A	E	G	N	N	A	R	A	N	I	T	C	R	N	N	A
O	N	Y	M	A	N	A	A	I	A	C	N	T	A	T	S	I
L	L	E	S	A	T	I	B	D	N	I	A	N	A	I	N	O

Test your general knowledge with this tricky crossword.

ACROSS

8. Stage dame famous for her role in *Odette* (4, 6)
9. Aphrodite's son (4)
10. Squirm, as if in pain (6)
11. "___ Girl," Madonna hit single (8)
12. George Eliot novel about a weaver (5, 6)
15. Meat from a young sheep (4)
16. Serious respiratory illness (10)
18. Fleetwood Mac's best-selling 1977 album (7)
19. Dispute, take exception to (7)
21. House that impressed Charles Ryder in an Evelyn Waugh novel (10)
22. Surname of "Buffalo Bill" (4)
23. Man as a species (4,7)
28. Ingredient of a martini (8)
29. Reddish brown variety of apple (6)
30. Natural source of lanolin (4)
31. Depleted part of the upper atmosphere (5, 5)

DOWN

1. Lewis Carroll creature sought by the Bellman (5)
2. 1935 Errol Flynn pirate film (7,5)
3. European headquarters of the Red Cross (6)
4. Mythical king of Argos killed by his wife (9)
5. Rolling Stones' lead guitarist (5, 7)
6. ___ Gershwin, composer of *Porgy and Bess* (6)
7. Biblical man swallowed by a whale (5)
13. Month in which Epiphany takes place (7)
14. Prospero's daughter in Shakespeare's *The Tempest* (7)
16. 1825 Pushkin play about a Russian tsar (5, 7)
17. December 28 Christian festival (9, 3)
20. Olympic sport comprising ten events (9)
24. Ornamental gilt brass (6)
25. Country south of Lebanon (6)
26. Daniel ___, *Robinson Crusoe* author (5)
27. 1958 Peggy Lee hit (5)

In each case, which is the odd word out?

1. VIXEN, DOE, COB, MARE

2. FACE, PLINTH, DIAL, ESCAPEMENT

3. ULNA, HUMERUS, TIBIA, RADIUS

4. BREAST, BUTTERFLY, BACK, MOTH

5. RED, ORANGE, YELLOW, BLUE

6. ROME, VENICE, ATHENS, FLORENCE

See if you can fit all the listed headgear back into the grid.

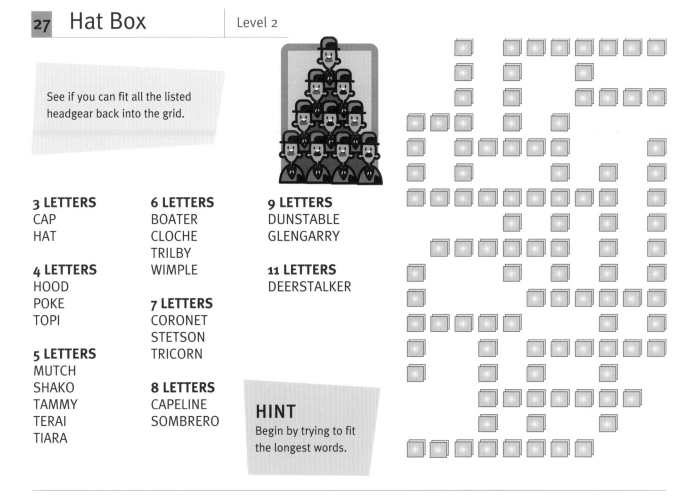

3 LETTERS
CAP
HAT

4 LETTERS
HOOD
POKE
TOPI

5 LETTERS
MUTCH
SHAKO
TAMMY
TERAI
TIARA

6 LETTERS
BOATER
CLOCHE
TRILBY
WIMPLE

7 LETTERS
CORONET
STETSON
TRICORN

8 LETTERS
CAPELINE
SOMBRERO

9 LETTERS
DUNSTABLE
GLENGARRY

11 LETTERS
DEERSTALKER

HINT
Begin by trying to fit the longest words.

---

28 You Wear It Well | Level 2

These questions are all connected to items of clothing. Try them for size!

1. Which female singer released an album called *The Red Shoes* in 1993?
2. At which African city was Desmond Tutu the archbishop from 1986–1996?
3. At which major sports tournament does the winner receive a green jacket as part of the prize?
4. Who sang the 1960 song, "Itsy Bitsy Teeny Weeny Yellow Polka Dot Bikini"?
5. During which war was the battle of Balaclava?
6. Who was Fred Astaire's dancing partner in the 1957 musical *Silk Stockings*?
7. Who played the lead role in the 1995 film *Devil in a Blue Dress*?
8. Which item of clothing takes its name from a 19th century trapeze artist?
9. What is the name of the famous character, an evil hypnotist, in George Du Maurier's novel entitled *Trilby*?
10. Who is the author of the famous rhyming *Cat in the Hat* books?

29

Dilemma

Level 2

These are ordinary crosswords — with a difference!
All the clues have been mixed up. Solve the puzzle by
working out which clues belong with which crossword.
We've given you two words to get you started.

ACROSS

4. Ran amok • Burning (6)
7. String of beads •
   Paid a bounty to (8)
8. Largest of plant forms •
   Covetousness (4)
9. Me, in person • Tilting
   playground ride (6)
11. Conspicuous wealth •
    Point out (8)
13. Dregs • Region (4)
15. Magnitude • Lifeless (4)
16. Fly high • Units of thermal
    insulation (4)
18. Close at hand •
    Item of footwear (4)
19. Wreaths of flowers and
    leaves • Country's
    representative abroad (8)
22. Stabbed •
    Science of morals (6)
24. Outer body covering •
    Bludgeon (4)
25. Rise and float in the air •
    The "E" in "EU" (8)
26. Hard tooth-coating •
    Dotes on (6)

DOWN

1. Unabashed •
   Pounding underfoot (9)
2. Plots • Contorted (7)
3. Entreaty • Relating to
   the mouth (4)
4. Make another offer •
   French goodbye (5)
5. Floating shipping
   hazards •
   Dealer in spectacles (8)
6. Forcibly remove •
   General destruction
   and disorder (5)
10. Fermented juice
    of grapes •
    Edible material (4)
12. Prolonging •
    Absorbed (9)
14. Passenger-carrying plane
    • Stocky terrier,
    often white-coated (8)
16. Elephant's long tooth •
    Land for building on (4)
17. Performance by a soloist
    • Moved (7)
20. Peeved •
    Seed of an oak (5)
21. Breakfast, lunch and
    dinner, for example •
    Full-length work
    of fiction (5)
23. Gas used to illuminate
    signs • Slender (4)

What am I?

My first is in JAGUAR and also BIG CAT,
My second's in GIBBON and also WOMBAT,
My third is in LIZARD but not in IMPALA,
My fourth is in LION but not in KOALA,
My fifth is in LEMUR but missing from MOOSE,
My sixth is in LEMMING but not in MONGOOSE,
My last is in CHEETAH and in KANGAROO,
My whole you might see if you visit a zoo.

30

Riddle

Level 2

Each of the first seven lines represents
a letter; can you solve the riddle?

The three words of each clue have a fourth word in common — and that's your answer. For instance, "Even, Tea, Tie (5)" would have the answer BREAK (break even, tea-break, tie-break).

ACROSS
1. High, Methodist, Service (6)
5. Ended, Plan, Season (4)
8. Golf, House, Sandwich (4)
9. Basket, Conger, Electric (3)
10. Dead, Leader, Memory (4)
11. Bone, Standing, Talk (4)
12. Cake, China, Set (3)
15. Evil, Glad, Lash (3)
18. Recorder, Sticky, Worm (4)
19. Code, Penalty, Surface (4)
20. Fire, Laughing, Natural (3)
21. Dance, Owl, Tithe (4)
22. Fan, Pony, Ox (4)
23. Dry, Sweet, Trifle (6)

DOWN
2. Bank, Home, Resort (7)
3. Bullet, Gloves, India (6)
4. Buddy, Bush, Oak (5)
6. Bird's, Egg, Mare's (4)
7. Bitten, Market, Performing (4)
13. Penguin, Purple, Roman (7)
14. Companion, Lad, Relationship (6)
15. On, Outside, Rail (4)
16. End, Far, Middle (4)
17. Eye, Meat, Snow (5)

In each case, which is the odd title out?

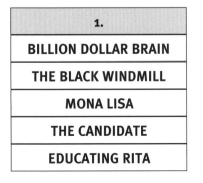

1.
BILLION DOLLAR BRAIN
THE BLACK WINDMILL
MONA LISA
THE CANDIDATE
EDUCATING RITA

2.
STAMBOUL TRAIN
A GUN FOR SALE
ENGLAND MADE ME
THE HUMAN FACTOR
EARTHLY POWERS

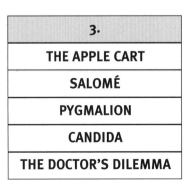

3.
THE APPLE CART
SALOMÉ
PYGMALION
CANDIDA
THE DOCTOR'S DILEMMA

In each case, fill in the missing word that will complete the phrase or term.

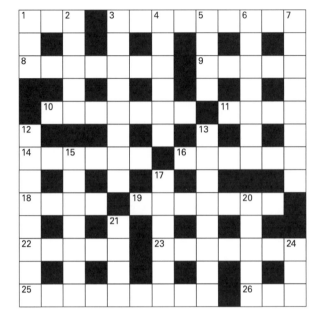

ACROSS

1. ___ glass (3)
3. ___ occasion (9)
8. ___ wrack (7)
9. ___ furnace (5)
10. ___ drain (7)
11. ___ deep (4)
14. ___ umbrage (6)
16. ___ bank (6)
18. ___ pond (4)
19. ___ lenses (7)
22. ___ run (5)
23. ___ glasses (7)
25. ___ crime (9)
26. ___ gloves (3)

DOWN

1. ___ reporter (3)
2. ___ blazer (5)
3. ___ ball (8)
4. ___ gardener (6)
5. ___ wedding (4)
6. ___ bath (7)
7. ___ leave (8)
12. ___ heels (8)
13. ___ cement (8)
15. ___ time (7)
17. ___ dancing (6)
20. ___ peas (5)
21. ___ B (4)
24. ___ bless (3)

34 Match the Meaning | Level 2

In each case, which of the four words is the synonym?

1. RAKISH — A. Jaunty B. Rude C. Streamlined D. Droll

2. DUPLICITY — A. Imitation B. Fraudulence C. Perjury D. Betrayal

3. FARCICAL — A. Ludicrous B. Wild C. Jovial D. True

4. FECKLESS — A. Capricious B. Clever C. Harmful D. Useless

5. INTUITIVE — A. Knowledgeable B. Automatic C. Instinctive D. Personable

6. QUIESCENCE — A. Silence B. Agreement C. Hopefulness D. Motionlessness

35 Second Thoughts | Level 2

In each case, fill in the missing word that will make a phrase, term or name.

DID YOU KNOW?
The world's first crossword was invented by Arthur Wynne in 1913.

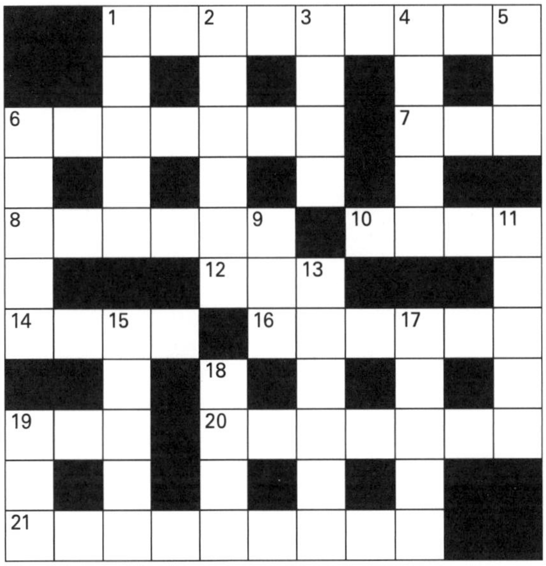

ACROSS

1. Seventy-six ___ (9)
6. Lost ___ (7)
7. Village ___ (3)
8. Rock ___ (6)
10. High ___ (4)
12. Battering ___ (3)
14. Out ___ (4)
16. Spin ___ (6)
19. Fishing ___ (3)
20. Public ___ (7)
21. Wine ___ (9)

DOWN

1. Skin ___ (5)
2. Stump ___ (6)
3. Root ___ (4)
4. White ___ (5)
5. Original ___ (3)
6. Designer ___ (5)
9. Raving ___ (3)
11. Snowy ___ (5)
13. Perpetual ___ (6)
15. Down ___ (5)
17. Identical ___ (5)
18. Tiger ___ (4)
19. White ___ (3)

36 Odd Man Out | Level 2

In each case, can you work out which is the odd word out?

1. **SEVILLE, OPORTO, BARCELONA, CORDOBA**
2. **BEETLE, COCKROACH, MITE, CICADA**
3. **TIARA, SOMBRERO, SHAKO, ESPADRILLE**
4. **TERRIER, WHIPPET, CORGI, MANX**
5. **BRUSH, DRESSER, BRAINED, MIRROR**
6. **RETINA, IRIS, CORNEA, COCCYX**

Answers on page 226

This is a normal crossword, but here, each letter represents a number. Can you work out which letter every number represents and complete the grid? We've given you three letters.

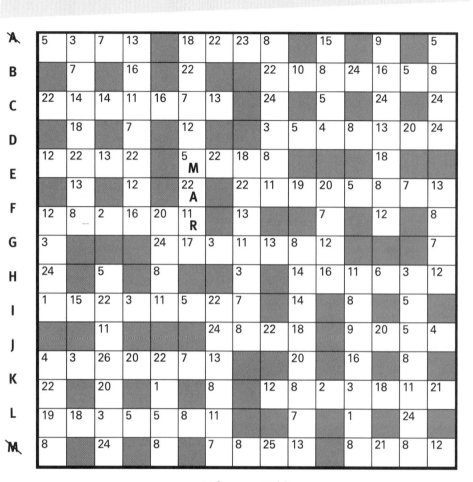

Reference Grid

1	2	3	4	5 M	6	7	8	9	10	11 R	12	13
14	15	16	17	18	19	20	21	22 A	23	24	25	26

HINT
The numbers that occur most frequently are likely to be vowels.

38 Common Bond | Level 2

If all these names are anagrams of their best-liked Bond films, can you name them all?

1. GREG DOLFIN

2. OLIVE TIKWALA

3. TREVOR DE WINSOOMER

4. ANTHEA DOIDERY

5. KAREN MOOR

6. DELTA IDLEVINE

39 Wine Box | Level 2

See how quickly you can fit all the listed words into the grid.

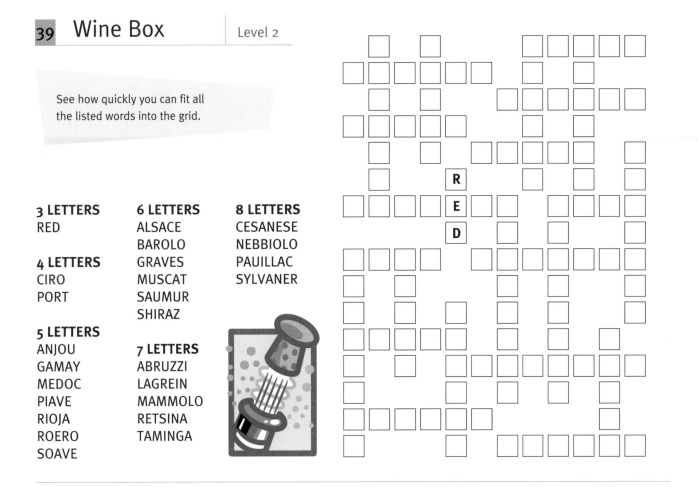

3 LETTERS
RED

4 LETTERS
CIRO
PORT

5 LETTERS
ANJOU
GAMAY
MEDOC
PIAVE
RIOJA
ROERO
SOAVE

6 LETTERS
ALSACE
BAROLO
GRAVES
MUSCAT
SAUMUR
SHIRAZ

7 LETTERS
ABRUZZI
LAGREIN
MAMMOLO
RETSINA
TAMINGA

8 LETTERS
CESANESE
NEBBIOLO
PAUILLAC
SYLVANER

---

40 Opposites Attract | Level 2

In each case, which of the four words is the antonym?

1. **EXPANSION** — A. Bankruptcy B. Slowness C. Insignificance D. Contraction

2. **CREATE** — A. Discourage B. Undermine C. Destroy D. Remove

3. **DISINFECT** — A. Stimulate B. Contaminate C. Brainwash D. Combine

4. **INAUSPICIOUS** — A. Useful B. Promising C. Joyful D. Spotless

5. **REPREHENSIBLE** — A. Irresponsible B. Culpable C. Guiltless D. Generous

6. **RETICENT** — A. Outspoken B. Obnoxious C. Polite D. Impetuous

Improve Your Word Power | Level 3

This is Level 3, where you'll find the puzzles are becoming a bit more difficult.

Puzzles 41–60

41 Jigsaw Crossword | Level 3

With the help of just three rows of Across clues, fit the blocks below into the empty grid to form a complete crossword.

ACROSS (ROWS)

1. Acknowledgment or praise
3. Not able to be erased
11. Deeds • Hard currency

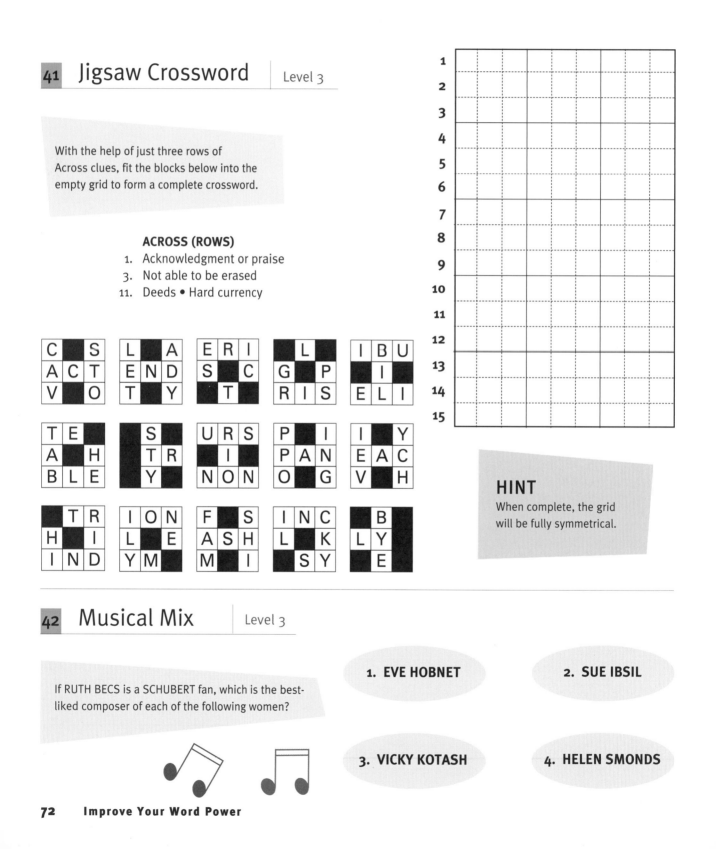

HINT
When complete, the grid will be fully symmetrical.

42 Musical Mix | Level 3

If RUTH BECS is a SCHUBERT fan, which is the best-liked composer of each of the following women?

1. EVE HOBNET

2. SUE IBSIL

3. VICKY KOTASH

4. HELEN SMONDS

43 Who Said What? | Level 3

Write the answers to the clues in the rows of the top grid, and the name of a famous person will appear in the shaded column of squares. Now transfer the cross-referenced letters from this grid to the lower grid to reveal something this person said.

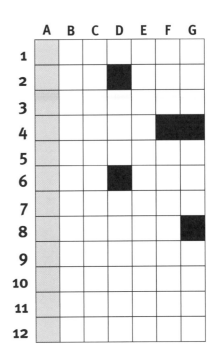

1. Cook's room
2. Tropical potato • Voice disapproval
3. Really hates
4. Concepts
5. Deliberately ducking questions
6. Unruly crowd • Dry, of wine
7. Middle East national
8. Nullify
9. Eccentric
10. Lumps of raw meat
11. Least lovely
12. Strong feeling

1B	■	3E	3C	5B	9E	■	2E	5A	8B	7D	■	11B	5G	8E	11G	4A	12G	8C	■	7C
11C	9A	12D	■	3B	9C	■	10A	7B	11D	3F	9B	■	4D	10C	2G	11A	10F	■	12B	2A
6C	5C	6G	1A	6E	12E	4B	12A	•	■	7E	1C	■	5D	10E	6F	6A	11F	■	9G	6B
1E	9F	5F	11E	■	9D	4C	1D	10B	2C	8F	■	2B	■	8A	7F	3D	5E	12C	1G	8D
12F	10D	4E	1F	3G	10G	7A	2F	7G												

44 Relatively Speaking | Level 3

How quickly can you answer these family-based questions?

1. Which well-known actor is the brother of Shirley MacLaine?
2. Which pair of brothers directed the 2000 film *O Brother Where Art Thou*?
3. Richard was the co-founder of a major publishing firm, while his daughter Carly is a famous singer. What is their surname?
4. Who wrote the 1969 novel *Travels with My Aunt*?
5. Which comedy actor played the *Father of the Bride* in the 1991 movie?
6. Who sang the 1972 song "Sylvia's Mother"?
7. Who starred as a singer on the run from the Mafia in the 1992 film *Sister Act*?
8. What was the nationality of the 20th century painter known as Grandma Moses?
9. What is the name of the constellation also called the Twins?
10. Woody sang of the American heartland, and his son Arlo had a hit with "Alice's Restaurant." What is their surname?

ACROSS ROWS

1. A marriage's sixtieth anniversary (7, 7)
2. Expose • Hatchet • Lake north of Ohio
3. Preserving plant • To a considerable extent
4. Jab with a lower joint • Intersecting points • Lowland areas
5. City home of Boeing aircraft • Hydro • Identical
6. Versatile players (3-8) • Neither's close follower?
7. Pre-tights legwear • Fishhook end • Workshy
8. De-select? • Printer's re-correction word • Pilot
9. Tries to put off • After tax • Deserve
10. Short version of "old" furniture? • Artificial international language
11. Unnecessary activity • Frozen water • Mythical giant • Arrest
12. Edgar Allan ___, author • Up-front payment • Impudence, cheek
13. Relaxation • Valuable stone • Disagreeable situation
14. Pigpen • Metal bar • Squint • States

DOWN COLUMNS

1. Web-footed bird • Beach grains • Curtains
2. In foolish fashion • Marsh plant • Food grain
3. Adolescent's spots • Parcel out • Verse, collectively
4. Claude ___, French painter • Tether • Added clause
5. Roasting chamber • Oodles! • Sinbad's magical bird • Self-esteem
6. Evil Roman emperor • Excessive desire • Percolated
7. John ___, early English poet • Any Scottish peak • Dance noisily
8. UK principality • Palm fruit • Ski slope
9. Greatly vex • Lose energy
10. Truck fuel • Mediating officer
11. Edgar ___, French painter • Foal's dad • Aberdeen ___, cattle breed

This is just like an ordinary crossword, except that thick black bars replace the black squares. Simply write your answers in the grid.

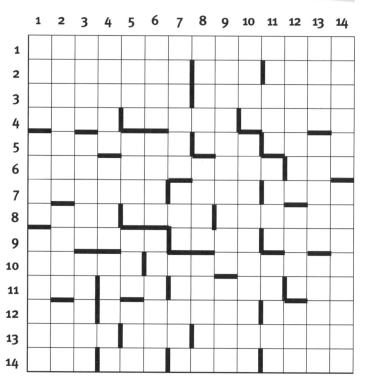

12. The Emerald Isle • Thomas ___, German novelist • Sleeveless garment worn by Arabs
13. Sudanese river • Grinding tooth • Ongoing score
14. Hot water spring • Elevates, dignifies

46 Odd Man Out — Level 3

Spot the odd one out in each of these sets of words.

1. SUCCESS, ARENA, BORROW, TORMENT
2. BLURB, ERSATZ, KAPUT, ZEITGEIST
3. REWARD, TRAP, STRESSED, CALL
4. BANANA, TEPEE, WIGWAM, COLON

In each case, only one of the three definitions is correct. Can you work out which one?

1. CARDOON
A. Mediterranean plant related to the artichoke
B. A jester's assistant
C. Strip of wood supporting a ship's figurehead

2. THRENODY
A. The practice of using a ouija board
B. A joke considered in poor taste
C. Mournful song for the dead

3. QUANDONG
A. Pouched rodent native to Argentina
B. Australian tree with peachlike fruit
C. Jury's period of consideration

ACROSS
1. PLAIN PEEP (9)
10. Kingdom (5)
11. Vessel, box (9)
12. Without artifice (9)
13. Small recess (5)
14. Radical (7)
16. RIP COAT (7)
17. Zero score (3)
18. In ___, on the journey (7)
20. Female of a pride (7)
23. Take a test again (5)
24. Wire walked on in circuses (9)
26. Drug which increases activity (9)
27. PAGER (5)
28. NEATER GIN (9)

DOWN
2. Submerge (7)
3. Very good indeed (9)
4. "___ Lane," Beatles song (5))
5. Inexperienced driver (7)
6. A GONER (6)
7. Quick (4)
8. Clown's one-wheeled transport (8)
9. Clergyman (6)
15. Send out radio waves (8)
16. Reptile related to the crocodile (9)
18. Common songbird (6)
19. USA MAST (7)
21. Eight-sided shape (7)
22. Sections of a play (6)
24. Sound of a plucked guitar string (5)
25. Egg shape (4)

48 Fruit Cocktail | Level 3

This is a normal crossword puzzle, but the clues in capitals are all anagrams of types of fruit. Can you unscramble them and solve the crossword?

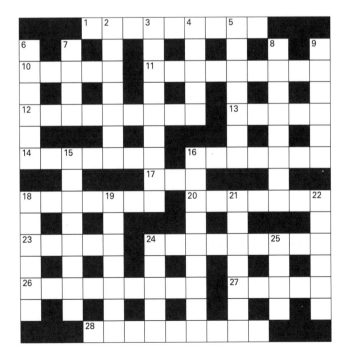

49 Two Tricky | Level 3

This is a codeword like the ones before, except this time we've only given you TWO letters to start you off. Can you fill in all the missing letters?

A	11	18	15	7	21	23	26	19	8		16	8	12	22	23	N
B	8			22		12		8		14		18			21	O
C	21		1	21	12	3		22		21	16	11	24		16	P
D	12	15	5	21		3	18	12	16	23		21	12	16	23	Q
E	25		13			24			5				22		13	R
F		12	11	21	6		23	1	21	21		16	7	13	2	S
G	18			10		16		5		15	19	21			18	T
H	4	21	12	19		23	21	12	15	5		12	7	13	22	U
I	9			12	6	21		8		18		2			24	V
J	21	14	13	8		1	5	21	24		5	24	2	22		W
K	15		3				12			15			12		18	X
L	23	18	18	8		16	24	8	11	5		16	22 N	12 A	11	Y
M	13		22	18	25	21		12		19	17	8	24		21	Z
	14			14		1		20		22		18			3	
	21	6	15	21	8		8	21	19	7	12	21	2	13	12	

Reference Grid

1	2	3	4	5	6	7	8	9	10	11	12 A	13
14	15	16	17	18	19	20	21	22 N	23	24	25	26

50 Match the Meaning | Level 3

In each case, which of the four words is the synonym?

1. BRACKISH A. Salty B. Slovenly C. Irritable D. Brittle

2. GUMPTION A. Strength B. Nous C. Bravery D. Tact

3. VESTIGIAL A. Crumbling B. Stubby C. Pious D. Residual

4. ARBITRARY A. Unrelated B. Hopeless C. Important D. Conscientious

5. ALACRITY A. Volume B. Boastfulness C. Briskness D. Selfishness

6. IMPERATIVE A. Bossy B. Enormous C. Likely D. Necessary

The answer to each clue is a six-letter word. Write the answer clockwise in the grid around its clue number. The first letter of each answer goes in the arrowed space, as in the given starter.

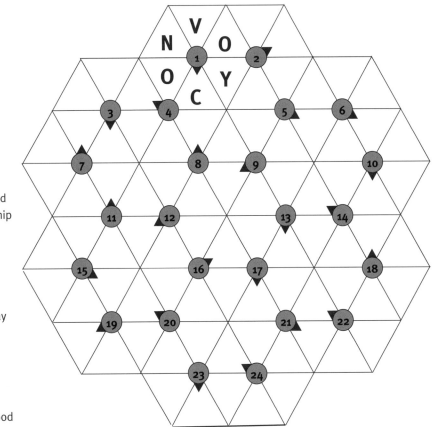

1. Line of trucks
2. Gulch
3. Indifference
4. Team game
5. Hold for ransom
6. Cartridge or fountain writing implement
7. Instant effect
8. Martial art
9. Arranged like spokes
10. Servile
11. Clandestine
12. Devoted adherent
13. Orange-shaped
14. Place of worship
15. Biting wit
16. Sufferer for a cause
17. Jump like lambs
18. Grand doorway
19. Short-haired hound
20. Try hard
21. Use a mouthwash
22. Swallowing food
23. Beginner
24. Swinging bed

52 Target | Level 3

See how many words of four or more letters you can find from the letters in the grid at right. Every word must contain the central shaded letter, and there is one nine-letter word. (No plurals—but "s" ending verbs are OK—no foreign words, no hyphenated words, no proper nouns.)

YOUR TARGET
25–34 words: not bad
35–44 words: very good
Over 44 words: amazing!

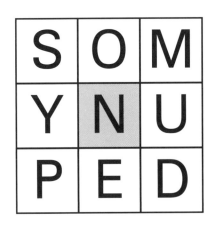

53 Backward | Level 3

Do this one the wrong way round! First, block in 28 squares in a symmetrical pattern to make a completed crossword. Next, number the squares crossword-fashion (1 to 37) allowing for words ACROSS and DOWN.

ACROSS
— Untruth
— Curved opening
— Mineral rock
— Perhaps
— Flood, sudden rush
— Turkish commander
— And not
— Worker's organization
— Male offspring
— Posted
— Reprimand
— Maiden name indicator
— High steep rock
— Grow old
— Climbing plant
— Every
— Friend
— Bulbous underground stem
— Irritable
— Part of a circle's circumference
— Begin, commence

S	T	A	R	T	I	C	L	I	F	F
P	A	L	E	A	G	A	I	N	O	R
O	R	E	A	L	E	L	A	N	E	E
K	E	Y	S	C	O	L	D	O	S	S
E	A	C	H	O	U	T	A	R	C	H
E	W	E	U	N	I	O	N	M	A	I
S	E	N	T	E	J	E	C	O	R	M
P	E	A	S	P	A	T	E	T	U	I
I	V	Y	A	L	E	E	L	S	O	N
L	I	E	R	A	G	E	M	A	R	C
T	E	S	T	Y	A	M	A	Y	B	E

DOWN
— Pour, flow copiously
— Reverence
— Country hotel
— Sphere
— ____ board, spirit communication device
— Telephone, ring
— Compete
— Overturned, upset
— Motor vehicle
— After-bath powder
— Move to music
— Speak, utter
— In new condition
— Road-surfacing material
— Theatrical entertainment
— Enemy
— Finely chopped meat
— Closes
— Addressed
— Word of agreement
— Beer

EXTRA CHALLENGE
Put the correct numbers against the jumbled clues on either side of the puzzle.

54 Riddle | Level 3

Each of the first seven lines represents a letter. Can you solve the riddle?

What am I?
My first is in FALCON and also in OWL,
My second's in SWIFT but not in FOWL,
My third is in STORK but not in SKY,
My fourth is in FULMAR but not in FLY,
My fifth is in CHICKEN but not in HEN,
My sixth is in CYGNET but not in PEN,
My last is in CHIRPS but not in SINGS,
My whole is a creature with feathers and wings.

In each case, which is the odd word out?

1. HOOVER, TAFT, STEVENSON, WILSON

2. LANZAROTE, FORMENTERA, TENERIFE, FUERTEVENTURA

3. OVERWHELMED, RASHLY, SOAKING, CURABLE

4. BIZARRE, ODD, HILARIOUS, FUNNY

5. HUSBAND, HUNTING, WORK, DAUGHTER

6. MADAM, TOT, SIR, DEED

---

56 Cryptic Challenge | Level 3

This crossword makes you think just a little bit harder—take your time over it!

ACROSS

1. Consumed with anger at first, but restrained (9)
8. In part of forest, reestablish plant (4)
9. Remember to fetch again (9)
10. Hold on to castle tower (4)
13. Cook part of fish right inside (5)
15. Agents capture the Spanish— it's disgusting (6)
16. Note, flower needed for church festival (6)
17. Polite way to ask for penny on the rent (6)
19. Inclined toward unproductive journalist (6)
20. Show contempt for national leader taken in by prophet (5)
21. Large bag for plunder (4)
24. Inelegant, wild, wild rose (9)
25. Pole among number returning home (4)
26. Brazen, like one who's had a close shave? (4-5)

DOWN

2. Sheep on river vessel (4)
3. Kitty is game! (4)
4. Controllers—they help to draw the line (6)
5. Fishing equipment to take on (6)
6. Apprehending the strikingly attractive (9)
7. Dopes dare to reform reckless criminal (9)
11. Making a suggestion that professional is showing off (9)
12. Part of shoe on container of big letters (5-4)
13. Gymnastics leader— girl is a tumbler (5)
14. Alter, change, but not at the moment (5)
18. Mystery of unruly gamine (6)
19. Church messenger devoured lamb joint first (6)
22. Oats scattered round covered walk (4)
23. Formerly attached to church (4)

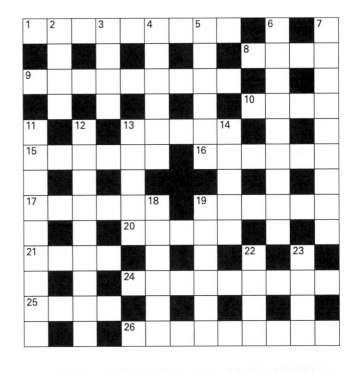

HINT

Sometimes a cryptic clue leads to a word that has two different meanings, and the clue gives both definitions. For example, "Search around for a type of polecat (6)." The answer is FERRET, which can mean both "search around" and "type of polecat."

We're only giving you two starter letters here, so you have 24 numbers
left to decode into the correct letter of the alphabet. Good luck!

Reference Grid

1	2	3 A	4	5	6	7 C	8	9	10	11	12	13
14	15	16	17	18	19	20	21	22	23	24	25	26

1. PROFUSE	A. Shallow B. Quiet C. Sparse D. Needy
2. LAX	A. Mercurial B. Intrigued C. Ostentatious D. Stringent
3. GREENHORN	A. Veteran B. Giant C. Believer D. Imposter
4. PERNICIOUS	A. Obstinate B. Harmless C. Assiduous D. Frequent
5. MOMENTOUS	A. Insignificant B. Pointless C. Ineffectual D. Incredible
6. PROBITY	A. Jealousy B. Kindness C. Generosity D. Iniquity

In each case, which of the four words is the antonym?

The black squares have to be added as well as the words. For a start, four black squares and four numbers have been inserted. The black squares form a symmetrical pattern.

HINT
A number in the grid will always indicate the beginning of an answer.

ACROSS
1. Facial spasm
4. Tallow
7. Eminent
10. Snug
13. Be present (at)
16. Gesture
18. Ocean
19. Speed
20. Arid
21. Expert
22. Plead
23. Chest bone
24. Sorcery
26. Prosecute
28. Handsome youth
29. Water channel
31. Stage makeup
34. Warehouse
35. Present time
36. Sty

DOWN
2. Baby
3. Dove's noise
4. Moist
5. Slow musical piece
6. Academic hat
8. Attempt
9. Secret, underhand
11. Vapor
12. Go by plane
14. Lukewarm
15. French painter
16. Small branch
17. Quarrel
23. Male sheep
24. Japanese emperor
25. Assistant priest
27. Historical age
30. Agent
32. Stitch
33. Fizzy drink

---

60 The Name Game | Level 3

Which Henry...

1. had six wives?
2. won the Nobel Peace Prize in 1973?
3. developed the moving assembly line for car production and sold a million cars in 1915?
4. wrote the novel *Tom Jones*?
5. received an Academy Award for Best Actor in 1981?
6. was a sculptor who died on August 31, 1986?
7. was an American poet who wrote "The Song of Hiawatha"?
8. was a philosopher who lived alone for two years on the shore of Walden Pond?
9. was a 17th century English explorer, mariner and adventurer?
10. shot to fame as Elliott in the 1982 film *E.T. the Extra-Terrestrial*?

Can you name the famous Henrys in the quiz?

Improve Your Word Power | Level 4

Welcome to the toughest level of puzzles—yes, they are as hard as they look!

Puzzles 61–80

61 Treble Chance | Level 4

We've given you all the answers—and more! You have to decide, in each case, which of the three words will fit in the grid to complete the crossword. One word has been put in as a start.

ACROSS

1. Jetty, Mirth, Hitch
4. After, Crawl, Scowl
10. Titular, Adjourn, Astound
11. Rayon, Spear, Satin
12. Lock, Rare, Limp
13. Director, Asbestos, Fidelity
16. Waiter, Kernel, Totter
17. Burrow, Fierce, Mallet
20. Catalyst, Handbook, Highbrow
21. Jump, Wide, Huge
23. Tonic, Aroma, Rumba
25. Entitle, Boiling, Archive
26. Grade, Steep, Sheer
27. Penny, Jewel, Three

DOWN

2. Injection, Enjoyable, Interpret
3. Town, Help, Tour
5. Cosmetic, Forceful, Comedian
6. Act, Wit, Why
7. Fillet, Wallow, Streak
8. Dross, Gnash, Unfit
9. Onus, Drop, Less
14. Tactician, Pirouette, Turquoise
15. Keyboard, Barbecue, Membrane
18. Tipper, Eleven, Emerge
19. Hover, Aside, Focal
20. City, Harm, Hate
22. Ache, Wife, Stub
24. Mar, Out, Now

62 Call My Bluff | Level 4

In each case, only one of the three definitions is correct. Which one?

1. PILEUM

A. Roman doorway
B. The largest bile duct
C. The top of a bird's head

2. TARTANA

A. Small covered wagon
B. Extinct horse of Central Asia
C. Lively Basque dance

3. COCKALORUM

A. The weight at the bottom of a pendulum
B. Wild party following a rodeo
C. Self-important little man

63 Elvis Lives | Level 4

Can you unravel these five Presley hits?

1. **SEES DOUBLE HUES**

2. **FAITHLESS METAL**

3. **UNRESTORED RENT**

4. **CUPID'S US MISSION**

5. **HYPHENATING CIRCLE**

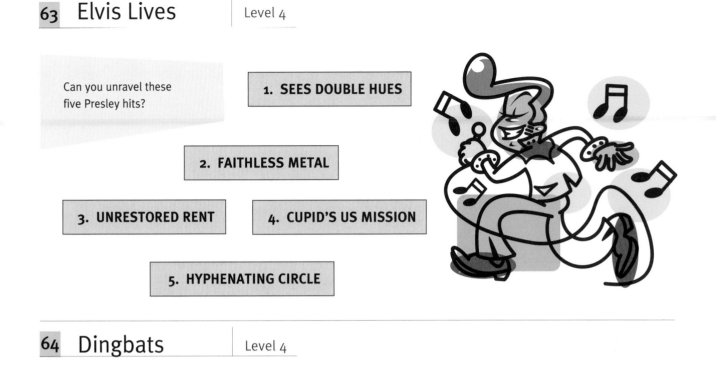

64 Dingbats | Level 4

In the weird world of words, a dingbat makes you think laterally to come up with a phrase, as shown in the example below. Can you solve the rest?

HINT
Thinking laterally—what does it mean, exactly?

| mind |
| matter |

Here the answer is "mind over matter."

GEGS

good all time

timing
tim ing

i   i
bag   bag

With the help of the Across clues only, can you fit the 35 pieces into their correct positions in the empty grid (which, when completed, will exhibit a symmetrical pattern)?

1. Section; error
2. Light beam
3. Alligator pear; notion
4. Schoolbag
5. Fish star sign; cure
6. Accommodate
7. Share out; sheepfold; incline
8. Impulse; region
9. Course taken; fireplace
10. Layperson
11. Sparkle; banishment
12. Wild Mexican horse
13. Topic; skilful
14. Single time; nibble
15. Portly; female rabbit; distinctive character
16. Core
17. Arm cover; run in
18. Annoying
19. Military squad; deer meat
20. First woman
21. Usual amount; alleviate

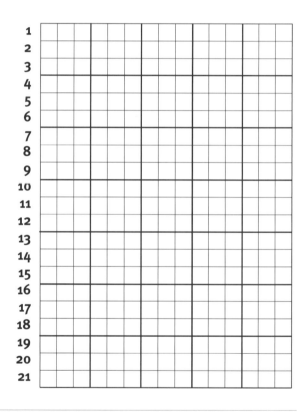

Hidden inside the paragraph at right are the names of ten items of furniture. Can you find them all? For example, "What's your address, Eric?" would hide the word DRESSER.)

Others of a similar nature will understand how my fear of flying means I haven't attempted much air travel. As the wide skies beckon and I step into the cabin, eternity stretches before me. My whole being seems disturbed, upset, teetering on the edge of collapse, not able to move. But as I lean toward Rob, everything becomes more bearable and in the midst of my panic, he's there to console me.

67 Bracer

The first part of each clue gives a six-letter answer, five of whose letters make up the five-letter answer to the second part, and four of which make up the four-letter answer to the third part. The unused letter from the first answer is entered in column A, and that from the second answer in column B. The two columns, when completed, spell out two architectural features.

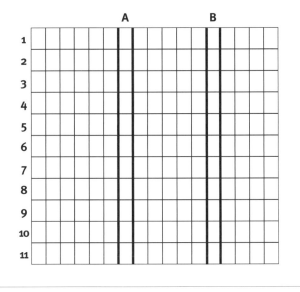

1. Large wood; worries; repose
2. Stay; US state; excavate
3. Young girl; entitled; pantomime lady
4. Masked, concealed; existed; told fibs
5. Was deficient (in); formed into a hard mass; pack of cards
6. Injuries; robust; whole; university teachers
7. Jewish state; intense beam; scorch, burn
8. Racket sport; fork prongs; mathematical function
9. Sleazy, corrupt; ___ Day, film star/singer; Diana ___, film star
10. Stretch of water; by the side of; ambition
11. Fiddle, contrive; approach, outlook; tilt

68 Spiral

Every answer (except the first) uses the last letter of the preceding answer as its initial letter, the chain thus formed following a spiral path to the middle of the grid. The diagonals spell two mollusks.

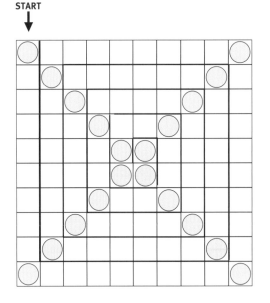

START

- Musical instruction to pluck strings (9)
- _____ Reed, late film star (6)
- Robin _____, Christmas card bird (9)
- Italian restaurant (9)
- _____ Lincoln, US president (7)
- Tune, air (6)
- Hue denoting cowardice (6)
- Without value (9)

- Commotion, excitement (9)
- Slender, slim (6)
- Radio (8)
- Traveled on snow (5)
- Twelve (5)
- Pen tip (3)
- Prejudice (4)
- Shine, gleam (5)
- Synthetic material (5)
- Information, TV bulletin (4)
- Male title (3)

69 Outfit | Level 4

With three blanks, three words and one letter as a start, can you fill out the grid with the words below?

HINT
The grid pattern is fully symmetrical, so other blanks can be calculated right away.

4	User	Ejected
Anil	Zulu	Heather
Aped		Heftier
Avid	**5**	Piloted
Done	Aztec	Rapture
Etch	Drape	Reissue
Gave	Equip	Tangent
Goes	Exact	Targets
Grey	Obeys	Unaided
Iron	Outer	
Lure	Skein	**9**
Mail	Vault	Adjourned
Odds		Airlifted
Ores	**7**	Exclusion
Rash	Bracket	Huskiness
Sank	Buttery	Keyboards
Star	Crowned	Shrinking
Stud	Dampish	Tap-dancer
Tear	Defrays	Unwelcome

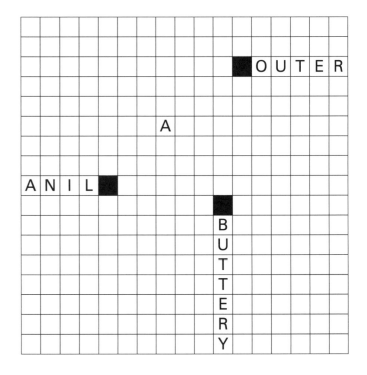

70 The Name Game | Level 4

Which Jane/Jayne...

Can you name the famous Jane/Jaynes in the quiz?

1 ...was the subject of a novel written by Charlotte Brontë in 1847?
2 ...won an Academy Award for best original screenplay for *The Piano*?
3 ...was Queen of England for only nine days?
4 ...starred alongside Marilyn Monroe in *Gentlemen Prefer Blondes*?
5 ...was an American frontierswoman whose real name was Martha Jane Burke?
6 ...was the third wife of King Henry VIII and mother of Edward VI?
7 ...was Christopher Dean's ice-skating partner?
8 ...was a major English novelist who wrote *Pride and Prejudice*?
9 ...is an American film actress and producer of exercise books and videos?
10 ...starred as Elaine in the TV series *Ally McBeal*?

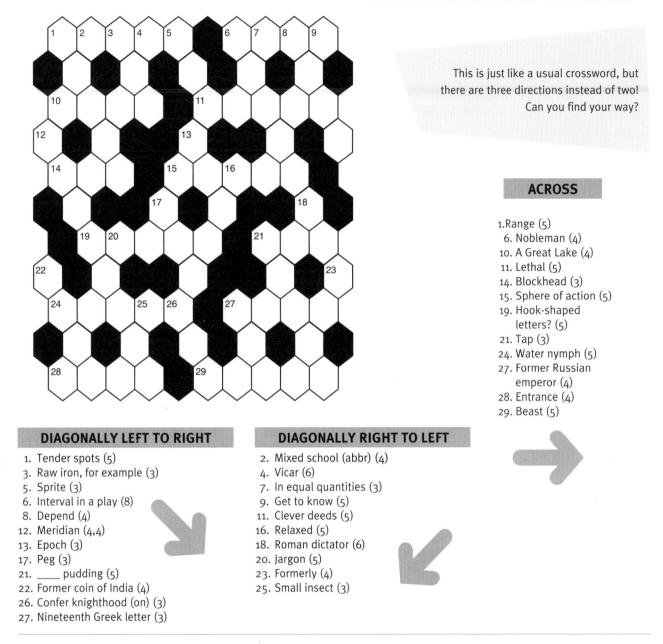

This is just like a usual crossword, but there are three directions instead of two! Can you find your way?

ACROSS

1. Range (5)
6. Nobleman (4)
10. A Great Lake (4)
11. Lethal (5)
14. Blockhead (3)
15. Sphere of action (5)
19. Hook-shaped letters? (5)
21. Tap (3)
24. Water nymph (5)
27. Former Russian emperor (4)
28. Entrance (4)
29. Beast (5)

DIAGONALLY LEFT TO RIGHT

1. Tender spots (5)
3. Raw iron, for example (3)
5. Sprite (3)
6. Interval in a play (8)
8. Depend (4)
12. Meridian (4,4)
13. Epoch (3)
17. Peg (3)
21. ____ pudding (5)
22. Former coin of India (4)
26. Confer knighthood (on) (3)
27. Nineteenth Greek letter (3)

DIAGONALLY RIGHT TO LEFT

2. Mixed school (abbr) (4)
4. Vicar (6)
7. In equal quantities (3)
9. Get to know (5)
11. Clever deeds (5)
16. Relaxed (5)
18. Roman dictator (6)
20. Jargon (5)
23. Formerly (4)
25. Small insect (3)

72 Opposites Attract | Level 4

In each case, which of the four words is the antonym?

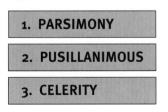

1. PARSIMONY — A. Stupidity B. Generosity C. Growth D. Federalism

2. PUSILLANIMOUS — A. Hedonistic B. Invigorating C. Gregarious D. Courageous

3. CELERITY — A. Slowness B. Anxiety C. Abbreviation D. Inelegance

Take your time over this toughie.

ACROSS

1. Tricky situation to graze (6)
5. Small tree to throw round a penny (7)
10. Burglar makes clarinets (9)
11. Inlaid during a tennis match? (5)
12. Good to get out of terribly rough time (4)
13. Wrecking steel car is the most obvious (8)
16. Upsetting, but a crime bug (9)
17. Wipe out part of camera section (5)
19. Deal with nice surprise (5)
20. Can anyone create vexation? (9)
21. Almost arrive with repairs and approves (8)
23. Capone manuscript for charity (4)
26. Row to right for ship (5)
27. Minion beneath the heather (9)
28. Veil for those with shy Kama, perhaps (7)
29. Flag officer? (6)

DOWN

2. Boil second vehicle, with relative (9)
3. Assist with a speculation (4)
4. Send out some of the mittens (4)
5. Satisfactory conclusion for community (10)
6. Soldier to watch sleuth (7,3)
7. Publish debatable point (5)
8. Understands when the courier arrives? (4, 3 ,7)
9. Somehow hit capable ally from A to Z (14)
14. Big instrument melted Turk, maybe (10)
15. Tot, together with friar, very close (3, 3, 4)
18. Nag ill nun again by rescinding (9)
22. Lacking newspaper I'm raising (5)
24. Slight advantage for border (4)
25. Garden flower almost from Dublin? (4)

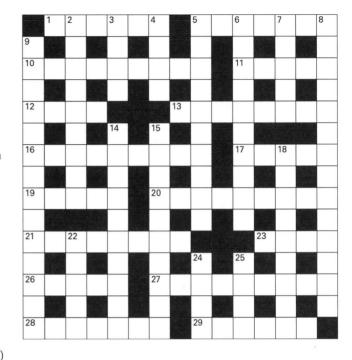

HINT

The answers to many cryptic clues are hidden inside the clues. For example, Fine stuff seen in capital city (4). The answer is Talc. The words *Fine stuff* define the answer, the words *seen in* tell you the answer is found somewhere within the two words *capital city*.

As in the puzzle on page 83, a dingbat makes you think laterally to come up with a phrase. Can you do the same for all of these?

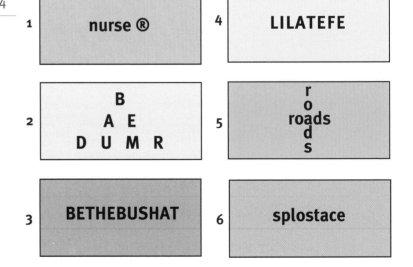

1. nurse ®

2. B
   A E
   D U M R

3. BETHEBUSHAT

4. LILATEFE

5. r
   o
   roads
   d
   s

6. splostace

Solutions to Radial clues (1 to 24) either start from the outer edge of the circle and read inward, or start from the inner ring and read outward to the edge (so they are all five-letter words). Solutions to Circular clues read in either a clockwise or counterclockwise direction around the circle.

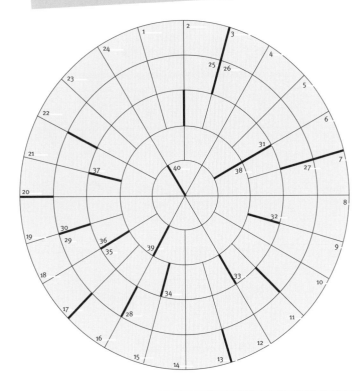

RADIAL:

INWARD
2. Values, assesses
3. Prescribed amounts
8. Monarch
9. Senior in age
11. Cut (gardening)
12. Per Ardua ad ___, RAF motto
13. Jeweled headband
20. Undercarriage
22. Foolish
23. River of Paris
24. Tartan skirts

OUTWARD
1. Manner
4. Long-necked bird
5. Fish basket
6. Board game
7. Packing box
10. Official positions
14. Worship
15. Paperwork (abbrev)
16. Snooped
17. Talk foolishly
18. Flower segment
19. Oyster gem
21. Species of duck

CIRCULAR:

CLOCKWISE
13. Look after
17. Annex or letter of the alphabet
20. Livelier
26. Singles
27. Take umbrage
30. Fish eggs
36. Label
37. Every twenty-four hours
38. Was told
39. Bury again
40. Abrasion

COUNTERCLOCKWISE
6. Toboggan
12. State firmly
25. Foreign
28. Celtic language
29. Consumed
31. Compass point
32. Sheltered side
33. Terminus
34. Food of the grass family
35. Intention

---

76 Odd Man Out   Level 4

1. **DILATORY, ADROITLY, TORRIDLY, IDOLATRY**

2. **ATE, FOR, NEW, WON**

In each case, which is the odd word out?

3. **INDEFINITE, PROLONG, ESTUARY, CANOPY**

4. **ALLOW, BORROW, CENT, FIST**

5. **TABLE, SELLING, NOTICE, FACETIOUS**

6. **CARTON, SETTEE, PANTRY, SPEECH**

Rhyming clue A leads to a solution beginning with A, clue B to one beginning with B, and so on through to Z. Having solved the clues, you must determine the only correct way to fit the answers into the grid.
This one is definitely for big brains only!

A. Back in early arts and how
   But not on straight and narrow now (6)
B. I'm to follow British still
   To upper limit, more would spill (4)
C. What spinal surgeons have to do
   Economies, to me and you (8)
D. Coin from the French, with feline on
   Or tube, once article has gone (5)
E. Put before bike or yard,
   Either way, you'll work out hard (8)
F. Almost free and nearly just
   If you're near Cannes, see it you must (6)
G. Let it out with left and right
   Sprinkly stuff makes make-up bright (7)
H. Part of ship, Northeastern English port
   And pal of Emu—the puppet sort (4)
I. Up above the earth so high
   Sort of fin light in the sky (2,6)

J. Passage here from A to B
   Smacking of frivolity (5)
K. I get one out of you. Explain
   Then, why none from champagne? (4)
L. Business so described's OK
   And so, not only crime may pay (6)
M. Blow it, miss, or go off form
   Or thing to keep your fingers warm (4)
N. This name is effeminate
   And in the main inadequate (4)
O. Theirs this simply cannot be
   Headless quite a time, we see (4)
P. Shakespearean adviser he! to royal Danes
   Then stabbed behind the arras for his pains (8)
Q. Not a lot of time in there—Just a snatch
   of lightning's glare? (5, 2, 1, 5)

R. Route beyond the thoroughfare
   Is not the place to stand and stare (7)
S. An address, perhaps to guarantee
   It's free in a democracy (6)
T. Right among the crooked touts
   They'll resolve their students' doubts (6)
U. Thus we stand, divided fall
   Hope Beckham's old mates are, after all (6)
V. I've a B reg, tell you what!
   This one's using words a lot (8)
W. Thrown beyond despised being
   In the grass it takes some seeing (8)
X. With treasure underneath that there
   HM Exports' task is clear (1, 5, 3, 4)
Y. Rye aid? No, more likely pot
   If foreign gangster's in the plot (6)
Z. The very top, the best one did
   In a dozen it has hid (6)

| 1. INVEIGLE | A. Exasperate B. Contend C. Cajole D. Complain |

| 2. IMBROGLIO | A. Brawl B. Entanglement C. Pattern D. Compendium |

| 3. PERNICIOUS | A. Rich B. Harmful C. Greedy D. Savage |

| 4. ABEYANCE | A. Obedience B. Servility C. Suspension D. Conversion |

| 5. CORPOREAL | A. Manageable B. Substantial C. Deadly D. Virtual |

| 6. TENEBROUS | A. Gloomy B. Shiny C. Nervous D. Excited |

In each case, which of the four words is the synonym?

A tough puzzle for expert solvers!

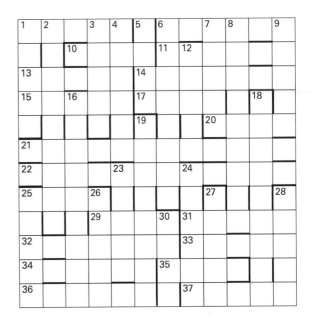

ACROSS

1. Know how to perform eastern combat (5)
6. From forest tree an injured lander (6)
10. Note yours truly, doctor (4)
11. Intertwined as ivy a caste member (6)
13. Aurally coarse fish (5)
14. Motoring club in the distance is an amazing event (7)
15. Orion star returns limb to one side (5)
17. Noble dear lad loses father (4)
20. Slack-sounding fruit (4)
21. Side of ditch neutralizes complaint (12)
22. Biblical book shows cake with seats I arranged (12)
25. Stir a log-roll (4)
29. Some Argentinian occipital bumps (4)
31. Score twice on behalf of heartless river (5)
32. I panic, a sort of Roman epicure (7)
33. Send chronological device back (5)
34. I tried to become more orderly (6)
35. Musical animals (4)
36. Backward American painter is like fat (6)
37. Aspect of the said fairies (5)

DOWN

1. Aurally pick up a gum tree! (5)
2. Questionable company girl raised in par (9)
3. Put off female animals outside (5)
4. Accommodation leased without starter for light meal (6)
5. Note clean up for carpel receptacle (4)
6. Pilot puts silly trivia in American chopper (8)
7. Faces many with defective sail (5)
8. Lift toe, rascal fumbles (9)
9. Even a bizarre obsolete birthmark (5)
12. Artist, back to front, on square screen (5)
16. Sugary compound is clued, go out (9)
18. Trio's cute rendition of metal work (9)
19. Funny bits, year book of animals long ago (8)
23. I'm embraced by bird with electronic picker (5)
24. Spenser's strike a very loud one? (6)
25. Nannies leave wartime group (5)
26. Some garlic itself is legal (5)
27. Accomplishes once the odd party comes first (5)
28. Old song is suitable, when heard (5)
30. Cane broken once in the North (4)

---

80 Figure It Out | Level 4

1. Which 1950s song begins with the words: "One for the money..."?
2. Which male actor played in the lead role in the 1970 film *Five Easy Pieces*?
3. Who recorded the hit single "Three Times a Lady"?
4. What was the name of the submarine captain in Jules Verne's novel *Twenty Thousand Leagues under the Sea*?
5. In which book of the Bible are the Four Horsemen of the Apocalypse mentioned?
6. Which US actress starred alongside Hugh Grant in the 1993 British comedy *Four Weddings and a Funeral*?
7. In the hit movie *Seven*, which actor played detective alongside Morgan Freeman?
8. Who recorded the 1976 song, "50 Ways to Leave Your Lover"?
9. Who, with Jane Fonda and Dolly Parton, made up the female threesome in the 1980 film comedy *Nine to Five*?
10. What is the name of the line of latitude that runs round the Earth at 23° 26´ south of the equator?

These questions are all linked to numbers in some way. Can you answer them all?

Expand Your Mind

This section calls into question the way in which we perceive the world around us. Can we always believe our eyes? Do our minds ever play tricks on us? And if so, why? Tackle the puzzles in this section and you'll soon discover that even to highly-developed senses and resourceful minds, things are not always what they seem.

OPTICAL ILLUSIONS

An illusion is defined as "a false conception or notion;" something which deceives us. In this section you'll find plenty of deceptive images, and you'll probably find that, however much you look at them, your mind will remain deceived. Take the picture below as an example. What do you see? The chances are that you'll be looking at a triangle, with its corners set in each of the pink segments. But actually, if you look closely, you'll realize that the picture consists only of the three pink shapes—the triangle itself is simply a figment of your imagination.

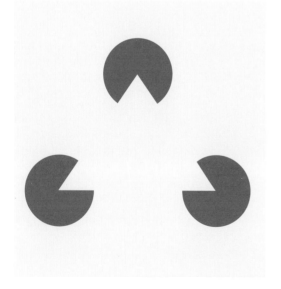

FILLING IN THE GAPS

So why do we imagine a shape that isn't there? In this example, the brain finds it hard to comprehend or categorize the three irregular pink shapes, which don't fit neatly with the simpler, more easy-to-recognize shapes that it prefers to perceive. So the brain fills in the gaps and creates an image that it can understand more easily. As a consequence, an imaginary triangle appears before our eyes—or rather, in our mind's eye; it doesn't exist on the page at all.

HOW DO YOU THINK?

Of course, not everybody's mind works in exactly the same way. Some optical illusions are perceived differently by different people. There are a number of famous illusions that can be perceived as one of two alternative images. In the example here, first published in 1915 by cartoonist W. E. Hill, do you see a young girl or an old woman? If you can see both, which do you see first? Studies have shown that younger people tend to see the image as a young girl, while older people see a picture of the elderly woman. This suggests that your brain interprets an image depending on your own experience. In this example, some people find it difficult to see both pictures, so if you're having trouble, read the clue opposite left, which should help.

ILLUSION CLUE: The young woman's chin is the old woman's nose.

SEE FOR YOURSELF

If you really want to find out more about how your own mind interprets images, the best thing to do is to get started with this section of puzzles! We've packed all sorts of visual tricks and problems into it. Some of them will challenge you to solve in your head a puzzle that you would normally see as a practical, hands-on problem. For example, each of the rope puzzles (e.g. puzzle 1) asks you to work out, just by looking at the picture, whether or not the twisted rope will become a knot when pulled. You are required to visualize in your mind the process of the rope being pulled in order to find the answer. The same is true of the cube puzzles (e.g. puzzle 6), where you must imagine putting the cube together, and how it will look when complete. You are likely to find such problems tricky at first, but that's why we've called this section "Expand Your Mind." By setting yourself a variety of visual challenges, you'll discover just what your mind is capable of.

A-MAZE YOURSELF

You'll also find a number of mazes in this section, and as usual, these will get gradually harder as you build your way up through the different levels. When solving a maze, your brain is forced to think ahead, to work out which direction you should take before you actually get there. You'll find this gets easier the more mazes you tackle.

We've also included a number of puzzles that ask you to look past the obvious way of doing things; you'll discover what we mean by this as you go along!

TAKING SHAPE

You might also want to keep some plain paper and a pair of scissors handy as you being this section, because there are a few tangram puzzles for you to solve. If you're not familiar with tangrams, you will find that the idea is fairly simple. Start with a variety of small shapes, and put them together to form the larger shape that you've been given on the page. In practice, the process is not so easy. If you're feeling ambitious, you can attempt to solve these in your head, but you might find it easier (and more enjoyable) to trace and cut out the shapes and put them together by hand. Either way, it's a lot tougher than it looks!

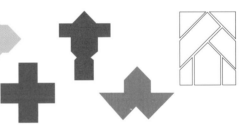

Shape up: tangrams can make an engaging practical puzzle.

TAKE YOUR TIME

Among the set of puzzles you're about to face, you are likely to find many that you will not be able to solve at first. A number of these puzzles will require careful thought, but we recommend that you don't give up too easily and check the solutions! As with many of the puzzles in this book, you may find that taking a break from a particular puzzle and returning to it later will help you see it in a different way, and will enable you to get past the mental block that's been hindering you.

PREPARE YOURSELF

Now you're ready to enter the world of visual puzzles. Remember to take them one step at a time. There's no need to rush. Good luck!

Expand Your Mind

Level 1

We're giving you the chance to find your feet on Level 1, where you'll be solving the easiest puzzles of the section.

Puzzles 1–20

1 Knotty Problem | Level 1

NO

If you pull both ends of this rope, will it form a knot?

2 Rambling Sentence | Level 1

Here's a maze with a difference. Starting at the top with the letter T, you must attempt to spell out a complete sentence by visiting every single letter in the maze once, and only once. Can you solve the puzzle?

HINT
If you take the correct route through the maze, your finished sentence will have four words.

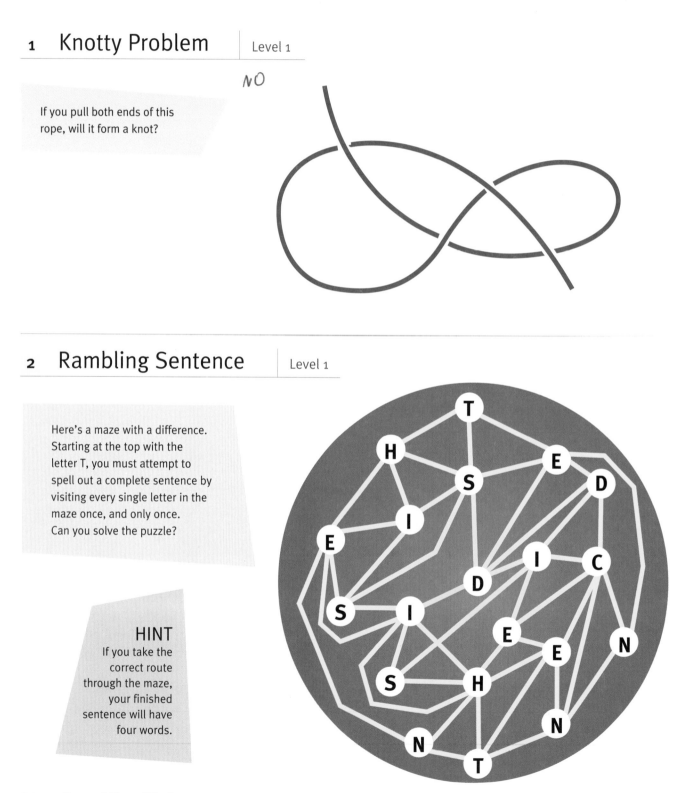

3   Glass Act

The four matches at right represent a glass. Can you put the cherry in the glass, moving only two of the matches?

HINT
The glass may not stay the same way up!

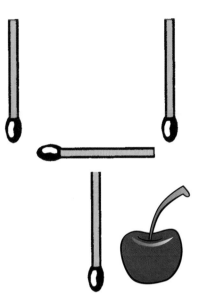

4   Circle Sizes

Which of the inside circles is bigger – the one on the right or the one on the left?

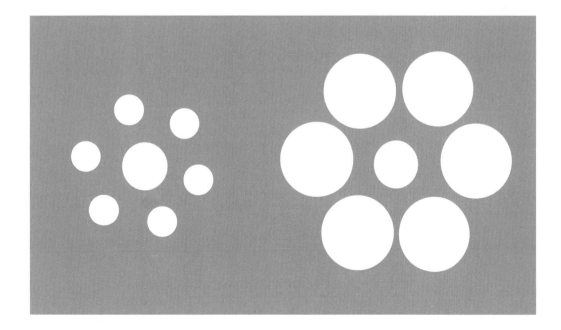

5 Going Dotty | Level 1

Here are nine dots in a square. Your challenge is to move only four of these dots so that you end up with a smaller square that has only three dots in each row and column. Can you do it?

HINT
The dots that change position will all be moving toward a common central point.

6 Cube Creation | Level 1

Which of the following cubes below can be made using the flat one laid out here?

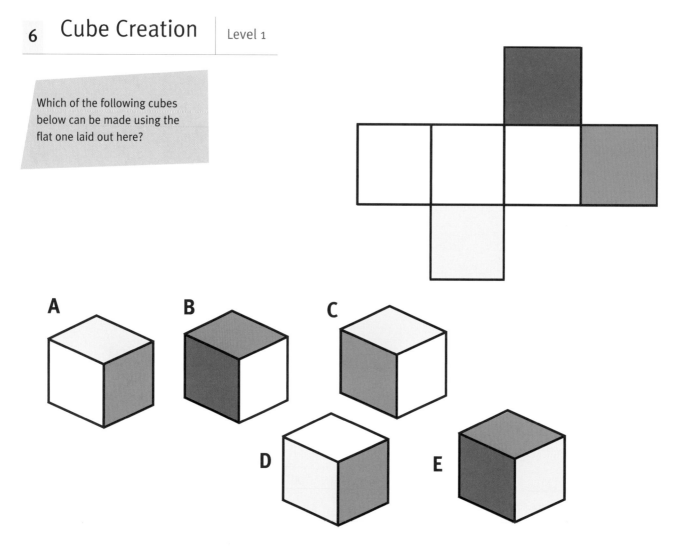

A

B

C

D

E

7 Camping Out   Level 1

On this campsite, each of the tents in the four corners would like some privacy and want to be separate from all the other tents. Meanwhile, the four tents in the middle of the camping area are a big group all together, and they would like to be kept apart from those other four tents. What's more, they are insisting that their area is square. You can only use four straight fences to keep everybody on the campsite happy—where should you place them?

8 Squaring Up   Level 1

For this puzzle, as with other puzzles of the same type in this section, you may want to recreate the given shapes on paper or cardboard in order to solve the problem. Here, you have six shapes, four identical to A, and two identical to B. Your job is to put the six shapes together to form one complete square. Give it a try!

2 X

4 X

B

A

9 Cross Purposes | Level 1

Using the shapes shown below, which make up a rectangle (trace and cut them out if you wish), can you first make a cross, then the other three given shapes?

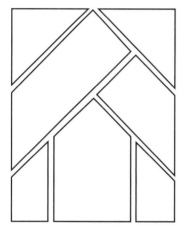

10 Coin Puzzle | Level 1

Imagine these circles are eight coins. The object is to make four stacks of two coins each in four moves. A move consists of jumping one coin over two coins and stopping on top of the next coin. The two coins that are jumped over can be next to each other or in a stack.

HINT
You might be trying to do this one in your head—it's a lot easier to grab eight coins and try it for real!

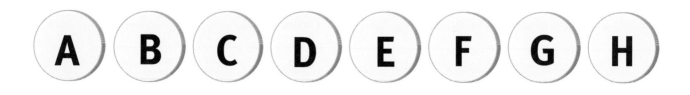

11 Counting Skills | Level 1

Do your eyes ever deceive you?
How many rods can you count
in the opposite figure?

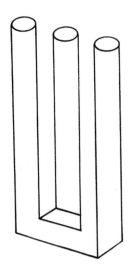

12 Thorny Maze | Level 1

Can you find your way
through this mass of
thorns and brambles
to the tasty looking
fruit in the center?
How quickly can
you get there?

13   Equal Shares | Level 1

A house stands on a square estate, as shown. Within the same estate are ten trees. Five siblings have inherited the estate. So they can all have an equal share of the property, they wish to divide up the land so they each have a piece of land of the same shape and size, making sure that each piece of land includes two of the trees on the estate. Can you divide up the area to fulfill their wishes?

HINT
Start by thinking about how the two trees nearest the central point of the square might be enclosed.

14   Turn It Down | Level 1

Look at the opposite discs. What is the smallest number that must be moved in order to make the triangle point downward?

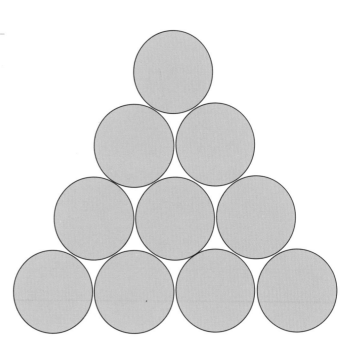

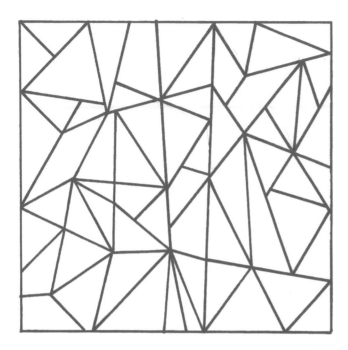

Somewhere in this picture there is a perfect five-pointed star. Can you locate it?

16 No Right Turn | Level 1

If you've ever gotten completely lost on a road because you couldn't make the right turn that you needed to, this maze is for you! You have to travel from IN to OUT, without making a single right turn. Can you manage it?

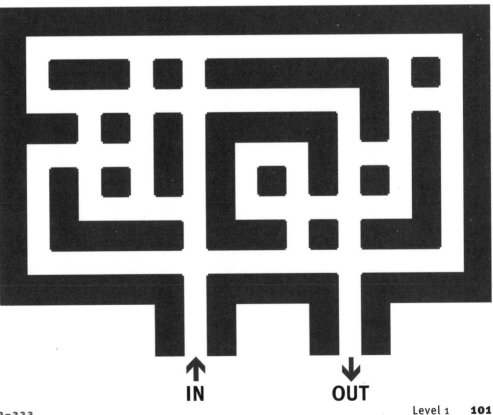

IN   OUT

17 Squaring Up | Level 1

You need 16 shapes (cut them out if you wish): there are four as shape A, four as shape B, and eight as shape C. Can you use them all to form a square?

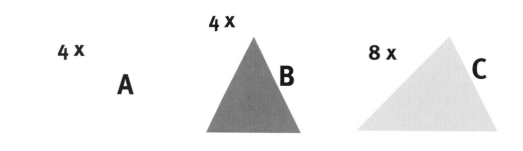

4 x

4 x

A

B

8 x

C

18 Snail Trails | Level 1

Imagine each of these pink dots are snails. These snails all want to escape from the grid, but none of them will cross the trail of another. In the end, each exits the grid at one of the squares marked with a number. The number explains how many squares the snail moved through to get out of the grid (not including the square they're in now). They can move horizontally or vertically but not diagonally. Can you draw in the path of each snail? Remember, the trails must NOT cross!

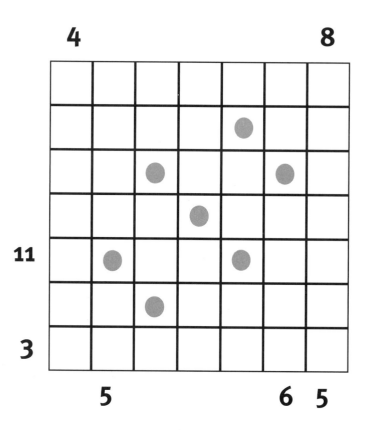

HINT
When you've completed the puzzle, every single square of the grid should have been used.

19 Going Straight Level 1

Take a close look at this picture. Are the thick lines straight or do they bend? Take your time to decide!

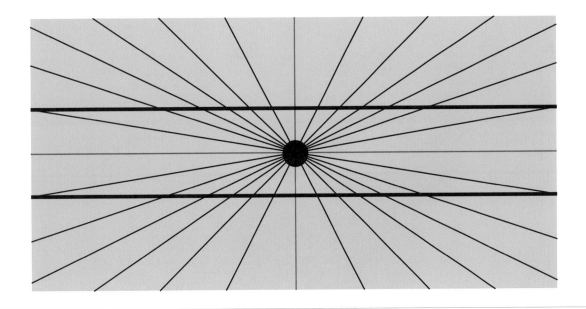

20 Letter Lines Level 1

Can you draw the following envelope in one single line, without retracing or crossing any lines, or lifting your pencil?

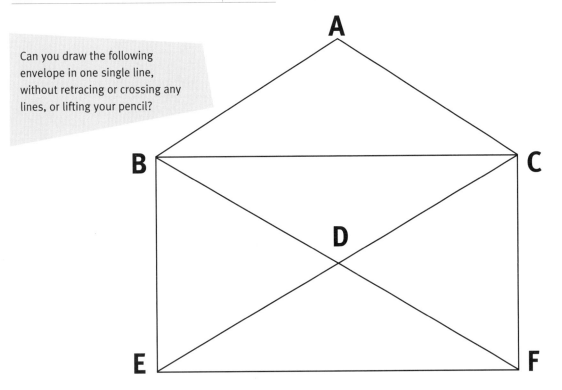

Expand Your Mind

Puzzles 21–40

Level 2

Now you've reached the start of Level 2, so don't be surprised if you find the puzzles are becoming a little bit tougher.

21 Knot a Problem? Level 2

If you pull both ends of this rope, will it form a knot?

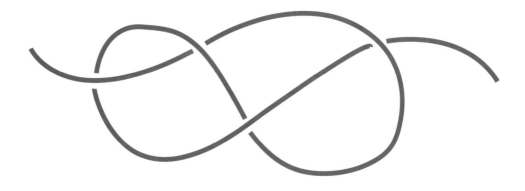

22 Jump Right In Level 2

Place six counters, three of each color, as shown. The object is to move the blue counters to spaces occupied by the pink counters, and vice versa. You may move a counter into empty adjacent squares, and jump over one counter at a time into an empty square.

HINT
The correct solution should take you exactly 15 moves. Can you find it?

23 Brain Trouble | Level 2

Read quickly through paragraph 1 and see how many letter Fs you can count. Then check the answers and see if you got it right. Read paragraph 2 just as quickly, and see if you notice anything wrong with it. If not, try reading it more slowly and you may spot a few errors.

2

MANY PEOPLE THINK THAT THAT OPTICAL ILLUSIONS ARE ARE TRICKS OF THE EYE, BUT THEY THEY ARE NOT. THEY ARE TRICKS TRICKS OF THE BRAIN – OUR EYES EYES SEE THEM AND OUR BRAINS BRAINS MISINTERPRET THEM.

1

RUFUS REACHED THE FINISHING LINE IN FRONT OF ALL OF HIS FRIENDS. HE WAS PROUD OF THIS FINE ACHIEVEMENT, ESPECIALLY SINCE HIS SPEED WAS THE FASTEST OF THE YEAR SO FAR.

24 Counting Up | Level 2

Count how many perfect squares of all possible sizes are hidden in the shape of the dots. The dots should be in the corners of the squares.

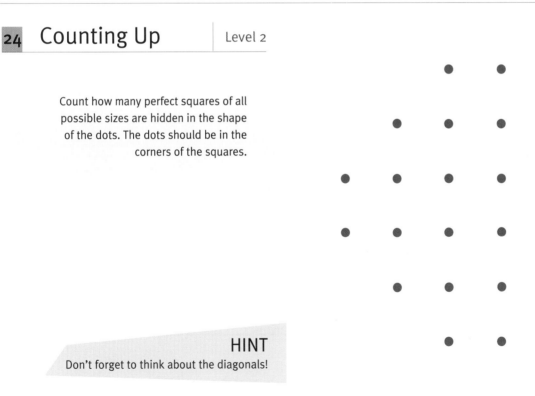

HINT
Don't forget to think about the diagonals!

25 | Twisting Triangle | Level 2

Take a look at this odd-looking triangle. How many pieces of wood do you think would be needed to construct it?

26 | Driving Test | Level 2

This is a driving test with a difference. Starting at the red dot, you must travel through every one of the 64 blocks in the square. But in doing so, your aim is to make as many turns on your journey as you possibly can. What is the maximum number you can make? You can finish your journey in any square you choose.

HINT
Use a pencil to test your routes, since you will no doubt need more than one attempt!

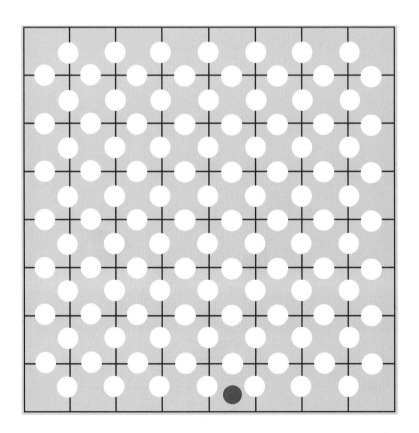

27

Chop and Change | Level 2

Lay out twelve used matchsticks or cocktail sticks on a table to form four equal squares as shown. Then try to remove and replace four matches so that you form three equal squares of the same size as the ones shown here.

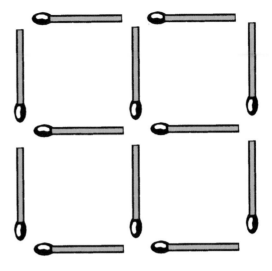

3-D Dilemma | Level 2

When the shape at right is folded to form a cube, just one of the following can be produced. Which one?

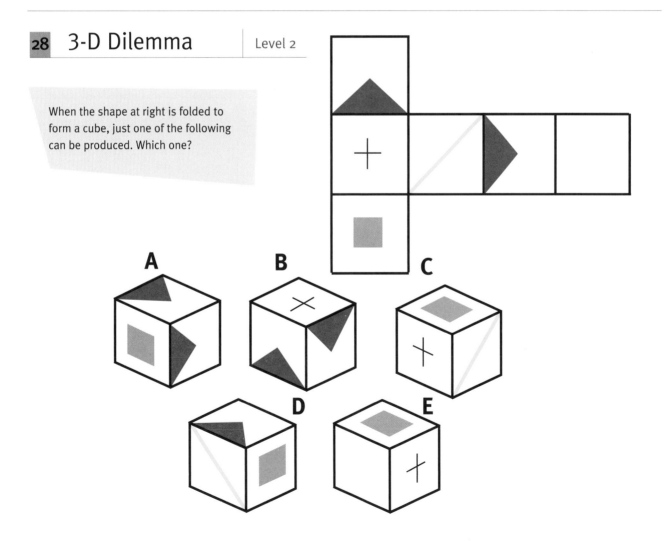

Cog Confusion | Level 2

Which of the four weights will rise
and which will fall when the handle
is turned as shown?

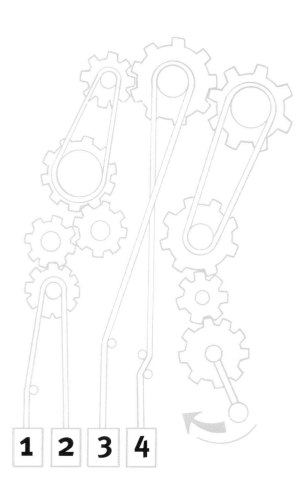

1 2 3 4

Straight Through | Level 2

Cross through all the dots using
four straight lines, without folding
the paper or taking your pencil off
the surface of the page.

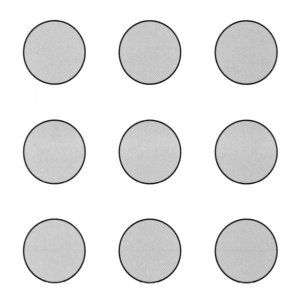

By the Lake

Level 2

Four wealthy men own cottages close to a lake. However, four campers have decided to pitch their tents in front of the cottages, closer to the lake. The cottage owners, wanting to keep the lake to themselves, decide to erect a wall to keep the campers out. They wish to keep each of their houses and the lake inside the wall, with the tents on the outside. How can they erect the shortest possible wall that will achieve this?

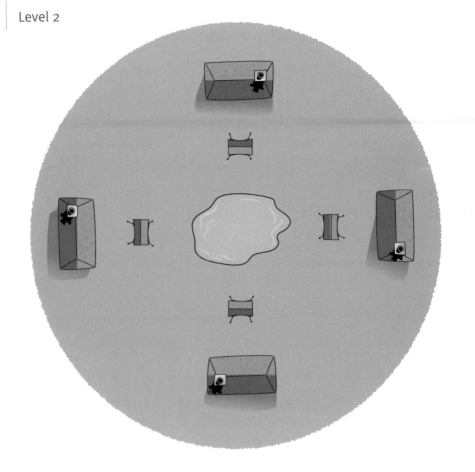

32

Building Blocks

Level 2

This is a tricky one! You have to create a triangle out of seven pieces, which you can trace and cut out of paper or cardboard if you like, in order to solve this puzzle. You'll need one piece shaped like A, three like B and three like C. With these seven segments, you must build an equilateral triangle; that is, a triangle whose three sides are all of equal length.

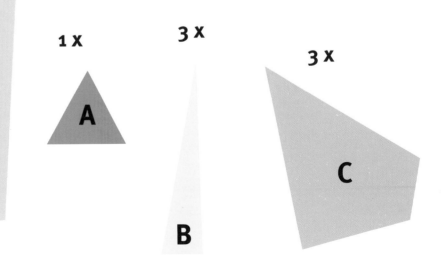

1 X

3 X

3 X

33 Vicious Circle | Level 2

This is a tricky puzzle, because there are ten shapes making up this circle, some with curved edges. Can you put the shapes together to make the three pictures shown? Trace and cut out the shapes to solve this puzzle if you wish.

34 Fair and Square | Level 2

Can you draw a perfect square around the figure at right so that each side passes through one of the crosses and none of the sides touches the figure? There's just one hitch—the lines of the square you draw must not be parallel to those of the existing square.

X

X

X

X

35 In and Out

Level 2

This is one maze you wouldn't want to attempt on foot! Luckily we're giving you the chance to solve it on paper instead. Starting at the bottom arrow, you must get to the tree at the center of the maze, then finish up at the other side. Try not to get too lost!

↑ OUT

↑ IN

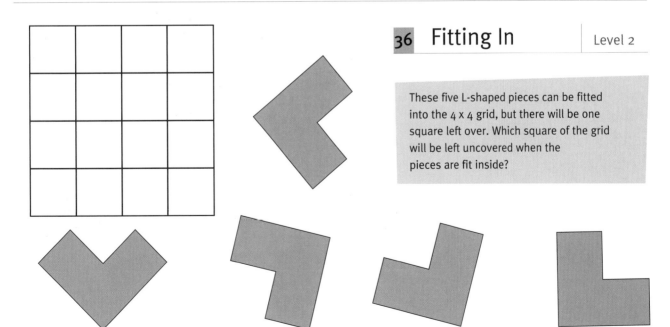

36 Fitting In

Level 2

These five L-shaped pieces can be fitted into the 4 x 4 grid, but there will be one square left over. Which square of the grid will be left uncovered when the pieces are fit inside?

37 Word Square | Level 2

Can you fit all of these six words into the 4 x 4 square?

AREA
BALD
BRAT
DAFT
DEED
LEAF

HINT
Some of the words will read the same across as down.

38 Fair Shares | Level 2

This sponge cake contains delicious fresh strawberries. A mother wants to divide it into four pieces for her children, so that each piece is of identical shape and size and contains three of the strawberries. How can she do this?

HINT
All the cuts the mother makes will consist of vertical or horizontal lines (rather than diagonal).

39 Pizza the Action | Level 2

Due to staff shortages, this pizza delivery boy has to make 21 deliveries in the same journey. To relieve the boredom, he has set himself the task that he will not travel along any road more than once. So, starting at point A, can you lead him to point B, passing through every one of the 21 delivery points, and never going over a road twice? Use the numbered points to describe the order you do it in.

40 Cube Confusion | Level 2

Stare at this cube for a few seconds. Is the blue dot on a front face or a back face?

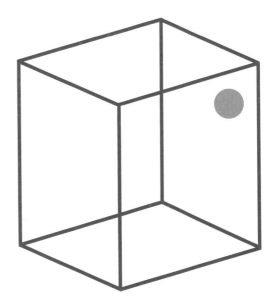

41 Shape Sorting Level 3

As with the other puzzles of this nature, you may want to trace and cut out the pieces making up the first shape in order to solve the puzzle. The 11 pieces below make up an oblong shape as shown. Can you rearrange them to make each of the other pictured shapes?

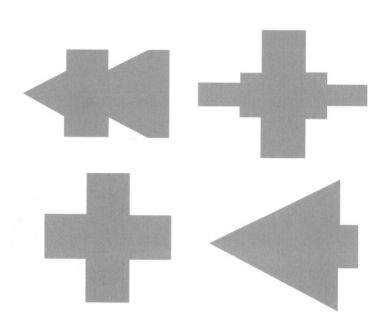

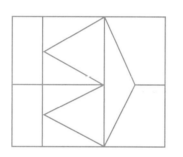

42 Star Seekers Level 3

Use 18 matches to create the pyramid shape pictured opposite. By rearranging six of those matches, can you form a symmetrical star?

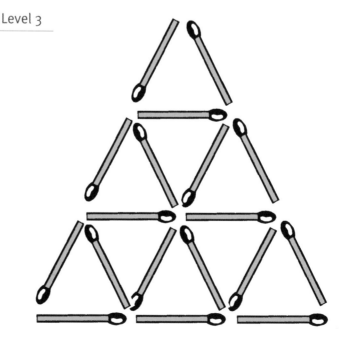

For this puzzle, you need 11 shapes as follows:
1 as shape A, 2 as shape B, 2 as shape C, 1 as shape
D, 3 as shape E and 2 as shape F. Then, you simply
need to make them into a square. Easy!

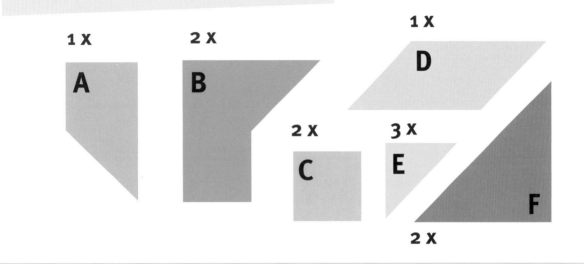

44 Middle Ground | Level 3

Look at the picture below.
One of the three dots is at
the exact center of the circle.
Which one?

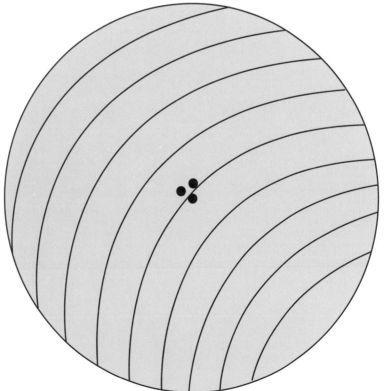

This puzzle consists of seven shapes that form a square as shown below. Trace and cut them out, then attempt to create the four different people pictures using all seven shapes each time.

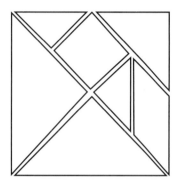

---

46 Double Squared | Level 3

Draw the shape at right, which consists of a smaller square on the end of another square four times its size, on a piece of paper. Then attempt to make two cuts to divide the shape in such a way that the resulting segments will, when arranged differently, form one perfect square.

Look at the ten cats within the circle. So they don't encroach on one another's territory, can you draw three smaller circles inside the bigger one, which will mean that each cat is in a separate segment from all the others?

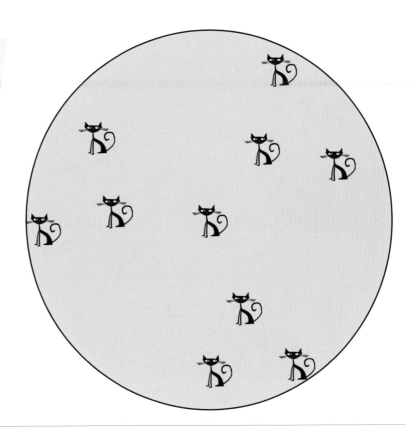

HINT
The circles you draw will all be of the same size.

48 It's Amazing! | Level 3

Get from the top to the bottom by spelling out AMAZING in horizontal or vertical steps — no diagonals!

A																			
M	A	Z	N	I	Z	I	N	G	A	M	A	Z	I	N	M	I	N	G	A	M	A	N	A	G	N

M	A	Z	N	I	Z	I	N	G	A	M	A	Z	I	N	M	I	N	G	A	M	A	N	A	G	N
A	Z	I	N	G	A	N	I	A	N	G	Z	I	A	M	A	Z	Z	A	N	I	Z	I	N	A	I
N	I	N	Z	A	M	A	Z	M	I	M	A	N	G	A	N	G	I	M	A	M	M	A	G	A	Z
G	A	G	A	M	Z	I	Z	A	Z	A	G	N	A	M	I	I	Z	A	G	A	Z	I	G	M	A
A	M	A	I	Z	G	N	G	A	M	A	Z	I	Z	A	Z	N	Z	I	N	A	G	N	N	A	Z
Z	A	Z	N	A	A	M	A	Z	I	N	I	G	N	I	I	Z	A	A	G	M	A	Z	I	N	G
I	A	I	G	M	G	N	I	N	G	A	N	M	A	Z	Z	A	M	M	A	N	I	Z	A	M	A
N	G	N	G	A	M	A	Z	M	A	M	G	A	M	I	N	G	A	I	Z	G	A	M	A	Z	I
G	A	N	I	Z	A	Z	I	N	Z	I	A	M	A	N	G	A	M	A	Z	I	N	G	Z	G	N

| | | | | | | | | | | | | | | | | | | | | | | | | G |

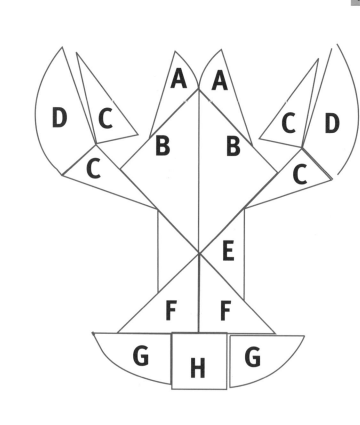

Trace this picture, cut out the 17 pieces, then try to make a square and a circle out of them.

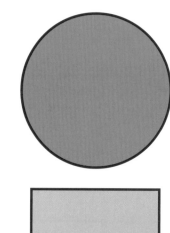

=

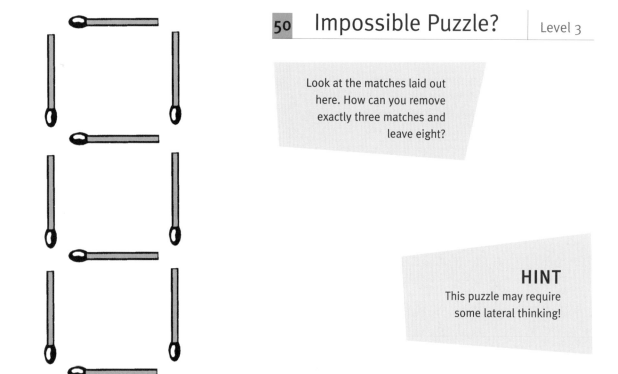

50 Impossible Puzzle? | Level 3

Look at the matches laid out here. How can you remove exactly three matches and leave eight?

HINT
This puzzle may require some lateral thinking!

51 Latin Cross | Level 3

Here, you'll need to trace five shapes, one exactly like shape A, one as shape B, and three as shape C. Then arrange them so they form a Latin cross, as shown.

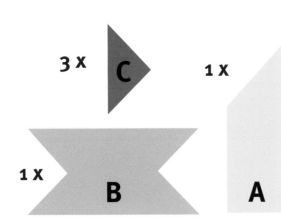

52 Tricky Triangles | Level 3

How many triangles are there in this figure?

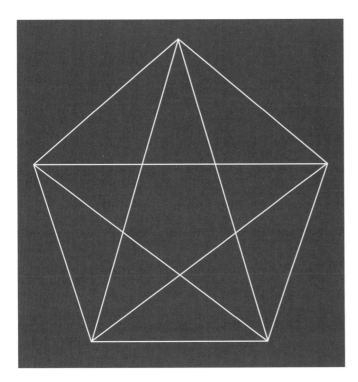

53 Knot Again!

This one's a trickier knot puzzle. So what happens if you pull both ends? Does it make a knot or not?

54 Cube Calculations

When the shape at right is folded to form a cube, it will make just one of the cubes below. Which one?

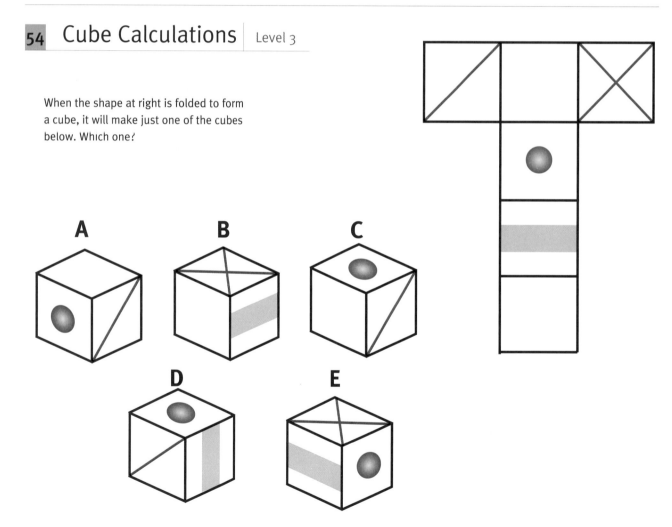

A

B

C

D

E

55 Perfect Match | Level 3

The shape on the left could fit on top of which of the five shapes A–E to form a perfect circle? Cutting them out is cheating!

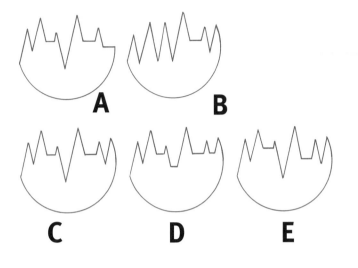

56 Canine Concerns | Level 3

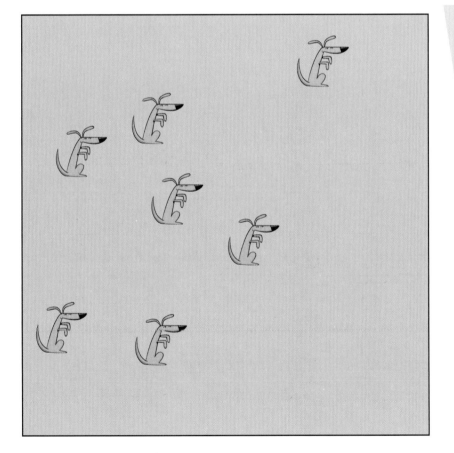

A man has been asked to look after seven dogs, but it turns out they all dislike each other. To keep them apart, he must place three straight fences across his field so that each dog has its own separate space. Can you help him?

HINT
Each dog's space will be of a different shape and size.

57 Hampton Court Maze | Level 3

Whether or not you've visited it for real, why not attempt to get through England's most famous maze, found in the gardens of Hampton Court. You must find your way to the middle (two dots) as quickly as possible.

58 Lost Matches | Level 3

Lay out 17 used matches or cocktail sticks so they form six equal squares as shown. Now take away five matches to leave just three squares.

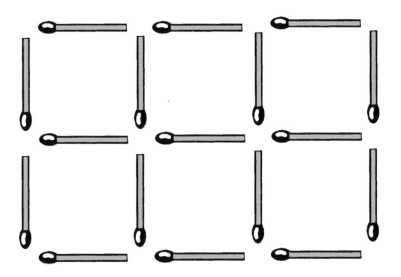

59 Greek Cross | Level 3

Draw or trace the shape of a Greek cross (as shown at right) onto a piece of paper or cardboard. Now, divide this cross using just two straight cuts so that the pieces, when put together differently, will form a square.

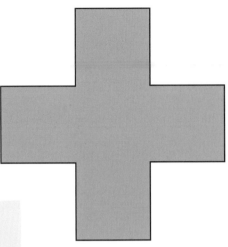

HINT
The two cuts you make will converge on a corner.

60 Broken Board | Level 3

A chessboard has been broken into eight pieces. Can you put those pieces back together to form a perfect 8 x 8 board? The easiest way to cut them out is from graph paper, or by drawing a grid of squares onto plain paper first.

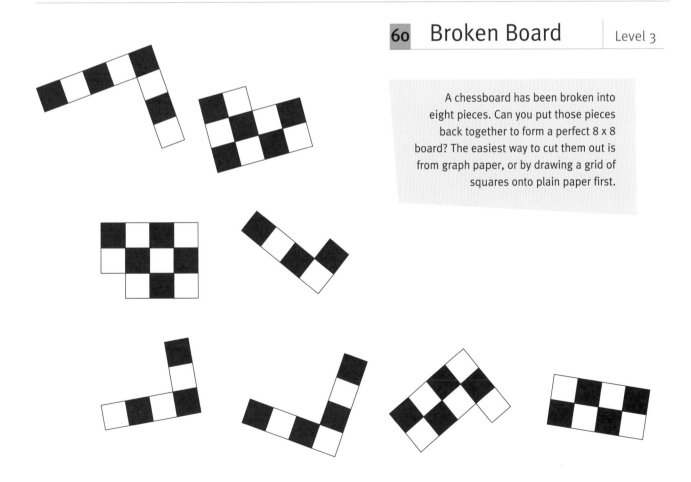

Expand Your Mind

Level 4

At last you've reached the final level—do you think you're up to the challenge?

Puzzles 61–80

61 Moving Stairway | Level 4

Take a look at this set of steps. Is the small dot at the front of the staircase or the back? And which way are the steps actually leading?

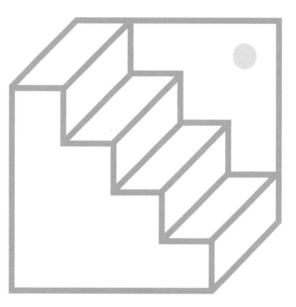

62 Where to Cross | Level 4

Look at the 64 dots in this square. Can you put a cross on eight different dots, so that no two crosses are on the same row, column, or diagonal?

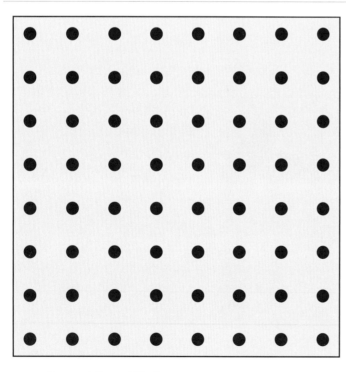

63 Hip to Be Square | Level 4

More cutting out required! You will need nine pieces, three as shape A, three as B, and three as C. Put them together to form one perfect square, or three smaller squares. You'll find it easier to create the three smaller squares. Making the bigger single square will be more satisfying. Take your time!

3 x

A

3 x

B

3 x

C

64 Clever Cogs | Level 4

Here's an ingenious coffee-pouring machine! Your job is to work out which way to turn handles A and B in order to pour a cup of coffee.

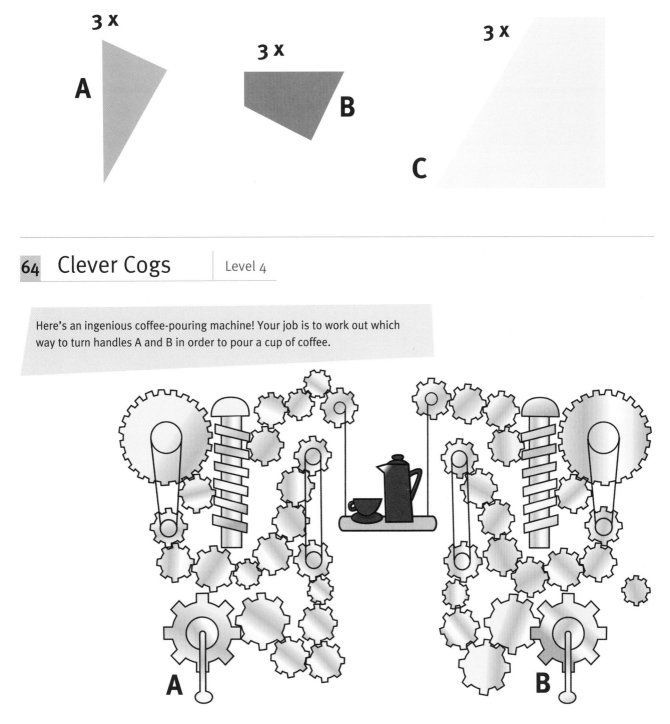

A

B

65 | Cherry Pie | Level 4

Another tasty dessert to divide up! This time there are four people who want a piece of pie, and each piece must be exactly the same size and shape. This would be easy enough, although they also each want one cherry on their piece, which makes things more difficult! Can you divide up the pie so that each of these four fussy people will have what they want?

66 | Pentominoes | Level 4

Pentominoes were invented by California mathematician Solomon W. Golomb. One pentomino consists of five small squares. There are 12 pentominoes in a set, as shown here. Use some graph paper to cut out the shapes yourself, then try completing the five tasks listed at right.

1. Using any four pentominoes, make a 4 x 5 rectangle.
2. Using any five pentominoes, make a 5 x 5 square.
3. Using any six pentominoes, make a 5 x 6 rectangle.
4. Using any seven pentominoes make a 5 x 7 rectangle.
5. Using any eight pentominoes, make a 4 x 10 rectangle.

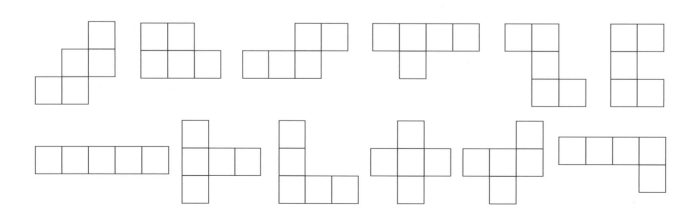

67 The Hexagon | Level 4

You'll need to cut out five shapes exactly like the ones shown. Then, simply make a hexagon out of them!

68 School's Out | Level 4

A student at a strict boarding school wants to escape for a night out. At the school, there are 145 doors, and only nine of them are closed (marked by blue blocks). The student (represented by the red dot) must get to the exit (letter E), but to ensure an alarm doesn't go off, there are certain rules he has to follow. First, to pass through a closed door, he must first go through exactly 8 open doors before each one. He doesn't have to go through every open door in the school, but he must go through every room and all nine closed doors. Can you help him enjoy an evening out on the town?

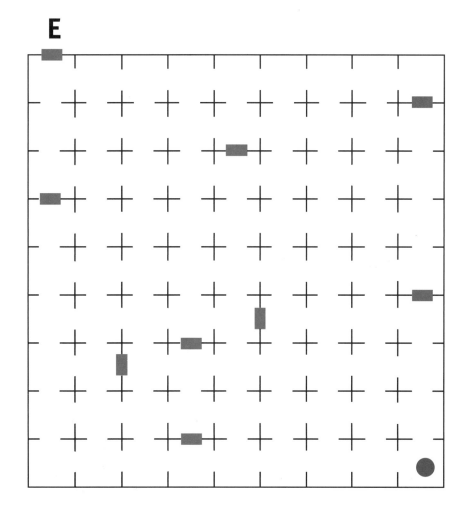

Can you find your way from the top left
arrow to the bottom right arrow?
How quickly can you get through?

70 Four Thought | Level 4

Lay out eight matchsticks or cocktail
sticks in a square as shown. Using
four other matchsticks, can you divide
the square into two parts of the same
shape and area?

71

Bits and Pieces | Level 4

A square is divided into eight pieces as shown at right—trace and cut them out if you wish. Then see if you can create the four given shapes using the eight segments.

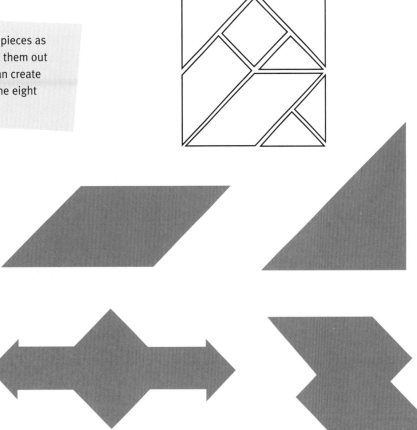

Two from One | Level 4

This is a tough one. Look at the shape of a Greek cross. Your job is to divide a Greek cross into the fewest number of pieces that will fit back together to form TWO Greek crosses of similar size. Good luck!

73 Constellations

Can you split up these stars
so there are five groups
of three within the square?
The areas in which each
group of stars is enclosed
should be more or less equal.

74 Five Cubed

Which of the five cubes
can be made from the
pattern shown?

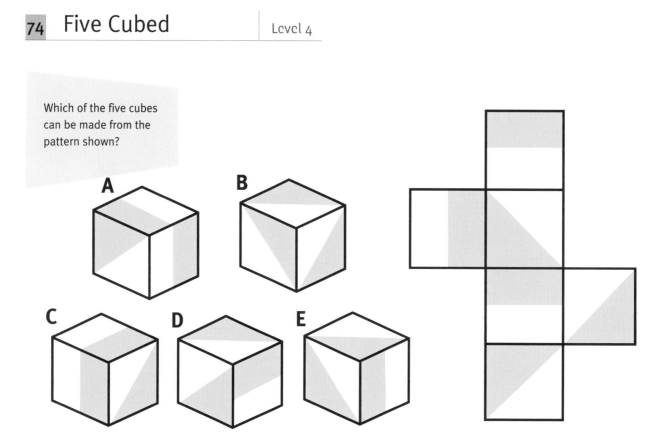

Match It Up | Level 4

Lay out 16 matches as shown. Now remove four of these matches to leave four triangles.

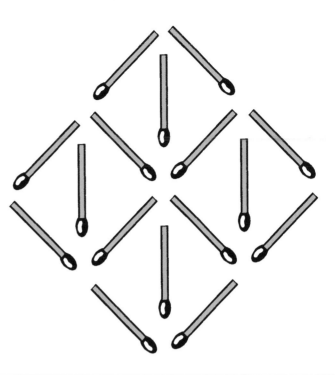

Can you get through this tricky maze, starting at the pink dot and finishing at the purple dot?

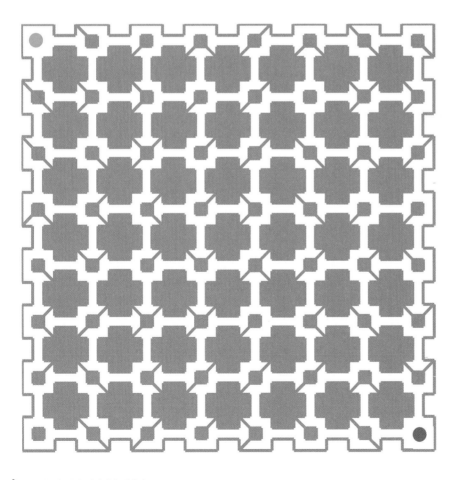

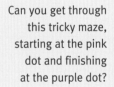

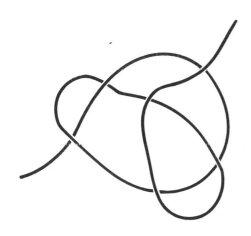

If you pull both ends of this rope, will it form a knot?

78 Happy Holidays   Level 4

Eight colleagues, living in eight suburbs of the same city (numbered 1–8), decide to take a break from work at one of the more attractive surrounding towns. The railway connections forbid them from traveling through each other's suburbs, or through the city itself, and they are obliged to stop at the first town they come to. Letters A–H represent the towns and the ends of all journeys. Colleagues 1–4 decide that they will all vacation at the same place, and so do colleagues 5–8, but colleagues 5–8 want to avoid the first group, and so decide to go to a place where 1–4 cannot go. Can you work out at which two places each group spends their vacation?

This time the square is made up of 7 segments. Cut out the shapes, then attempt to recreate the 5 figures using those shapes.

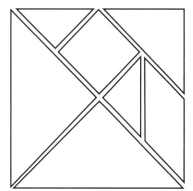

This is a version of the popular sliding-block puzzle. Cut out eight squares of paper numbered 1–8. Set them out as shown in A, with an empty space at the bottom right-hand corner. Your task is to move one block at a time into the empty space so that eventually the numbers are arranged in consecutive order, as in grid B. How quickly can you do it?

A

3	2	1
4	5	6
8	7	

B

1	2	3
4	5	6
7	8	

Reason It Out

Our powers of reasoning are much like any of our other problem-solving skills—the more they are used, the more efficient they become. In this section you'll find a variety of puzzles that require you to reason your way to the answer. There are likely to be a number of different ways of doing so, and although some may take you longer than others, the most important thing is to reach the correct answer, rather than how you get there. By the time you've made your way through the first couple of levels, you should notice an improvement in your powers of reasoning. You are training your brain every step of the way!

NUMBER TROUBLES

If you've already had a glance through this section, you'll notice that it includes a lot of puzzles based on numbers. But don't make the mistake of assuming that mathematical prowess is of ultimate importance here. The majority of these puzzles are testing your powers of deduction rather than your powers of multiplication or division! Take a look at the problem below, which is solved using algebra. Although these puzzles can look complex, they are really based on logic, and are often much simpler than they might seem at first glance. However, if you get stuck on such a problem, don't just resort to checking the solutions; you can always use trial and error to reach the correct answer.

IT'S ELEMENTARY

PIZZA PIECES

Here's a simple example of algebra being used to solve a puzzle. There are many examples of this type of puzzle in the pages to come, so if you're not familiar with this method, reading through the example may help.

Some very hungry children are eating pizza. By reading the clues below, can you work out how many slices each had?

1. Amy, Belinda and Carrie ate 24 slices between them.
2. The number of slices eaten by Amy and Belinda together is the same as the number eaten by Carrie.
3. The number of slices eaten by Belinda and Carrie, when added together, is equal to five times the number that Amy ate.

If Amy's number of pizza slices is A, Belinda's number of slices is B and Carrie's number of slices is C, from each of these statements we can make the following conclusions:

1) $A + B + C = 24$
2) $A + B = C$
3) $B + C = 5A$

Now can you work out who ate what? Check the workings (opposite page, at bottom right) if you get stuck or to see if you got the answer right.

Many children spend hours inventing codes so that they can share secret messages with their friends. It's just as much fun when you're older! With a little imagination, it's possible to create a simple code that can be extremely difficult to crack. In this section there are many such codes to test your deductive powers. Often they require you to think laterally rather than searching for the obvious answer. It may take you a long while to figure some of them out, but don't give up too easily. Often the solution to these problems will come to you in a split second of inspiration!

REST YOUR MIND

Have you ever been completely stumped by a puzzle, and despite struggling for hours, you've had no progress? Then the next day, after a good night's sleep, you go back to it and suddenly the answer is staring you in the face? Bear this in mind when you tackle this section. If you do find yourself struggling with a puzzle, and begin to feel frustrated with it, the best thing you can do is leave it for a while, preferably overnight, and come back to it. Often the solution will seem obvious in the morning. This is because by sleeping, you are giving your body and mind time to rest, and are allowing new ideas time to take shape in your head. Just as important, you've interrupted the train of thought that was previously leading you nowhere. Return to the puzzle refreshed and ready to look at it from a different angle, and your chances of success will be much greater.

Taking a break from a tricky puzzle will refresh your mind.

DON'T JUMP IN!

Sometimes, by thinking about how to solve a puzzle before actually jumping in and attempting it, you can save yourself lots of time. There might just be a pattern to your answer that makes it that much easier to solve. A German mathematician proved this point when, as a 7-year-old schoolboy, he was asked to add together all the numbers 1–100. To his teacher's surprise, he found the answer in record time. When asked how he'd done it, he replied that he'd noticed that the total of the first and last number of the series always came to 101, i.e. 1 + 100 = 101, 2 + 99 = 101, and so on. So he'd simply multiplied the number 101 by half the amount of numbers, which was 50, to get to the result 101 x 50 = 5050. By looking carefully at the problem, he'd found a quick and simple solution. Some puzzles in this section do involve a mathematical pattern in this way (e.g. puzzle 32), while many of the codes and sequence puzzles conceal other types of patterns. Most importantly, there are plenty of puzzles that will prove themselves much simpler with the aid of a little forethought.

GIVE IT A GO

Many of these puzzles look or sound complicated. Don't be put off. It's all too easy to take a first look at a problem and decide you can't solve it, but often it's just a case of finding the correct way to tackle it, and then it becomes simple. Start these puzzles at the beginning, and build up your confidence, along with your brain power, as you make your way up to the trickiest challenges at Level 4.

PIZZA PIECES SOLUTION
If A + B = C (no. 2), then we can change the first equation to read C + C = 24, or 2C = 24, so C=12. So Carrie ate 12 pizza slices. If B + C = 5A (no. 3), we can also change the first equation to read A + 5A = 24. So 6A = 24, and A = 24/6, so A = 4. Now if A + B = C (no. 2), we know that 4 + B = 12, so B = 12 - 4, so B = 8. Belinda ate 8 pizza slices and Amy ate 4.

Reason It Out

Level 1

The easiest puzzles are in Level 1.
These should prepare you for the
tougher levels to come...

Puzzles 1–20

1   Weighing Up | Level 1

How many apples are needed to make
the third pair of scales balance?

2   Age Difference | Level 1

By reading the facts below, can you work out
the ages of siblings John, Carol and Tony?

1. John, Carol and Tony's combined ages amount to 48.
2. John's age plus Carol's age equals Tony's age.
3. In six years' time, Tony will be twice Carol's age.

How old are they all now?

3 What Comes Next? Level 1

What number do you think should come next in each sequence?

A) 1, 2, 5, 10, 17, 26, 37, ?

B) 100, 81, 64, 49, 36, 25, ?

C) 324, 433, 542, ?

HINT
For puzzle C of this group, look carefully at the digits that make up each number, and how they relate to each other.

4 Circular Sums Level 1

Your job here is to insert the numbers 0–11 in the circles, using each number only once. We have assigned a value to the numbers 0–11 in the list below. The idea is that, for any particular circle, the sum of the numbers in the circles connected directly to it adds up to the value allocated to the number inside the circle. Feeling lost? Take a look at the example and it should make more sense.

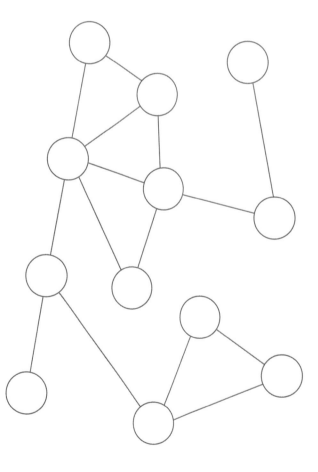

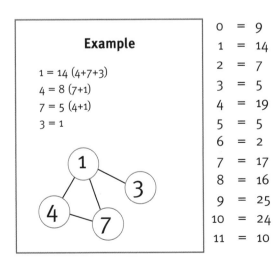

Example

1 = 14 (4+7+3)
4 = 8 (7+1)
7 = 5 (4+1)
3 = 1

0	=	9
1	=	14
2	=	7
3	=	5
4	=	19
5	=	5
6	=	2
7	=	17
8	=	16
9	=	25
10	=	24
11	=	10

5 Secret Message | Level 1

There are lots of codes and secret messages within this section, and many of them require a lot of thought, so we're starting you off with a fairly easy one. Can you find the secret message in this letter?

dearest oli via,

how is your l ittle bro ther? much recov ered hope fully. Y ou are both in o ur thou ghts and prayers.

james

6 Planet Plus | Level 1

These three planetary names contain ten different letters, so a different digit can replace each one. Can you replace the letters with numbers to create a legitimate sum, using each of the digits 0–9? No number is allowed to start with a zero and we would like you to enter the solution with the largest possible EARTH.

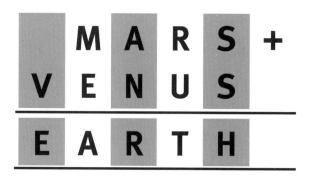

MARS +
VENUS
———
EARTH

HINT

Use an additional piece of paper for your calculations. You might want to use a pencil, since it could take a few attempts to work this one out!

7 Red or Blue? | Level 1

A bag contains five red balls and five blue balls, and five of these ten balls are pulled out of the bag at random. What are the odds that the five balls will be the same color?

HINT
Before you start working, bear in mind that the odds of pulling a red or blue ball out of the bag are 1 in 2.

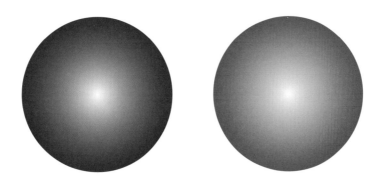

8 Swamp Hopping | Level 1

Imagine the grid at right is a huge swamp, which is impossible to walk through but you need to cross. Luckily there are stones placed at various points around the swamp, and if you can locate these before you start, you can cross the swamp safely. The trail of stones may go up, down, right or left but never diagonally. In the grid, each square has either one stepping stone or is a deadly swamp. The number in each square shows how many stones there are in that square and the four which are adjacent. When you've located all the stones, you should be able to mark in the one safe route that will take you from side A to side B.

A

3	3	4	3	3	2	1	1	2	1	2	2	4	3
3	3	2	2	2	2	1	1	3	3	2	3	4	4
3	1	2	2	3	3	3	2	4	3	3		3	4
3	3	2	3	4	3	3	2	3	3				3
4	2	3	2	3	2	3	2	4	3	3	3	2	3
3	3	2	3	3	2	3	3	3	2	2	2	2	2
3		4	3	4	2	3	3	3	2	1	2	0	2
2		2	3	3	2	2	2	3	3	3	3	3	2
3	2		1	4	3	3	3	3	3	4	3	3	3
2	3	1	1	2	2	1	1	1	2	1	2	1	1

B

HINT
The blue squares are definite swamp patches, so beware of them. Looking at these squares should help you get started.

9 Lost Causes | Level 1

A group of absent-minded people take a vacation. By the time they arrive at the resort, various losses have occurred, as recorded below. Nobody ended up with more than one of the listed items. Can you work out what percentage of the vacationers have lost all four Items?

OF THE VACATIONERS:

70% have lost their luggage

75% have lost their tickets

80% have lost their traveler's checks

85% have lost their wallets

10 Pyramid | Level 1

Each number in this pyramid is the sum of the two numbers on the adjacent bricks below it. From the numbers that have been put in place, can you work out what each of the others must be?

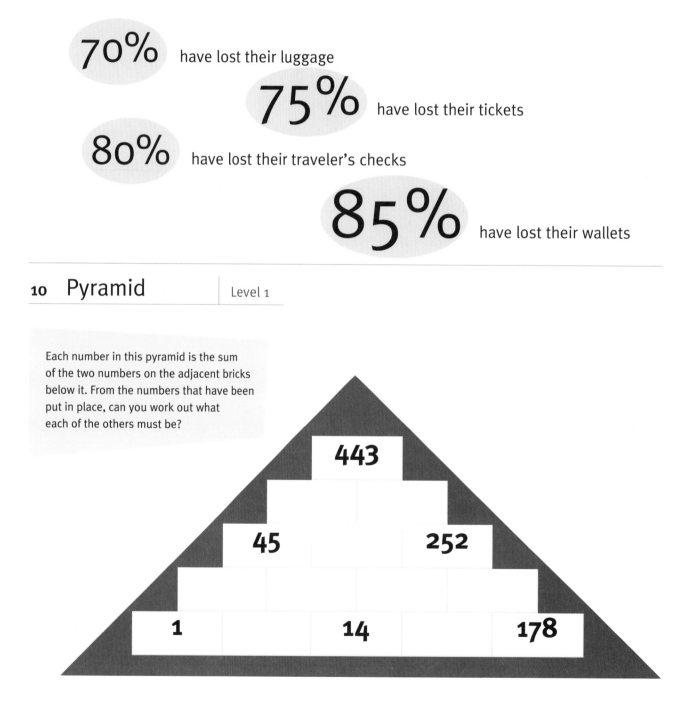

443

45   252

1   14   178

Elvis Presley was responsible for the quotation at right. Can you work out what he said?

.OT EVAH TNOD UOY
ENIL YM NI .CISUM
TUOBA GNIHTYNA
WONK TNOD I

---

12 Word Wonder | Level 1

See how quickly you can solve these word puzzles.

A

Which of the four-letter words on the right belongs with those on the left?

ABLE	ISSUE	EXIT FLEA LORE
ECHO	ULTRA	OKAY ONCE
INTO	?	

B

Which of the words below the line belongs with those above it?

| DOOR | POOL | TIME |
| DRAY | STOP | ? |

| BARD | CALM | SLIP |
| BOOT | EASY | SPRY |

C

Of these twelve words, which two do not fit with the others, and why?

DEFER	DIRECT	STORE	PLEASE
SHELF	ROAST	FLESH	LASTED
ASLEEP	SALTED	CREDIT	FREED

13　Know Your Numbers | Level 1

Test your mental arithmetic with this number challenge!

1. An average apple weighs 4oz. How many apples can you expect to get in a 2lb bag?

2. Peaches are packed into trays of 40 but 5% are still bruised in transit. How many damaged peaches will there be in 9 trays?

3. A hotel fries 3 dozen eggs, boils 1½ dozen, and poaches 15. How many eggs have been cooked?

4. One lap of a running track is 400m. How many laps are run in a 10km race?

5. There are 15 cookies in a box. If 27 children are to be given 2 cookies each, how many boxes must be bought and how many spare cookies will there be?

6. How many seconds are there in 5 hours?

7. Add together the number of edges of a box (i.e. one face of a box has four edges), the number of sides in a hexagon, and the number of degrees in a right angle.

8. A trained athlete's resting heartbeat is 52 beats/minute. How many times does his heart beat each hour?

9. If vowels are each worth 25 and consonants are each worth 18, what is the difference in value between "exercise" and "bicycles"?

10. How many complete revolutions of the clock face does a minute hand make each day?

14　Starstruck | Level 1

Here's a drawing challenge for you—but don't worry, you don't need to be artistic, just thoughtful! The challenge: draw a figure made up of ten straight lines. Somewhere along these lines there are nine dots, and there must be three dots along every single line.

HINT
Give yourself a few attempts to solve this puzzle— you're not expected to get it right the first time, but it will be rewarding when you've done it!

E.G.: Here are five dots along two lines:

15 Urgent Message | Level 1

This is the rail fence code, used during the American Civil War. This message could have been sent from Robert E. Lee to Ulysses S. Grant before their historic meeting in 1865. What does it say?

**p a n n t s r e d r l a e o d i e
l n i g o u r n e p e s h l f r**

---

16 To the Nines | Level 1

Each square should contain a nine-letter word, starting from any letter and moving either up, down, or across but not diagonally. Can you fill in the two missing letters and find the nine-letter word in each square?

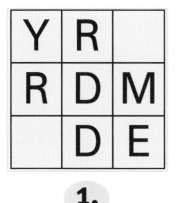

1.

2.

3.

17 Mother and Daughter | Level 1

By reading the facts below, can you work out the age of mother and daughter?

Six years ago the mother was three times as old as her daughter.
In 36 years the mother will be 1.5 times as old as her daughter.
How old are they both?

HINT
Try solving this puzzle as an algebraic equation, using X and Y as the numbers to work out. For example, start by saying "Let X = mother's age, and let Y = daughter's age."

18 Name the Day | Level 1

Simply calculate the answers to the clues and a famous historical date will appear in the shaded squares across the middle.

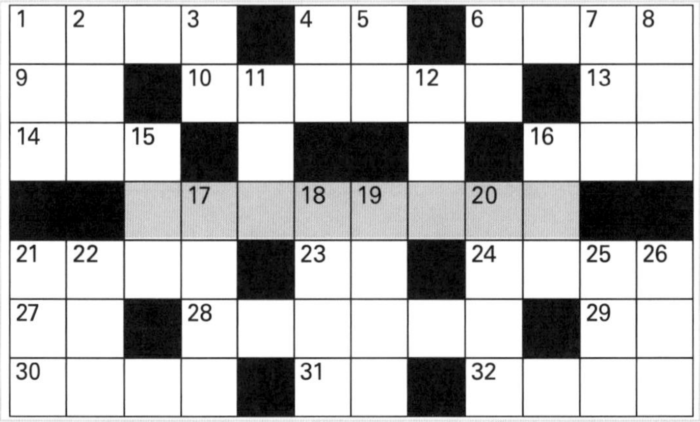

Across

1. $2^5 \times 3^4$
4. $5^{11} \div 5^9$
6. 199 X 36
9. 8352 ÷ 87
10. 614 X 706
13. Square root of 5929
14. 29 X 22
16. 31 X 21
21. 21^3
23. Cube root of 6859
24. 397 X 21
27. 11223 ÷ 129
28. 703^2
29. Cube root of 2744
30. 112 X 43
31. Square root of 1849
32. 113 X 48

Down

1. $14^2 + 10^2$
2. 9571 ÷ 17
3. $7^2 - 5^2$
4. Cube root of 12167
5. 3942 ÷ 73
6. Square root of 5476
7. $5^2 \times 3^3$
8. 81954 ÷ 174
11. $6^3 + 145$
12. 31 X 27
15. 31 X 13 X 2
16. 24161 ÷ 37
17. 439 X 14
18. $2^3 \times 893$
19. 90381 ÷ 47
20. 14333 - 6438
21. 41 X 24
22. 38642 ÷ 139
25. Square root of 97344
26. 31 X 24

19 Figure-Fit Level 1

Can you fit the square pieces into the jigsaw block so that each line across and each line down has the total shown at the end?

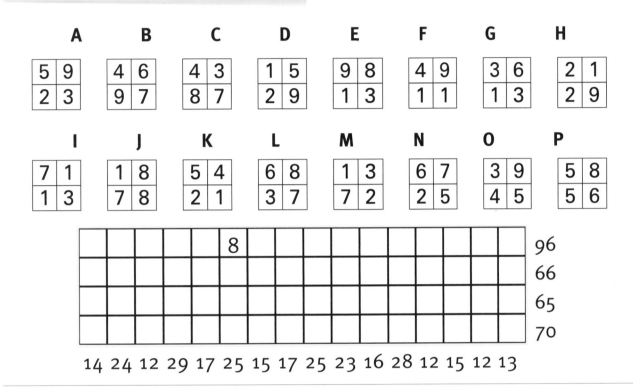

20 Add-a-Number Level 1

In each of these sums, can you insert the same number twice to make the calculations correct? Note: Numbers can only be added before the equals sign, not after!

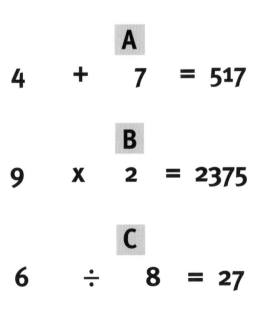

A

4 + 7 = 517

B

9 X 2 = 2375

C

6 ÷ 8 = 27

HINT
For sum A, you'll need to insert a two-digit number twice. For sum C, you'll have to think harder than for the other two. No more clues, I'm afraid.

Reason It Out

Puzzles 21–40

Level 2

Welcome to Level 2, in which we'll be stepping the puzzle difficulty up a gear. Can you handle it?

21 Quick Getaway | Level 2

Detective Dee Cipher watched her suspect's best friend examine these two grids and suddenly speed away in his car. In his haste they fell onto the road. Can you help the detective work out the message?

22 Magic Square | Level 2

In the opposite grid, can you insert the remaining numbers from 1–25 into the blank squares so that each horizontal, vertical, and diagonal line totals exactly 65?

	16			
				2
17		12		22

23   Code Among Thieves   Level 2

One criminal passes a message to another while detained by police detectives. Following this, the suspect refuses to say a word. Can you crack the code and work out exactly what the message says?

D,OYJ OD FRSF/ YJRTR

OD MP RBOFRMVR

SHSOMDY ID/ FP MPY

VPMGRDD SMUYJOMH/

24   Pyramid   Level 2

You may find this pyramid puzzle harder than the one in the previous level—that's the idea! As before, each number is the sum of the two numbers on the adjacent bricks below it. From the numbers in place, can you work out all of the others and complete the pyramid?

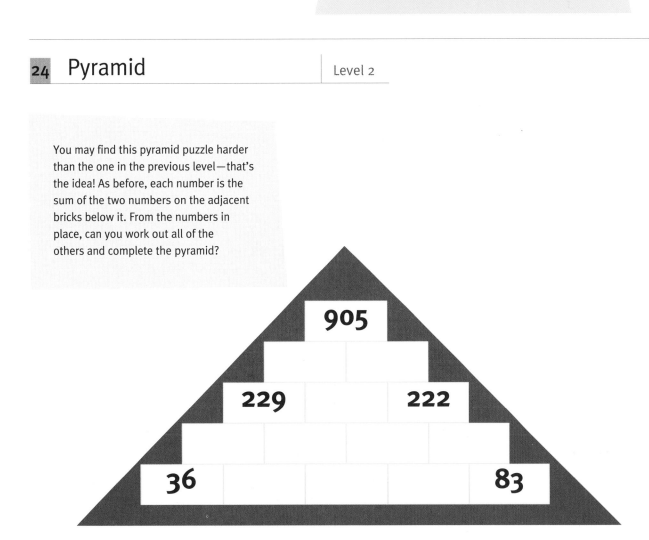

25 Master of Words | Level 2

Mastermind is a simple but classic game played in many parts of the world. One player has a group of four pegs, each a different shade, and places them in a particular order, unseen by the opponent. The opponent then guesses the order of the pegs, making one guess at a time. After each guess, the first player tells the opponent how many pegs are of the right hue but in the wrong place, and how many are the right shade and in the right place (but not which pegs this applies to!). We've adapted the game so that it uses words instead of shades. By looking at your opponent's comments on the words guessed below, can you find the correct word with the fifth guess?

		✔✔	✔
Guess 1	**NEED**	1	1
Guess 2	**LAWN**	1	2
Guess 3	**LEAN**	0	2
Guess 4	**WEAL**	1	1
Guess 5	_ _ _ _		

Key
Right letter, right place = ✔✔
Right letter, wrong place = ✔

26 Age Concern | Level 2

James wanted to set a confusing problem for his friend Tom. Can you help Tom solve the puzzle?

HINT
To solve this one using algebra, start by naming the amount of years ago that the two met as x. Then, name James' current age as j, and Tom's current age as t. The first phrase of the first sentence then gives you the following equation:
$t - x = 3(j-x)$. Work out what the next phrase tells you in the same way, and you'll be halfway there.

“ Tom, let's suppose that you were three times my age when we first met, and that now, I am the age that you were then. When I am three times my present age, our combined ages will add up to exactly one hundred. If these facts were all true, how old should we each be today? ”

27 Circular Sums | Level 2

This is the same as puzzle number 4, but more difficult! Remember that the sum of the numbers in a circle connected directly to it equals the value corresponding to the number in that circle, as given in the list. Check back to puzzle 4 for the example if you're not sure.

0	= 17	7	= 26
1	= 11	8	= 17
2	= 6	9	= 11
3	= 12	10	= 10
4	= 21	11	= 32
5	= 12	12	= 18
6	= 29		

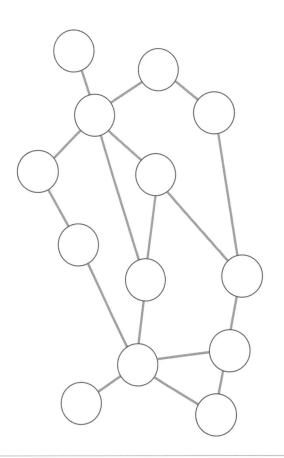

28 Outcast | Level 2

Can you work out which number doesn't belong in group 1, and which word is the odd name out in group 2?

1
8432
7963
6696
3972
5840
9657

2
JAMES
SIMON
KAREN
ALEX
SUSAN
SAUL

29 Know Your Numbers | Level 2

A slightly harder number challenge than the previous quiz. Are you up to it?

1. Yellowstone National Park has an area of 2.2 million acres. The Kruger National Park in South Africa has an area of 20,000 square kilometers. Which is larger?

2. Which of the following numbers is divisible by 17?
   a) 16,252
   b) 15,497
   c) 18,218

3. You have landed on the planet Vog. On leaving your spaceship, you are faced with 390 staring, unfriendly eyes. Unlike humans, who regularly have two eyes, the Vogans are creatures with 3, 6, 7 or 10 eyes. Checking that your V45.6 specter gun is in its holster, you see that there is an equal number of each type of Vogan. Can you calculate how many of each type of Vogan you may have to kill?

4. What number comes next in this series: 5, 9, 17, 33, 65?
   a) 112   b) 129   c) 131   d) 108   e) 116

5. Young Sarah's brother is one and a half times as old as she is. In four years' time, she will be three quarters of his age. How old are Sarah and her brother now?

6. You've gone shopping for a dinner party. The ingredients for the main course cost twice as much as the ingredients for the appetizer, and the appetizer costs twice as much as dessert. The total cost is $21. How much did the ingredients for the appetizer cost?

7. If 6 cups of coffee and 3 muffins cost $15, and you can buy 3 cups of coffee and 9 muffins for the same $15, how much will it cost you to buy 14 cups of coffee?

8. What are the symbols missing from this equation?   ((4 ? 8) ? 5) ? 7 = 13.4

30 Making Magic | Level 2

Can you create your own magic square? Just fill each of the numbers 1–9 into the square at right, ensuring that each horizontal, vertical, and diagonal line adds up to the number 15.

31 Number Maze | Level 2

Starting with any hexagon on the left-hand side, moving forward at each go, try to work your way to the other side. At each step, you must follow the instruction for that column (such as x 4). There are, of course, dead ends. Can you make it through?

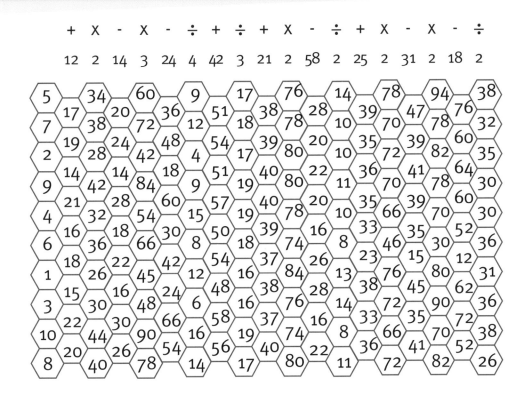

+	X	-	X	-	÷	+	÷	+	X	-	÷	+	X	-	X	-	÷
12	2	14	3	24	4	42	3	21	2	58	2	25	2	31	2	18	2

32 All the Squares | Level 2

Look at the chessboard opposite. How many perfect squares of all sizes can be found altogether on the board? If you work this one out systematically, you should notice a pattern in your workings, which makes the answer easy to calculate. What is it?

33 Ray of Hope

Sir John Trevanion was an English cavalier of distinction, who, having fallen from grace, was locked away in a castle. While awaiting his doom, he was handed the following letter, and shortly afterward he asked to pass an hour in private repentance in the chapel. When the jailer came to pick him up, he was nowhere to be found. By reading the letter, can you work out how he escaped?

HINT
Pay close attention to the punctuation of the letter, and keep the number three in mind.

> *Worthie Sir John:—Hope, that is ye beste comfort of ye afflicted, cannot much, I fear me, help you now. That I would saye to you, is this only: if ever I may be able to requite that I do owe you, stand not upon asking me. 'Tis not much that I can do; but what I can do, bee ye verie sure I wille. I knowe that, if dethe comes, if ordinary men fear it, it frights not you, accounting it for a high honour, to have such a rewarde of your loyalty. Pray yet that you may be spared this soe bitter, cup. I fear not that you will grudge any sufferings; only if bie submission you can turn them away, 'tis the part of a wise man.*
>
> *Tell me, an if you can, to do for you anythinge that you wolde have done. The general goes back on Wednesday. Restinge your servant to command—R T.*

34 Fruit Cocktail

From a bag containing the items of fruit listed here, four fruits are picked out at random. What are the chances that all four of these are cherries?

10 cherries

4 strawberries

3 plums

HINT
This puzzle requires the same solving strategy as puzzle 7 on page 139.

Set Square | Level 2

In this grid, all of the blank squares should contain numbers under 10. All you have to do is insert the correct number into each square so that all the calculations shown are correct. Simple!

6	x	3	÷		=	9
+		+		x		+
	+		÷	4	=	
-		-		÷		÷
	-	5	x		=	
=		=		=		=
7	-		-		=	

Number Jumble | Level 2

By looking at this sequence of numbers, can you work out what number should come next?

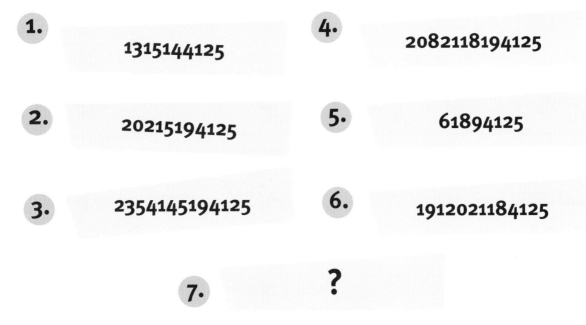

1. 1315144125

2. 20215194125

3. 2354145194125

4. 2082118194125

5. 61894125

6. 1912021184125

7. ?

Weight and See

Level 2

Looking at the three sets of scales shown here, can you decide how many hats would be needed to make the third set of scales balance?

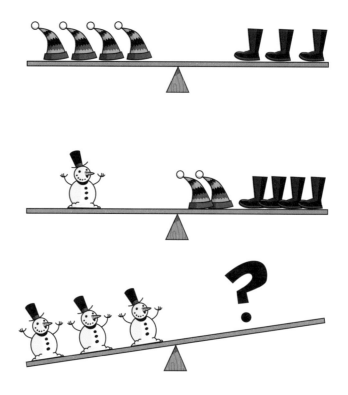

38

Hidden Words

Level 2

Each of the sentences below conceals a hidden word within the theme indicated by the heading. Can you find them all?

FRUIT

1. When he saw his daughter climbing the ladder, he ordered her to come to the bottom at once.
2. The flippant tone of the doctor angered the woman, who had been waiting to see him for over an hour.

CURRENCIES

3. Knowing he only had twenty minutes to pack, Ronald emptied the contents of his drawers into the suitcase and threw his passport on top.
4. As the play ended, the audience rose and cheered to show their appreciation of a flawless first night performance.

HERBS

5. The cell phone he called went straight to the answering machine, although he was reluctant to leave a message.
6. "Do not let this terrible piece of prose mar your feelings about the book as a whole," instructed the teacher.

EUROPEAN COUNTRIES

7. On all accounts, we deny responsibility for the disappearance of the cream cakes.
8. While climbing the mountain, we found ourselves in serious danger many times.

MUSICAL INSTRUMENTS

9. During the interview, Simon hoped nobody noticed the loud rumblings from his stomach.
10. Due to a lack of finances, the couple had to cancel lots of upcoming social events.

FURNITURE

11. The perspiring woman mopped her brow, declaring, "There's not much air in this place!"
12. "This concealer is just the job if you want to hide skin blemishes," explained the heavily made-up clerk.

39 Round and Round | Level 2

Can you decipher this sentence?
The winding spiral is there to help you. Work out
exactly how and you should find the puzzle
simple enough to solve!

OYDID UTI RAL? PD NIF HES

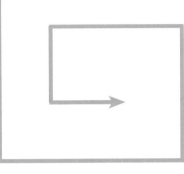

40 Number Master | Level 2

We have already tried the Mastermind game using
words instead of hues. This time we're using numbers!
If the boxes show the guesses from number 1 downward,
can you work out what the mystery number should be,
and write it in the blank squares in each case?

Key
Right number, right place = ✔✔
Right number, wrong place = ✔

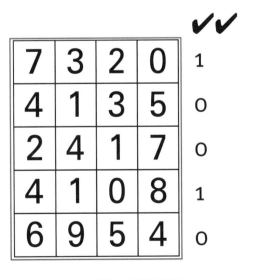

9	5	7	7	2	0
3	7	1	2	0	3
5	7	3	9	0	2
1	3	6	7	2	0
4	0	8	1	0	1

7	3	2	0	1	1
4	1	3	5	0	1
2	4	1	7	0	2
4	1	0	8	1	2
6	9	5	4	0	1

Reason It Out

Level 3

Now that you've reached Level 3, it's time to work those brain cells just a little bit harder!

Puzzles 41–60

41 Know Your Numbers | Level 3

At this level the number quizzes are getting a lot trickier.
You should allow yourself more time to solve this set of questions.

1. A journey takes 5 hours in total. The average speed over the first 3 hours is 58mph while the average over the last 2 hours is only 43 mph. What is the average speed for the whole journey?

2. Jason wishes to change $245 into £ sterling. If the rate of exchange is $1=64p and the bank charges 2% commission, how much to the nearest penny will he receive?

3. A farmer estimates that it costs $450 to feed 10 horses for 9 days. How much will it cost to feed 12 horses for 7 days?

4. The sum of Kim and Joe's ages is 13 years. Next year their ages will be in the ratio 3:2. How old are they at present?

5. On joining a gym Carries weighs 175 pounds. To achieve her target weight she needs to lose 16% of her present weight. What is her target weight?

6. In a sale, after a reduction of 10% the price of a DVD player is $162. How much would you save on the original cost if you bought it?

7. What is $83\frac{1}{3}\%$ of $\frac{4}{5}$ of 573?

8. A frog is two meters from the edge of a pond. He always hops exactly half the distance between himself and the pond. How many hops will it take him to reach the water?

42 Magic Square | Level 3

Again, you need to place the numbers 1–25 in the square so that each row, column and diagonal adds up to 65. This time, we've put in even fewer numbers to help you. Hope you like a challenge!

	24			
		13		
11				9

43 Cryptograms | Level 3

A cryptogram is a type of code where each of the letters represents a different letter of the alphabet, in a completely random fashion. Here are two quotes from famous people. Can you work out what they are saying?

HINT
Try working out where the small words in a sentence might be — AND or TO or THE — to get you started with the first few letters.

1. **IADUD FUD IPL BRTGN LW GRUDSILUN RT IAD IADFIDU; IALND PAL IARTB IADV FUD QLG FTG IALND PAL FUD SDUIFRT LW RI.**

Rhetta Hughes

2. **FJVV OYEE SCWAMS, FAUR JU EHCZ JU TSHTES ISJM YR RIMHAZI RISYM KSSR YCURSJW HK RISYM QMJYCU.**

John Philip Sousa

44 Master of Words | Level 3

Like puzzle 25 on page 148, here is the game of Mastermind played with words. By looking at the results of the first four guesses below, can you find the correct word with the fifth guess?

		✔✔	✔
Guess 1	**ROBE**	1	2
Guess 2	**NEAR**	0	2
Guess 3	**LEAN**	1	0
Guess 4	**ACRE**	1	0
Guess 5	_ _ _ _		

Key
Right letter, right place = ✔✔
Right letter, wrong place = ✔

45 Arrow Number | Level 3

Each number already in the grid shows the sum of the digits (one per square) in the line whose direction is shown by the arrow. There are no zeroes. In any sum, each digit can only appear once. For example 8 cannot be completed with 4 + 4. A sequence of digits forming a sum can only appear once in the grid. For example, if 8 is 5 + 3 then another 8 cannot also be made up of 5 + 3, or 3 + 5; it must contain a different set of digits, such as 7 + 1 or 6 + 2. Can you find the unique solution?

	6 ▾	20 ▾	27 ▾	4 ▾		31 ▾	13 ▾	14 ▾
12 ▸					19 / 6 ▾			
38 ▸			8			4		
	13 ▸			12 ▸			12 ▾	14 ▾
19 ▸		5			20 ▸			
19 ▸					20 ▸	9		

46 Number Master | Level 3

You've tried this one before (puzzle 40 on page 155), but don't get too confident. This time there are five digits in each case instead of four. Can you work out the mystery numbers and write them into the answer boxes?

Key
Right number, right place = ✔✔
Right number, wrong place = ✔

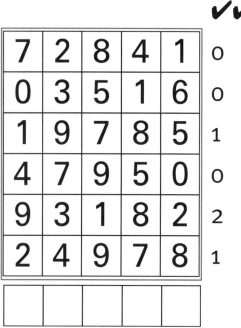

					✔✔	✔
7	2	8	4	1	0	3
0	3	5	1	6	0	2
1	9	7	8	5	1	2
4	7	9	5	0	0	1
9	3	1	8	2	2	2
2	4	9	7	8	1	2

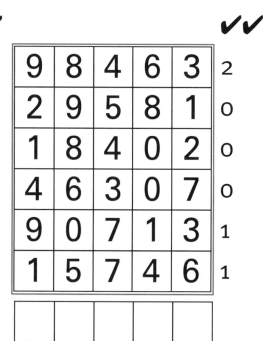

					✔✔	✔
9	8	4	6	3	2	0
2	9	5	8	1	0	2
1	8	4	0	2	0	2
4	6	3	0	7	0	3
9	0	7	1	3	1	1
1	5	7	4	6	1	1

47 Logi-Fit

Each numbered hollow square has space for four words, entered across and down, as in a crossword. From the clues, can you work out the only place for each word and so complete the grid?

CLUES

Square 1: None of the words begins with L or D.
Square 2: None of the words begins with P or T.
Square 3: None of the words begins with G or T.
Square 4: None of the words begins with G, L or P.
Square 5: None of the words begins with D or G.

DALLY	GATED	LAPEL	PANEL	TANGY
DEBIT	GRASP	LOCUS	PARED	THIRD
DREAD	GREAT	LOGIC	PETAL	TOPIC
DUCAL	GRILL		PETIT	
DUMPS			PRIED	

48 Ben and Jen
Level 3

In **1988** Ben was over ten years **older** than Jen, and the **difference** between the square of their ages was exactly **1988**. Can you work out exactly how old they each were in that **year?**

49 Multitalented | Level 3

You might have noticed that if you multiply the number 5 by itself, the result ends in the number 5. This is also the case for various other **numbers** (apart from the obvious 0 and 1), including 6 (the result being 36). If we look at two-digit numbers that when squared have the same last two numbers as we started with, we find this applies to 25 (the result being 625) and 76 (resulting in 5,776). For **three-digit** numbers, there are 625 (309,625) and 376 (141,376). However, there is only ONE four-figure number to which this rule applies. Can you work out what this is?

HINT
You could try algebra to work this out — but you might find a quicker way using a calculator!

50 What Comes Next? | Level 3

In each case, your job is to work out what comes next...

1. What letter should come next in this sequence?

A, S, O, N, D, J, F, M, ?

2. Which country should follow these four?
Choose from the list of countries in the box.
ARGENTINA, ENGLAND, ITALY, OMAN

TANZANIA
URUGUAY
VIETNAM
YEMEN

3. Which number should replace the question mark to finish this sequence?

23 8 1 20   3 15 13 5 19   14 5 24 ?

51 Secret Society | Level 3

The following code is given to people who wish to join a secret society. If they can crack it, they can claim membership. You might find this code tricky, but the crucial clue lies in the hint given opposite. So, would you be able to become a member of this society?

HINT
SECURITY is of paramount importance.

OYRMR AN JHFX JHR LPSFAOX VJMNR OYSH YSMUHRNN JI YRSMO SHU OYSO AN NJIOHRNN JI YRSU.

I MJJNRQRFO.

---

52 Sum Way Down | Level 3

In the top line, the circles A to E are to be filled with two digits each, using between them each digit 0–9 only once. So, in the first picture, 0, 1, 3, 5, 6 and 9 all need placing. From then on, the number in each circle is the sum of the digits in the two circles that are above it and joined to it by a line. Therefore, circle F will contain the answer to 7 + 4 + 8 + 2. Given the numbers already in position, can you complete the picture?

HINT
When filled in correctly, the circles will contain fifteen different numbers.

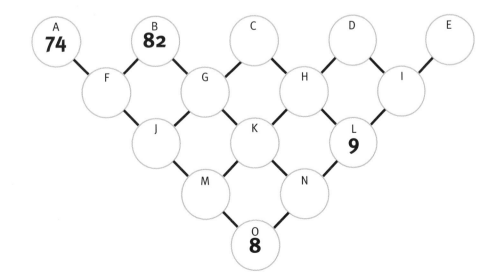

Out of This World | Level 3

Each alien symbol has a value in the range of 1 to 8, and has the same value wherever it occurs. The numbers around two edges give the total of the values in each row or column. Can you work out the correct value for each symbol that will give these totals?

2 7	3 2	4 1	3 4	3 2	2 8	4 3	2 8	
								41
								23
								43
								34
								19
								48
								36
								21

---

54 Briefcase Blunder | Level 3

Jimmy has forgotten the combination to his briefcase. Luckily, he'd written down various facts about it when he first decided on the code. By reading these, can you help him work out the five-digit combination, then write it into the squares?

Clues

1. The second digit is a result of the third and fifth multiplied together.
2. Three of the digits are different prime numbers.
3. The first digit is one less than the second.
4. The first digit is equal to the third and fourth added together.
5. The second and third digits added together have the same total as the first, fourth and fifth digits added together.

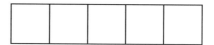

55   Even Odds   Level 3

Here's another magic square, but this time the total of each row, column and diagonal is a staggering 285! We've put in all the even digits in rows 1, 3 and 5 and the odd digits in rows 2 and 4. How quickly can you complete the square?

	24	4		2
		7	33	39
2	48	4		8
9	9	1		3
6		8	84	0

56   Misfits   Level 3

Which number is the odd one out in group A, and which doesn't fit in group B?

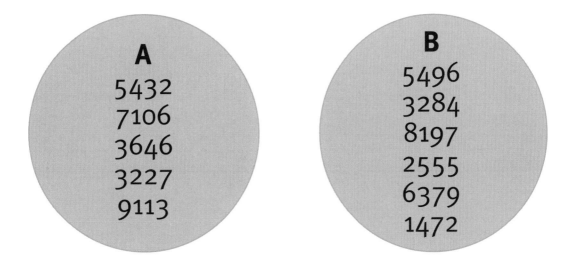

A
5432
7106
3646
3227
9113

B
5496
3284
8197
2555
6379
1472

57 | Pan Magic | Level 3

This magic square can be completed using the numbers from 10 to 34 inclusive. To give you a start, the digit 3 has been entered everywhere it occurs as well as all the multiples of three. Can you complete the square so that the five numbers in each row, column and diagonal add up to the total? The problem is that this time we're not going to tell you what number that is!

	3			3
	21		30	12
33			24	
		3	3	15
	15		27	3

HINT
It may help to know that this square is PANMAGIC, which means that *every* diagonal line of five numbers, like the example in the picture below, adds up to the mystery total.

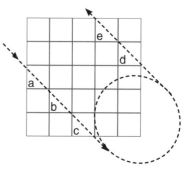

58 | Wine Wonder | Level 3

The advertisement outside this wine shop is also a neat addition sum. If we tell you that E is 8 and that each different letter has a different value, can you find out what the wines are worth?

HINT
TxTxT=ROT
OxOxO=E

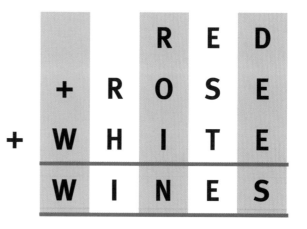

Here's a trickier version of the set square you solved earlier. Can you fit the right numbers into the blank squares so that each of the sums in the grid is correct? In each row and column, the contents of the first five squares make up one sum, and the contents of the last five squares make up a different sum.

	+		=		-	22	=	
÷		+		-		-		-
	+		=	38	-		=	
=		=		=		=		=
	+	42	=		-		=	46
+		÷		-		-		+
52	-		=		÷	5	=	
=		=		=		=		=
	÷		=	11	X		=	

Bearing in mind the facts below, can you work out the current ages of the father, mother and son?

HINT
The easiest way to solve this puzzle, as for previous puzzles of this kind, is to use algebra.

1. The combined ages of the mother, father and son total 100.

2. In nine years' time, the father will be twice as old as the son, and the mother will be one year older than the father is now.

3. How old are they all today?

| Level 4 | Well done—you've finally reached Level 4—the most mind-boggling puzzles start here! |

61 The Missing Link | Level 4

This is a Codeword puzzle, like the ones you'll have come across in the Word Power section of this book (eg puzzle 23 on page 63). Can you work out which number represents each letter of the alphabet? In this puzzle, all Across words marked with dots can be placed after the unnumbered shaded missing link word (green squares) to make another word or phrase. All Down words with dots can be placed before the missing link word in the same way. For example, if the shaded word was TIME, one of the Across words might be TABLE (as in TIMETABLE, and one of the Down words might be LIFE (as in LIFETIME). As you discover which letter is represented by a number, record them in the reference grid, and cross them off the list of letters outside the main grid.

Grid:

14•	5	24	7	4	15	16•	20•	22•	4•	10•	20•	18•	15•
A 2•	14•	2•	18•	1•	12	5•	22	2	1	24	6	13	2•	N
B 5•	14	14	13	18	14•	15•	18	26	21	5	2	4	15•	O
C 17•	21	14	18	22	25•	22•	12	14	14	24	7	2	5•	P
D 18•	21	1	20	18	18•	1	11	2	5	10	25•	24	1•	Q
E 20•	18•	13•	14•	15	•	15	18	5	15	13	5•	22	13	R
F 24	4	16•	24	18	15		2	24	10	8	7•	4	18	S
G 14	12	5•	1	2	18	22		15	14	4	8•	2	7	T
H 14	18	10•	25	21	22	2	18	•	14	16•	18•	7•	7•	U
I 14•	5	20•	18	24	5	4	14	18•	2	2	7	18	8•	V
J 24•	17	5	19	1	7	4	8•	5•	15	14	20	13	15•	W
K 23•	5	13	12	18	5	15	24•	15•	4	4	8	15	4•	X
L 18•	7	5	3	18	3	18	15•	4	20•	22•	4•	16•	22•	Y
M 25•	5•	22•	23•	7•	18•	14•	18•	15	18	9	18	10	2•	Z

Reference Grid

1	2	3	4	5	6	7	8	9	10	11	12	13
14	15	16	17	18	19	20	21	22	23	24	25	26

62 Create-a-Sum | Level 4

Complete the sum so that each of the numbers 1–9 appears in one of the nine squares above the line, ensuring that the solution to the addition is correct. How quickly can you solve this one?

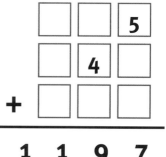

63 Numerocross | Level 4

This tricky grid must be filled with numbers rather than words. Can you complete it?

ACROSS

1. From a set of three different numbers the following are formed by multiplying the numbers in pairs: 28,782, 80,730, 42,435. This answer is one of the original numbers (see also 4 across and 11 across)
4. See 1A. This is another of the original numbers
6. The sum of all the integers up to and including 167
7. The difference between consecutive cubes. The sum of the digits is 16
9. The square root of 280,900
11. See 1A. This is another of the original numbers
12. Two fifths of 5 down
13. Twice 12A
14. An even palindromic number whose digits add up to nine
16. One of two numbers is five times the other and their product is 68,445. This is one of the numbers (see also 18A)
18. See 16A. This is the other number.
20. The sum of all the whole numbers up to and including 359
21. The sum of all the whole numbers that divide exactly into 245 (including 1 and 245)
22. Two numbers differ by two. This is the difference between their squares (the digits in the answer total 15)

DOWN

1. Two numbers differ by two. This is the difference between their squares. The sum of the digits is a square number
2. A prime number
3. The difference between the squares of two numbers that differ by three. The digits in the answer total 9. The last digit is 3 times the first
4. The sum of the squares of all the whole numbers up to and including 10
5. 1/0.002
8. One of two numbers whose sum is 53,069 and whose difference is 18,987 (see also 10D)
10. See 8D. This is the other number
15. The difference between two consecutive cubes. The digits total 19
16. The product of two primes that differ by two
17. One of two numbers is 1.5 times the other and their product is 387,096. This is one of the numbers (see also 18D)
18. See 17D. This is the other number
19. The sum of all the whole numbers that divide exactly into 369 (including 1 and 369)

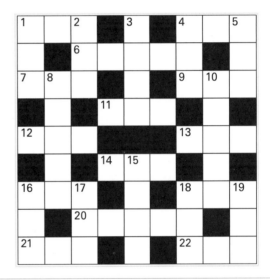

64 Cookie Crumbles | Level 4

In a family, there are five children, Brad, Katie, Tommy, Jack and Sam. They've found a pack of cookies in the cupboard and before their parents return home, they've eaten every one. But they didn't share them equally! By reading the facts below, can you work out how many cookies each child had?

1. Katie had the same amount of cookies as Jack and Brad put together.
2. Sam had two less cookies than Katie.
3. The two children who ate the least number of cookies were the only ones who ate the same number each.
4. Tommy had one more cookie than Sam.
5. Nobody ate more than six cookies.

65 Musical Note | Level 4

This note has fallen out of what looks like a violin case, carried by a suspicious-looking man late one evening. What does it say? The hint below should help.

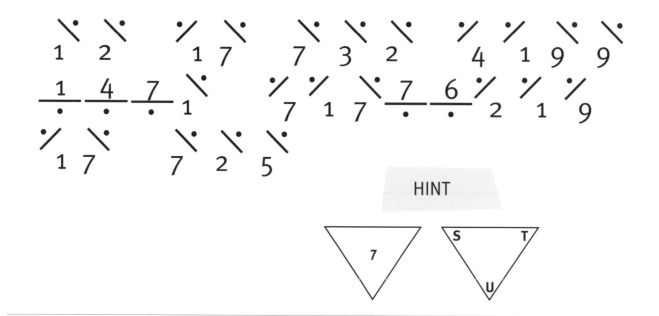

HINT

66 Number Cross | Level 4

Get a grip on these tricky clues and complete the crossword grid. In each case, A and D refer to Across and Down clues.

HINT
Historical clue:
Death of Shakespeare—
the year can be read in the lightly shaded squares.

CLUES

1A = 122 x 5A
5A is a prime number
6A = 101 x 4A
1D = 101 x 5D
2D is a square number
3D = 4A x 2D

EXTRA CLUE: Numbers 7, 8 and 9 do not appear in the solution.

Circular Sums | Level 4

Like the previous puzzles of this type, the sum of the numbers in the circles directly connected to it should equal the value corresponding to the number in that circle. If you can't remember exactly how to solve them, look back to puzzle 4 on page 137 for an example.

0 = 1	7 = 39
1 = 29	8 = 13
2 = 27	9 = 5
3 = 24	10 = 12
4 = 24	11 = 10
5 = 24	12 = 7
6 = 6	13 = 19

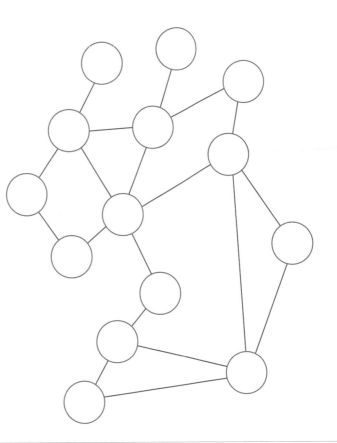

68 Number Master | Level 4

This is the same as the previous Number Master puzzles, but it's tougher because you have to work out the answer with fewer guesses to go on. See how you do.

Key
Right number, right place = ✔✔
Right number, wrong place = ✔

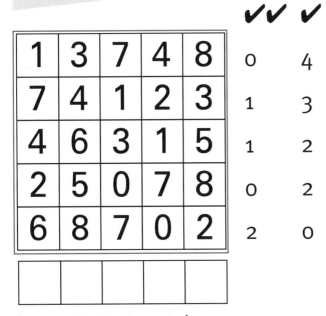

✔✔	✔
1 3 7 4 8	0	4
7 4 1 2 3	1	3
4 6 3 1 5	1	2
2 5 0 7 8	0	2
6 8 7 0 2	2	0

✔✔	✔
0 2 8 1 3	1	2
3 6 5 0 9	0	3
6 2 0 8 9	0	3
3 0 7 5 6	2	1
2 8 6 9 3	1	1

Here's your trickiest number quiz yet. Can you solve it?

1. The cost of a meal for 5 people is $120. They add 10% as a tip for the waitress. How much must each person pay in total if they share the cost equally?
2. Simon wins $2,000 in a lottery. He decides to share the money between his grandchildren in the ratio of their ages. If Sophie is 9 and Ellie is 7, how much will each child receive?
3. The sum of 9 consecutive numbers is 189. What are the numbers?
4. Which offer represents the better value—two x 16 oz bars of Belgian chocolate at $12.45 per bar or eight x 4 oz bars at $3.75 each?
5. Last year Tom was exactly 6 times as old as his son; this year he is exactly 5 times as old as his son. What will their ages be next year?
6. Will buys a bag of potato chips and 2 cans of cola for $1.51 and Hannah buys 2 bags of potato chips and a can of cola for $1.25. How much will Polly have to pay for 1 bag of chips and 1 can of cola?
7. Ten people at a meeting each shake hands with everyone else present. How many handshakes will there be in total?
8. The sum of the ages of the three children in a family is 34. What will be the sum of their ages in 3 years' time?

---

70 Weight Bearing | Level 4

Looking at the picture below, how many marbles will be required to balance with the toy car?

71

Number Squares

Level 4

These get a bit tougher each time — and of course this one is the hardest! Can you fill in the missing numbers so that every number in the square is correct? In each row and column, the contents of the first five squares make up one sum, and the contents of the last five squares make up a different sum.

	-		=	7	+		=	
+		-		X		-		+
	÷	3	=		+	35	=	
=		=		=		=		=
25	+		=		X		=	84
+		+		+		X		-
	+	51	=		-	19	=	
=		=		=		=		=
	+		=	94	-		=	

72

Master of Words

Level 4

As with the previous puzzles of this type, see if you can find the mystery words on the fifth guess. You might find these a bit harder than the earlier puzzles!

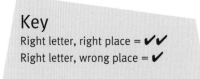

Key
Right letter, right place = ✔✔
Right letter, wrong place = ✔

		✔✔	✔
Guess 1	**S O N G**	0	3
Guess 2	**G O L D**	1	0
Guess 3	**D U E T**	0	1
Guess 4	**G U T S**	2	1
Guess 5	_ _ _ _		

		✔✔	✔
Guess 1	**L I L O**	1	1
Guess 2	**L O B E**	0	3
Guess 3	**L I O N**	0	1
Guess 4	**B A I L**	2	0
Guess 5	_ _ _ _		

As with previous puzzles of this type, each number already in the grid shows the sum of the digits in the line whose direction is shown by the arrow. Remind yourself of the rules by reading through the opposite list, then try this harder version.

RULES RECAP:
There are no zeroes. In any sum, each digit can only appear once. For example, 8 cannot be completed with 4 + 4. A sequence of digits forming a sum can only appear once in the grid. For example, if 8 is 5 + 3 then another 8 cannot also be made up of 5 + 3, or 3 + 5; it must contain a different set of digits, such as 7 + 1 or 6 + 2.

	4	27	24	17		27	9	16
24					12 / 11			
43	1					5		
	11			9			11	9
16					24			
24			2		12	7		

By looking at the top sequence of numbers, can you fill in the missing number in the two rows beneath, following the same principle?

A	69,282	1,728	112
B	59,317		180
C	26,377		

75   Logi-Fit | Level 4

As previously, each numbered 5 x 5 square has space for four words. From the clues given, can you work out the only place where each word can possibly fit?

CLUES

Square 1: None of the words begins with E or V.

Square 2: None of the words begins with E, G or V.

Square 3: None of the words begins with G or S.

Square 4: None of the words begins with S or V.

Square 5: None of the words begins with G or T.

EASEL	GAULT	SILLY	TACKY	VAGUE
EQUAL	GRASS	SPILL	TIGER	VAULT
ETHIC	GRAZE	SUGAR	TIMES	VENUE
	GREAT		TONAL	VENUS
			TOPIC	
			TROUT	

(grid with numbered squares 1, 2, 3, 4, 5)

---

76   Word Addition | Level 4

In this sum, each different letter represents one of the digits from 1 to 9 (there is no zero). Each letter, of course, stands for the same digit in each column. As there are two possible answers, which one gives you the largest BRAIN?

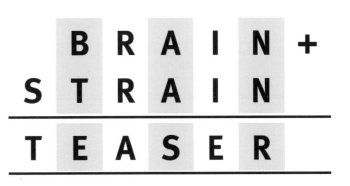

$$\begin{array}{r} BRAIN + \\ STRAIN \\ \hline TEASER \end{array}$$

This works exactly like the previous puzzle of this type. In the top line, the circles A to E are to be filled with two digits each, using between them each digit 0–9 only once. Therefore, in the top line, 1, 2, 3, 5, 6 and 8 all need placing. From then on, the number in each circle is the sum of the digits in the two circles that are above it and joined to it by a line. So the sum of the digits in circle B, + 4 + 7 (circle C) will equal 22 (circle G). Can you complete the puzzle?

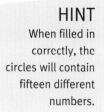

HINT
When filled in correctly, the circles will contain fifteen different numbers.

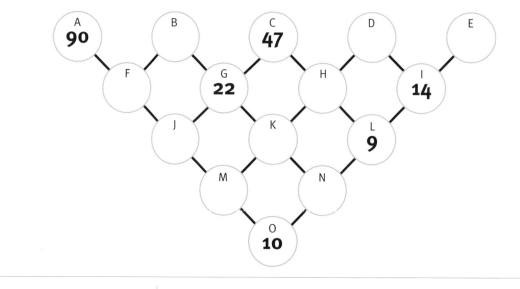

As before, each letter represents a different letter of the alphabet. Can you decode these quotations?

Reference Grid

A	B	C	D	E	F	G	H	I	J	K	L	M
N	O	P	Q	R	S	T	U	V	W	X	Y	Z

1. VRQYL GRQ'D NEL MOCCSQYWW, NED SD GSBB COL DMY WOBOISYW
RP O BOIKY IYWYOITM WDOPP DR WDEAL DMY CIRNBYV.

Bill Vaughan

2. WTIR OQEA TAR ARNGKEKRI QEG DRRA IYZARM DH OQR DIZSSZEAO
NIZORI ZA OQR RMZOTI'G UQEZI.

Lord Camrose

79 Each Way | Level 4

By correctly placing in the grid the answers to the clues, a palindromic number can be developed in each Across and Down line. A palindromic number reads the same backwards and forwards (example: 3,553). A few digits have been placed to start you off.

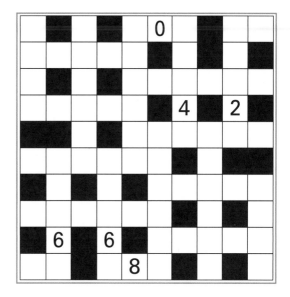

$111^2 =$

$43^3 - 3140 =$

$2,837^2 - 2,820^2 =$

$42^3 - 516^2 + 481^2 =$

$(12^2 + 4) \times 303 =$

$(22^2 - 31) \times 159 =$

$10,841^2 - 10,808^2 =$

$11^2 \times 455 =$

$(350 \times 271) - 1 =$

$4,000^2 - 3,879^2 =$

80 Hang-Maths | Level 4

This is a game along the lines of the classic hangman. You might want to play it with a like-minded friend. One player makes up a step, whether it's the addition of two or three numbers, or a long multiplication, subtraction or division. Instead of asking if a digit occurs anywhere, a player might ask, "Is there a 5 in the tens column?" and so on. The setter then fills in ALL occurrences of that digit in that column. If no such digits occur, a piece of the hangman is drawn (full hung man shown below!). In this example of a long multiplication exercise, the digits asked for have been filled in and the only other questions asked reveal that: there is no 2 or 8 in the ones column. It is now possible to complete the multiplication without further mistake. Can you do it?

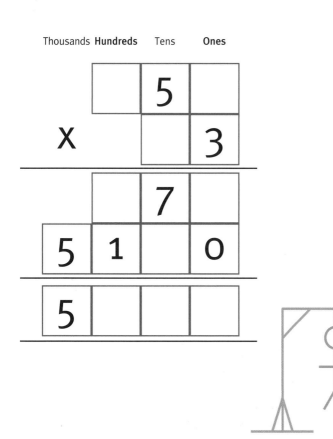

Think Logically

Logic is a strange phenomenon. We all think we are logical; we all assume others are as well. Yet logic is taught in very few schools, and poor logic or even inverted thinking can fool many of us.

In the puzzles that follow, you are invited to let logic alone be your guide. You won't need to search your memory to find some obscure fact, but you will need to put two and two together and come up with exactly four. If you feel the need to use guesswork, you must be doing something wrong!

Most of the puzzles are self-explanatory, but a few will be that much easier with a little explanation. Read through these guidelines before you start out.

PICTURE-FORMING PUZZLES

Tsunami

Your aim is to color in certain squares in the grid to form a picture. The only clues you have are the numbers at the end of each line. These tell you, in order from top of left, the number of colored squares in each block. Each block of colors is separated by at least one white square. So 2 6 means there are two colored squares followed by one or more empty squares, followed by a block of six colored squares. Solving the puzzle depends on your ability to cross-reference these clues and apply logical deduction. When you've finished, a picture will be revealed.

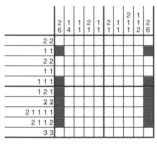

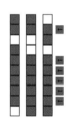

As a start, the left-hand column (2, 6) can be colored in only three ways:

Whichever is correct, the squares next to the arrows must be colored in, so we have one square of the 2 and five of the 6. This filling can be repeated in column ten.

Now look at the second row across (1, 1). The two single blocks have been colored so the rest of this line must be empty. You can place an X in each cell of this row to show this. Continue in this way, cross-referencing rows and columns as you go, until the picture is complete.

Enigma

These puzzles have numbers inside the grid, rather than around the outside. Apart from the 1's, each of the other numbers is half of a pair. Your task is to join the pairs so the number of squares

in the path is exactly the same as the numbers you are linking together. So two 6's would be connected by a path of exactly six squares—this path includes the two squares at each end containing the numbers. These paths linking pairs of numbers must not cross each other or themselves so each path is unique.

ENIGMA PUZZLE

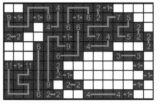

ENIGMA LINES

ENIGMA SOLUTION

The best way to proceed is to draw a line across each cell in a path when you are logically sure you have it right. The filling in can be done when all the paths have been completed. The 1's can, of course, be filled in right away. Then, you can work your way up through the 2's, 3's, etc. The example diagrams explain the idea.

GENERAL LOGIC PROBLEMS

With the puzzles known as "logic problems," the idea is to carefully read the statement of the problem in the introduction, and then consider the clues. Next, you enter in the chart all the information immediately apparent from the clues, using an X to show a definite "no" and a ✓ to show a definite "yes." Look at this example problem:

EXAMPLE

Three children live on the same street. From the two clues given below, can you discover each child's full name and age?

Clues

1. Miss Brown is three years older than Mary.
2. The child whose surname is White is 9 years old.

Working it out:

Miss Brown (clue 1) cannot be Brian, so you can place an X in the Brian/Brown box. Clue 1 tells us that she is not Mary either, so you can put an X in the Mary/Brown box. Miss Brown is therefore Anne, the only possibility remaining. Now place a ✓ in that box in the chart, with corresponding X's against the other possible surnames for Anne.

If Anne Brown is three years older than Mary (clue 1), she must be 10 and Mary, 7. So place ✓s in the Anne/10, Brown/10 and Mary/7 boxes, and X's in all the empty boxes in each row and column containing these ✓s. The chart now reveals Brian's age as 9, so you can place a ✓ in the Brian/9 box. Clue 2 tells us that White is 9 years old too, so he must be Brian. Place a ✓ in the White/9 box and X's in the remaining empty boxes in that row and column, then place a ✓ in the Brian/White box and X's in all the remaining empty boxes in that row and column. You can see now that the remaining unfilled boxes in the chart must contain ✓s, since their rows and columns contain only X's, so they reveal Green as the surname of 7-year-old Mary.

SOLUTION:
Anne Brown, 10
Brian White, 9
Mary Green, 7

You'll find a lot of logic problems in different formats throughout this section, some without a straightforward chart to fill in, so you'll need to keep your wits about you and use your powers of deduction to the maximum. The more logic problems and puzzles you try your hand at, the quicker and sharper your logical abilities will become. So get solving!

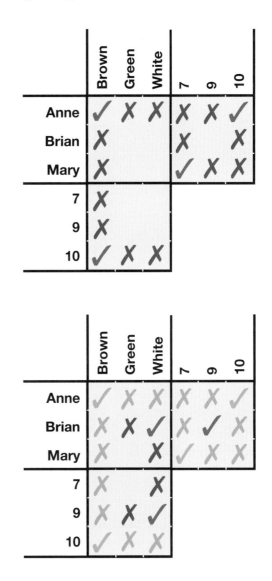

Think Logically

Puzzles 1–20

Level 1

Welcome to the first logical level! We've started you off with some of the easier puzzles, just to help you get the idea.

1   Explorers | Level 1

This factual logic problem concerns three explorers, the places they explored, and the years in which they did so. Can you follow in their logical footsteps and discover who went where?

1. Australia was explored by Europeans some time after the death of James Cook.

2. The 1795 exploration was not of New Zealand and wasn't made by Sturt.

3. Mungo did not make his explorations in the year 1828.

4. Park explored the River Niger.

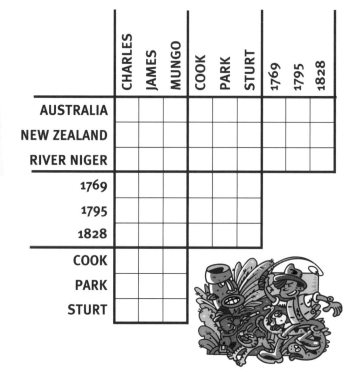

	CHARLES	JAMES	MUNGO	COOK	PARK	STURT	1769	1795	1828
AUSTRALIA									
NEW ZEALAND									
RIVER NIGER									
1769									
1795									
1828									
COOK									
PARK									
STURT									

PLACE EXPLORED	FIRST NAME	SURNAME	YEAR

2   Drink Up! | Level 1

Four friends are settling down to enjoy a drink after a hard day's work. Can you supply each of them with the correct beverage?

1. The whisky and soda is not for Sam.

2. Lisa's gin is not with tonic.

3. Tom has ginger ale but not in vodka.

JULIE

BRANDY	GIN
VODKA	WHISKY
BITTER LEMON	GINGER ALE
SODA	TONIC

TOM

BRANDY	GIN
VODKA	WHISKY
BITTER LEMON	GINGER ALE
SODA	TONIC

LISA

BRANDY	GIN
VODKA	WHISKY
BITTER LEMON	GINGER ALE
SODA	TONIC

SAM

BRANDY	GIN
VODKA	WHISKY
BITTER LEMON	GINGER ALE
SODA	TONIC

3 In Conclusion I | Level 1

The author Lewis Carroll was also a pioneer in logic. These examples in elementary thinking are based upon his book *Symbolic Logic Part I*. In each case he invites readers to examine his statements and write down the logical conclusion or conclusions that follow. We have done the same here. By looking at the statements, can you form reasonable conclusions in each case, as shown in the example?

HINT:
Reality does not apply here, so it is perfectly reasonable, as concluded in the example, that cats may be chickens and either animal may understand French!

EXAMPLE:
All cats understand French.
Some chickens are cats.

CONCLUSION...**Some chickens understand French.**

A
All ballet dancers are athletic.
Some athletic people are football players.

CONCLUSION..

B
All politicians are people we trust.
All politicians are liars.

CONCLUSION..

C
All successful university students are teetotallers.
All young university students are heavy drinkers.

CONCLUSIONS 1 ....
2 ....

3	4	4	0	2	3
0	2	4	1	1	1
4	1	1	3	2	0
3	0	2	2	4	3
3	1	4	2	0	0

0					
1					
2					
3					
4				✓	
0	0	1	2	3	4

4 Domino Search | Level 1

The 15 dominoes from 0-0 to 4-4 have been laid out in a rectangle. Can you draw in the lines to show where each domino has been placed? Use the check grid to mark each domino as you find it. We've located the 4-4 domino in the top grid (shaded and checked off) to help you.

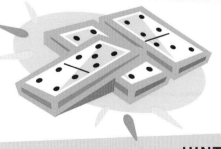

HINT:
It'll make things easier if you look for the "doubles" dominoes first.

2	3	1	4	3	3
4	0	2	2	4	4
2	0	0	0	1	3
0	1	2	3	4	1
0	4	1	1	2	3

0					
1					
2					
3					
4					
0	0	1	2	3	4

5 Seascape I | Level 1

Do you remember the old game Battleship? These puzzles are based on that idea. Your task is to find where the vessels are placed in the diagram of the sea. Some parts of ships or sea squares have already been filled in. The number next to each row or column tells you the number of occupied squares in that row or column. The ships may be positioned horizontally or vertically, but no two ships are in adjacent squares horizontally, vertically or diagonally.

Aircraft Carrier

Battleship

Cruiser

Destroyer

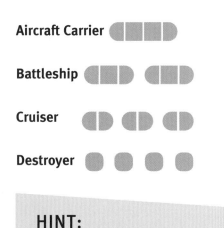

HINT:
The wavy blue lines indicate a sea square—a space which contains no ships.

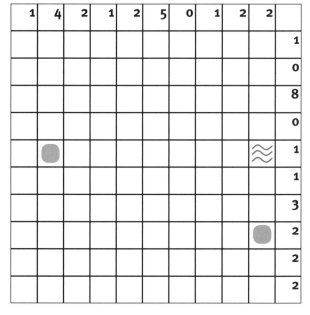

1	4	2	1	2	5	0	1	2	2	
										1
										0
										8
										0
	●								≈	1
										1
										3
								●		2
										2
										2

6 Hedge Your Bets | Level 1

Can you draw the boundary lines on this estate so that each plot is the same size as each of the others and each contains a house, a cat, a dog and a tree?

7 Truth Will Out | Level 1

Everything has its opposite: good has evil, truth has lies and the Keystone Kops have Snuffy's Gang—the most inept bunch of criminals ever to carry out a smash-and-grab raid and get away with handfuls of broken glass. When caught, as they inevitably are, Harry, Basher, Clogger and the rest always follow Snuffy's orders and tell a mixture of truths and lies in the vain hope of confusing the questioning detectives so that the facts cannot be exactly pinned down. It's not usually successful. Can you solve these cases just as the police had to?

CASE ONE

Even in early youth they used this trick to try and wriggle out of a spot of petty shoplifting. They made these statements:

'Arry: Basher distracted the shopkeeper. Snuffy took the sweets.
Basher: 'Arry took the sweets. I didn't distract the shopkeeper.
Snuffy: Basher was not the lookout. 'Arry distracted the shopkeeper.

In this case, one of them told the truth and the other two lied completely.

Can you work out who did what?

CASE TWO

Next time, the gang stole a shopping bag only to find it was full of empties being taken to the bottle bank. Later, they claimed:

Snuffy: I snatched the bag. 'Arry didn't run off with it.
'Arry: Snuffy snatched the bag. I ran off with it.

In this case, one has lied completely and the other has told one truth and one lie. An eyewitness, Mandy, was known to tell the truth half the time and lie the other half.

Mandy: 'Arry took the bag. Snuffy ran off with it.

Can you now work out who did what?

8 Film Bluff | Level 1

David Nivea has invited five film fans to a showing of NEWT GLASGOW, another of those films which so nearly became great! From this shot of the audience and the clip of clues below, can you work out who is sitting in which seat?

1. John Wane is somewhat blocking the view of the person directly behind him.

2. The person with **Jack Lemon** is not **Ava Gardener**.

3. Clint Eastward is sitting directly behind **Jack Lemon**.

4. Meryl Streak's escort is sitting on her right.

Row

K

L

M

N

Seat   24   25   26   27

9 Match Point | Level 1

Lay out 15 used matches or toothpicks in this spiral pattern. Now move just three of them to make two squares.

HINT:
One square may be inside another!

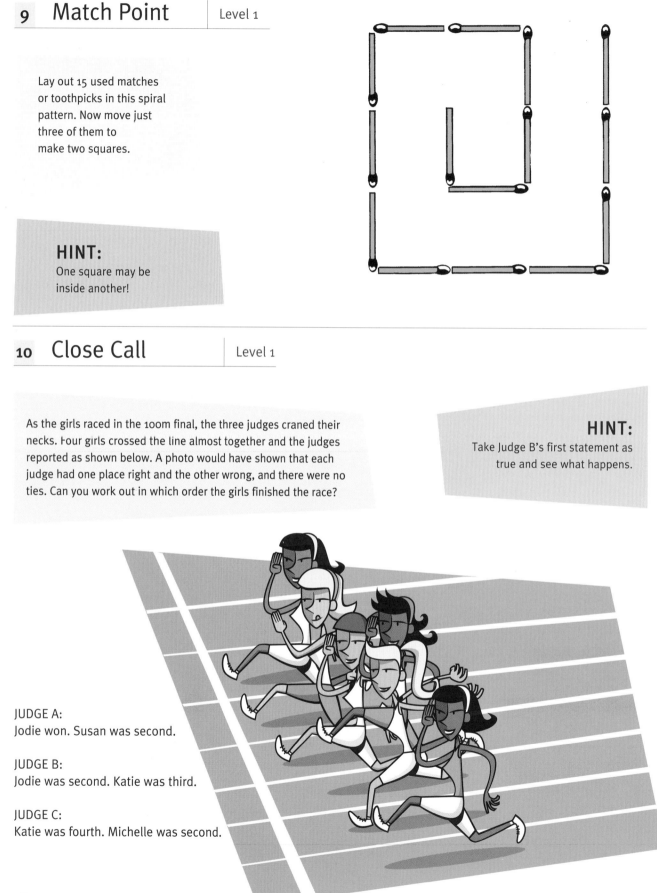

10 Close Call | Level 1

As the girls raced in the 100m final, the three judges craned their necks. Four girls crossed the line almost together and the judges reported as shown below. A photo would have shown that each judge had one place right and the other wrong, and there were no ties. Can you work out in which order the girls finished the race?

HINT:
Take Judge B's first statement as true and see what happens.

JUDGE A:
Jodie won. Susan was second.

JUDGE B:
Jodie was second. Katie was third.

JUDGE C:
Katie was fourth. Michelle was second.

11 It's Your Move | Level 1

HINT

If Crosses go first, there is a simple strategy for Noughts that assures he/she will not lose. You might want to work out what it is before you start playing!

Most adults wisely give up playing Noughts and Crosses (tic-tac-toe), knowing that each game should be a draw if both players play perfectly. A simple extension of Noughts and Crosses is called **Diagonal Three**. In this case, the first player to have three of his/her marks in a row LOSES the game. The three marks do not have to be next to each other, as shown in the grid below, where player X loses.

Below is an empty grid, so you can try playing the game against an opponent.

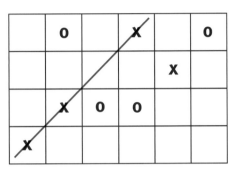

12 Ace in Place | Level 1

The cards Eight to King of each suit, together with the Ace of Hearts, have been placed in a five by five square. Figures and letters showing the values—8, 9, 10, J, Q, K and the suits—Hearts, Clubs, Squares and Diamonds—have been placed at the end of each line across and down. With the Ace in place and the fact that the two cards shown at the top left belong in the pink shaded squares, can you work out the unique place for each card?

13 Snuffy's Gang | Level 1

Having discovered that colophony, the resin from pine trees, is much in demand in a wide range of domestic products, the inept Snuffy decided to put his gang to work. One would chop down the tree, another strip the bark and the third would collect the resin. As usual, the enterprise came to a sticky end and at the police station the gang could only try their trick of mixing truth and falsehood, in the hope of causing total confusion. When questioned, one told two lies, another one truth and one lie, and the third, weakly, two truths. Can you put two pairs together correctly and work out who did what?

Basher:
Clogger stripped the bark.
Snuffy chopped the trees down.

Clogger:
Basher collected the resin.
I chopped the trees down.

Snuffy:
I chopped the trees down.
Basher stripped the bark.

14 Cone-fusion | Level 1

Four youngsters have just bought an ice cream, each from a different vendor. Can you work out the kind each chose and from whom it was purchased?

1. Rachel's is made by Rico's. Luigi's is vanilla and is not Vince's choice.

2. Alec's ice cream is not mint.

3. A girl chose the chocolate cone. The one sold by Antonio's is not coffee.

4. A girl bought from Luigi's store.

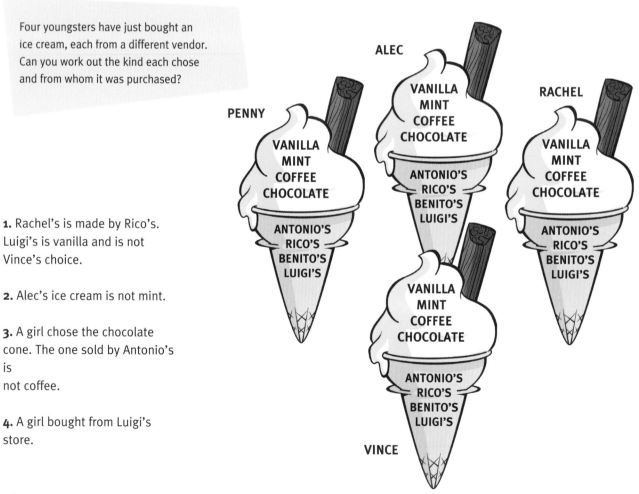

Mike wants Jim to help him in the back garden. He would like to place four stones, each of them at an equal distance from the other three. Jim explains that it would be difficult to do this on the patio, but he can easily do it in the garden. How does Jim plan to achieve this?

16 Cobra Level 1

This is a Tsunami puzzle. The numbers outside the rows and columns of this grid tell you how many squares to shade. When you've finished, you will have created an amazing picture! For further instructions on solving the Tsunami, turn to pages 176–177.

HINT:

Your finished picture should resemble a snake— but don't worry if you can't see it appearing until the final stages of your solution!

This is an Enigma puzzle. Your task here is to join the pairs up so that the number of squares in the path is exactly the same as the numbers you are linking together. So two 6's would be connected by a path of exactly six squares—this path includes the two squares at each end containing the numbers. These paths linking pairs of numbers must not cross each other or themselves so each path is unique. Do it correctly and you'll end up with a picture. For further instructions on solving this type of puzzle, turn to pages 176–177.

HINT:

Do this right and the results will be well worth it! But as with the Tsunami puzzle on page 185, don't worry if your picture doesn't start to come together until you're nearing the end.

			5	4	4	12			8				3		3	
		5						11				11		2	2	
		3			2	2			4	4			4			6
						8	3			5	8					
		3	2			6		3					4	4		
		2	1	6		12	1				8					
				1						5			4		6	
				1						6			4			
	4		4		3		3	7		4		6			4	
4		4			1					5		4	10			
3		3	3		3	8						7				
			3	10	5						7				6	
3		3											10			
	3	3	3		4	4	5				5	4				
		2	2		10			7				4			11	
		1					8			11			6			
			9			9										
		3						3		3		2		3		3
	3	7		7			9				9	9	2		9	

Of the eight Kings and Queens in a standard pack of cards, four are lined up here. In these clues, TO THE RIGHT/LEFT means NEXT DOOR, and not anywhere beyond.

There's a King to the right of a King.
There's a King to the left of a Queen.
There's a Queen to the left of a King.
There's a Queen to the right of a Spade.
There's a Spade next to a Spade.
There's a Club to the left of a Heart.
There's a Club to the right of a Spade.
Can you identify each card?

19 Pick One

Here are three boxes of chrysanthemums. Labels on the outside of each box are supposed to show the colors inside. Unfortunately, every label is on the WRONG box. Without looking inside, you take one flower from the left-hand box and immediately know which flowers are in EVERY BOX. What is the color of the flower you picked?

20 Pick-pockets

Level 1

Following the disastrous kidnapping escapade, when the gang were forced to pay the parents to take back their obnoxious offspring, Snuffy and two of his minions tried their hand at a spot of pick-pocketing. The idea was that one would fake a slip in front of the mark, another would lift the wallet and the third would walk off with it. It was unfortunate that at their first attempt the one making the getaway wouldn't cross the road as the sign said **Don't Walk**. At the police station, the gang decided that the only hope was to tell a mixture of lies and truths as usual. This time, they agreed that the best liar would tell lies all the time; the next best would lie half the time and tell the truth the other half, and the worst liar would tell the truth every time. From the statements given, can you work out who did what, and what sort of liar each of them is?

'Arry: Snuffy took the wallet.
I ran off with it.

Clogger: 'Arry faked the slip.
Snuffy took the wallet.

Snuffy: 'Arry ran off with the loot.
Clogger faked the slip.

Think Logically

Puzzles 21–40

Level 2

Welcome to Level 2! You'll find the puzzles are getting a little harder, and you may need longer to work these out.

21 Whoops!

Level 2

Mrs Ficklefingers is the daily help for the Markham family, who have suffered badly this week with her somewhat clumsy attempts to free the house of dust. Fortunately, she had a day off on Wednesday but on each of the other days some article or other, all of different ages, was broken beyond repair. The conclusions from clue 1 have been entered for you— can you complete the grid?

1. The article that was 50 years old was broken on Tuesday. It was not the ornamental glass from the dining room.

2. The ashtray was broken on Thursday but not in the hall.

3. Monday saw disaster in the lounge but it was neither the vase nor the article that was 5 years old.

4. The 10-year-old article did not come from the dining room, nor was it the lamp.

	5 YEARS OLD	10 YEARS OLD	50 YEARS OLD	100 YEARS OLD	ASHTRAY	GLASS	LAMP	VASE	DINING ROOM	HALL	LOUNGE	STUDY
MONDAY			✗									
TUESDAY	✗	✗	✓	✗		✗			✗			
THURSDAY			✗									
FRIDAY			✗									
DINING ROOM			✗		✗	✓	✗	✗				
HALL						✗						
LOUNGE						✗						
STUDY						✗						
ASHTRAY												
GLASS		✗										
LAMP												
VASE												

DAY	ARTICLE'S AGE	BREAKAGE	ROOM

22 How Few?

Level 2

What is the smallest group of people you could have that contains all these family relationships?

AUNT MOTHER

BROTHER NEPHEW UNCLE

COUSIN NIECE FATHER

DAUGHTER SISTER SON

23 Ferry Nice

Strolling along the river bank, three courting couples saw an inviting restaurant—on the other side. On their side was a small rowboat, clearly only capable of taking two at the most. This meant someone would be rowing back. No girl, however, was willing to be either in the boat or on the shore with either of the other two men unless her own boyfriend was also present. Can you sort out a plan so that they can all get across the river and into the restaurant for dinner?

24 Stall Order

On this market stall, fruit and vegetables always alternate along the rows and down the lines (left and right are as you look at the stall). The yams are in the same line down as the broccoli, which are further right and higher than the bananas, which are higher and further left than the cherries, which are immediately above the peas, which are two lines below the watercress, which is to the right of and in the same lines across as the cauliflower, which is lower than the dates, which are in the same line down as the apples, which are higher than the grapes, which are lower than and to the right of the lychees, which are immediately to the right of the radishes, which are higher than the figs, which are not in the same line across or down as the turnips, which are higher than the kumquats, which are in the same line across as the onions—which we've put in for you. Can you fill in the names of the other fruit and vegetables in the spaces where they each belong?

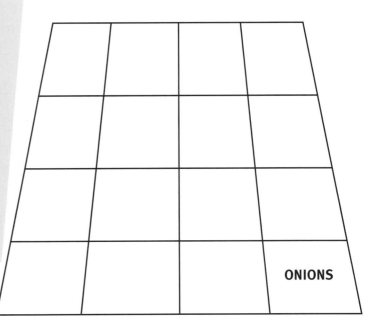

As with the previous ship-placement puzzle on page 180, your task is to find the vessels in the diagram. Three sea squares (where there are no ships) and one destroyer have been placed for you. A number next to a row or column refers to the number of occupied squares in that row or column. Remember that the boats may be positioned horizontally or vertically, but no two boats are in adjacent squares, even diagonally.

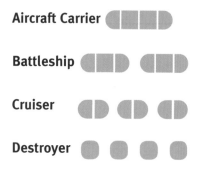

Aircraft Carrier

Battleship

Cruiser

Destroyer

HINT:

Once a ship has been located, you can shade in all the squares around it as empty, as no ships are located directly next to each other. So start by shading the eight squares around the destroyer in the puzzle at right.

2	1	1	3	2	1	3	2	1	4	
										0
	●									2
						≈				3
										2
										1
										6
										1
			≈							1
						≈				4
										0

R.I.P.
Edwina Proud
Died 07/28/92
Buried 07/27/92

26 Grave News   Level 2

A gravestone reads as shown on the left. If there was no error or crime involved, can you explain this apparently impossible situation?

When Clarissa, Melissa and Larissa were summoned to the boss's office at ten in the morning they knew that their previous night's crimes had been found out. On their way to see him, they decided that they would neither lie completely or tell the absolute truth about what had happened. Instead, they would tell the truth half the time and lie the other half, to try to deflect blame from any one person. So, when Mr Smothers asked them what they had to say about the missing stamps, gold pen and petty cash, each gave one true statement and one false one. Can you help Mr Smothers deduce who stole what?

Clarissa: Melissa took the cash. Larissa took the pen.

Larissa: Clarissa took the cash. I took the stamps.

Melissa: Larissa took the pen. Clarissa took the stamps.

HINT:

One of the above statements is not actually needed to solve this puzzle—it's just there to confuse you!

---

28 Cube Route | Level 2

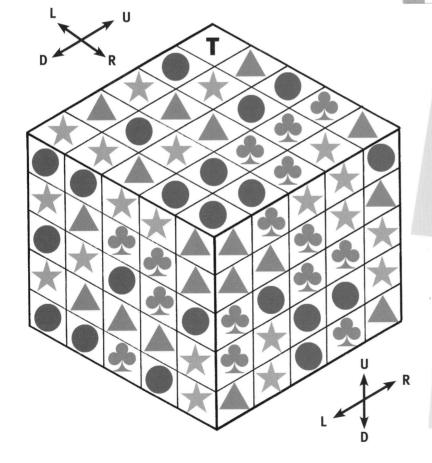

Can you find a way to climb this cube from the top to the bottom? Your base camp is one of the squares along the bottom two edges (which is your first problem!) and the top square is the one marked **T**. To help you find the one path, the symbols on each face have a meaning—Up, Down, Right or Left. The symbols have the same meanings on each face.

HINT:

To solve this correctly, you'll have to visit each of the three faces on the cube.

As with the puzzle on page 179, here we're using Lewis Carroll's game of logic to make conclusions from a number of statements—this time slightly more difficult. In each case, can you come to the correct conclusion?

HINT:

In puzzle A, you may be tempted to make the conclusion: Jerry Holler's songs are never tedious. But is this conclusion logically valid? Does it follow from the proposition? If not, what conclusion do you come to? Then try the other puzzles.

A
Jerry Holler's songs never last five minutes.
A song that lasts five minutes is tedious.

CONCLUSION...

B
No boys under 18 are admitted to the disco.
All groovy dancers have purple hair.
None of those not admitted to the disco have rings through their noses.
None but those under 18 are not groovy dancers.
NOTE: Only the boys are being discussed here.

CONCLUSION...

C
Everyone who is sane can solve logical puzzles.
No lunatics are fit to serve on a jury.
No politicians can solve logical puzzles.

CONCLUSION...

30 Domino Search | Level 2

A standard set of dominoes has been laid out, using numbers instead of dots for clarity. Using a sharp pencil and a keen brain, can you draw in the lines to show where each domino has been placed? You may find the check grid useful; cross off each domino as you find it. To give you a start, domino 3/6 has been placed.

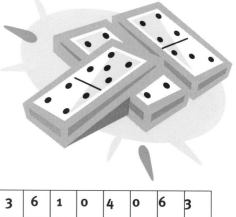

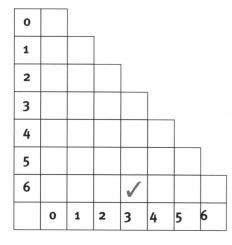

3	6	1	0	4	0	6	3
0	2	5	3	6	1	1	2
0	4	6	6	2	5	3	1
5	3	3	6	0	4	6	4
1	4	1	2	0	2	4	5
0	2	5	4	4	2	3	5
3	5	1	0	1	2	6	5

31 Die Spotting   Level 2

From the logical layouts given, can you work out which number belongs with the third line of dice?

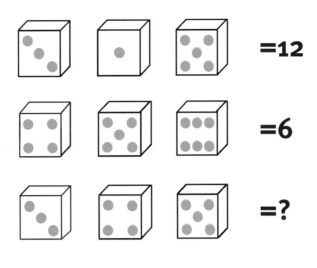

=12

=6

=?

---

32 In a Jam   Level 2

Tickle your taste buds and sample the delights in each kitchen as these ladies prepare their jam, sponge cakes and sweets. Who's making what?

KELLY

BLACKBERRY	PLUM
RASPBERRY	STRAWBERRY
CARAMEL	LEMON
ORANGE	VANILLA
COCONUT ICE	FUDGE
NOUGAT	TOFFEE

JAM

CAKE

SWEETS

AUDREY

BLACKBERRY	PLUM
RASPBERRY	STRAWBERRY
CARAMEL	LEMON
ORANGE	VANILLA
COCONUT ICE	FUDGE
NOUGAT	TOFFEE

JANE

BLACKBERRY	PLUM
RASPBERRY	STRAWBERRY
CARAMEL	LEMON
ORANGE	VANILLA
COCONUT ICE	FUDGE
NOUGAT	TOFFEE

JAM

CAKE

SWEETS

SONIA

BLACKBERRY	PLUM
RASPBERRY	STRAWBERRY
CARAMEL	LEMON
ORANGE	VANILLA
COCONUT ICE	FUDGE
NOUGAT	TOFFEE

1. Audrey is not the one cooking a caramel sponge while also making plum jam; and neither Audrey nor the lady doing these things is making nougat.

2. Jane is making a lemon sponge, and the fudge maker an orange sponge, but neither lady is making blackberry jam.

3. Sonia is making raspberry jam, but she is not the cook making both the vanilla sponge and the coconut ice.

33 Equal Measures | Level 2

Tony took two friends on a celebratory picnic, where they discovered that they had 15 fluid ounces of champagne, and each wanted an exact third. The only containers available were, in addition to the full 9-oz and 6-oz, a 7-oz cup and a 4-oz jar. There was no way to pour and measure parts of a container, either all the contents of one vessel were poured into another or a vessel was filled from part of the contents to another. Since the champagne was part of a toast, they all wanted their 5-oz share at the same time.

Can you pour correctly to give three shares in 8 pourings?

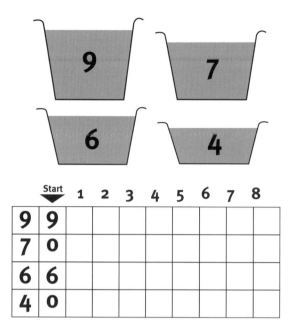

	Start	1	2	3	4	5	6	7	8
9	9								
7	0								
6	6								
4	0								

34 Logi-Squares | Level 2

Each square in each of these bigger squares must be shaded either blue, green, orange, pink or yellow. Each line, across and down, must have each of the five colors appearing once each. Also, every shape, shown by the thick lines, must also have each of the five in it. From those given, can you fill in the rest?

HINT:
If you have no crayons, simply write the initial of each color in the squares instead.

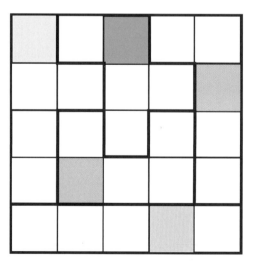

35

In Conclusion III   Level 2

More from Lewis Carroll's game of logic. As with the previous In Conclusion puzzles (eg page 179), can you form logical conclusions, which have used all of the evidence, from the propositions below?

A
Punks are illogical.
Nobody puts pins through his or her nose who wants to get a job.
Illogical persons put pins through their noses.

CONCLUSION...

B
None but the brave deserve rewards.
Some boasters are cowards.

CONCLUSION...

C
No sober person climbs trees.
Jenkins is always bruised.
No person who does not climb trees is always bruised.

CONCLUSION...

---

36   Dragon   Level 2

This is an Enigma puzzle like the one on page 186. As before, you must join the pairs up so that the number of squares in the path is exactly the same as the numbers you are linking together. However, this is a special enigma puzzle, in which red squares must be joined to another red square, blue squares to a blue square, and so on. Use red, blue, green and black pencils or pens. For more instructions on solving this type of puzzle, turn to pages 176-177.

HINT:
Remember that the 1's can be filled in right away. Then you might find it easiest to work your way up through the 2's, 3's, and so on.

2			10						11				10								12					
2		10				15			12			11					12							14		
		11		10	11		10				3		2	2	12		1		3		8					
			2	2							8	3			1		10	3	12	1			14			
							8	3		2	2	1				1	12			8	10					
		15	6			6			6	3	2	2		4		13	5							1		
	5			15				6		4	2	2	13					4								
15	5			16	1		3		1		15	3	4		5				4	1						
					7		2	3	4		3			4	1	16		16			10		2			
	2	2	1	5			3	2	4	1				6			3		3		1		2			
			1	5		3	3	3		2	2		5	4				1	1					10		
4	16	16				3					5	6			6		4				3					
	2				7	3	3		4		3	4	7		3			2	2	4			3	10		
	2		3	3		2	3			3	3				6	3		1	6		1		16			
4		3		3	2	15		9		3		4			4			1		1						
	3		12	2	1		9		10	16		3			11		4	16	4	1		6	1	2	2	
16	3			2		14			1				3	7		1		10			4	6				
1		3		1	4			3			6						11		6	10		4			6	6
2	2			2	2		1		5				4		5		4									3
1		3		2	2	4	2	2		3	3		10		4			4				14				
2	2	2		3	5		5				1	3						2	2	10		14				3
2	1		12		3			5			1	6	16		1	5				4	1					15
1		5			5	5	5		14		13	1		13								4	3	10		
	17	1	3		3	5		3	1							11		6	10		4					
		6	5			3	5	1	1	5		5			1	1		5		10	4		3			
				6	4		2	2	5	5				1	7		6			5						
				8			5	2	6			6						10			3					
	5		10	17		4	8	2	2									15	15		3			5		
					1			2		5	1		7		4		4									
2	2		5			10	16				5		16					15	5							

---

37 Tentackle | Level 2

Eight children are camping, two to each tent, and some have given us a couple of clues as to how to find them. The trouble is that their directions are as bad as their cooking, and in each case only one direction is true, while the other is an exact opposite, so that East should read West, etc. Directions are not necessarily exact, so North could be North, Northeast or Northwest. To help you, Andy is already tucked into a sleeping bag in his tent.

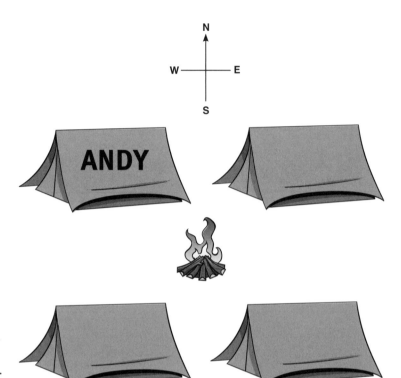

Bill says: I'm North of Glen and West of Freddie.
Gary says: I'm South of Tom and East of Glen.
Kevin says: I'm South of Andy and east of Freddie.
Joe says: I'm North of Freddie and West of Andy.
Freddie says: I'm South of Gary and West of Kevin.
Glen says: I'm North of Bill and East of Joe.

38 Take Route | Level 2

The idea here is that you must work out the route of a meandering line which will take you from square A to square B. Sounds simple enough... but you must make sure that the numbers outside the grid indicate the total number of squares occupied by the line in that particular row or column. Can you find the correct route that takes you through this grid?

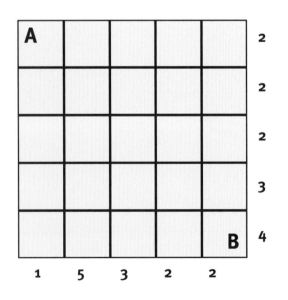

39 Per-lease State! | Level 2

A street accident involving four men has taken place, but sadly their recollections of the incident are rather hazy. Three of the men made statements, but each of them lied twice, and told the truth once, about who was playing which part in the scene. Can you work out who owned the cart, who drove the car, who was the pedestrian and who rode the bicycle?

BEN:
I was selling apples from my cart.
John drove the car right into it.
Aaron fell off the bicycle.

JOHN:
Ben walked straight out across the road.
Dennis rode his bicycle in front of the car.
It's not my apple-cart.

DENNIS:
Ben is lying about John being in the car.
John was hit by the car as he stepped out into the road. It's not my apple-cart.

40 Seat Yourself | Level 2

Six couples are about to sit down to dinner; Mrs A is already in her place, at seat 9. The hostess has made the five decisions that are listed below. By reading them, can you work out who will sit where at the table?

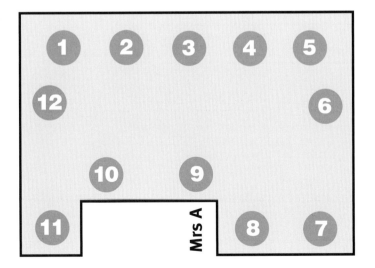

1. A wife and her husband will be seated next to each other (i.e. 10 is next to 11 or 9).

2. Each lady will sit opposite a man.

3. Mrs C will be opposite Mr B.

4. Mrs D will be on Mrs F's right.

5. Mrs E will be on her husband's left.

Think Logically

Level 3

Puzzles 41–60

Don't be put off if this lot take a while to solve—remember, your brain power is improving as you go!

41 Beret Truth | Level 3

Five French tunnel diggers each wear either a red or a blue beret. Emerging from the dark, each has lit a match and, for the moment, can see what the other four are wearing, but does not know whether his own hat is red or blue. It happens that those wearing red speak the truth and those wearing blue are lying. From the statement made by each man, can you guess which beret he wears?

JACQUES: I see 3 red and 1 blue.

PIERRE: I see 4 blue.

HENRI: I see 4 red.

CLAUDE: I see 1 red and 3 blue.

FRANCOIS: I see *****
(inaudible—the whistle blew!)

1 The coffee mug is directly above the camera, which is immediately left of the foot spa. None of these is in an end box.

2 The golf ball's box number is even and three higher than the box containing five hundred dollars, which is not number 1.

3 The apple is directly below the pot of jam. The dishcloth is immediately to the right of the boat, which has a box number twice that of the one containing tonight's star prize—a HOLIDAY!

42 Take Your Pick | Level 3

Come on, try your luck! Every one of these 10 boxes contains a prize, the usual mixture of star and booby prizes! First, pick one of the numbered boxes, then read the clues opposite to work out what you've won. Can you win the holiday?

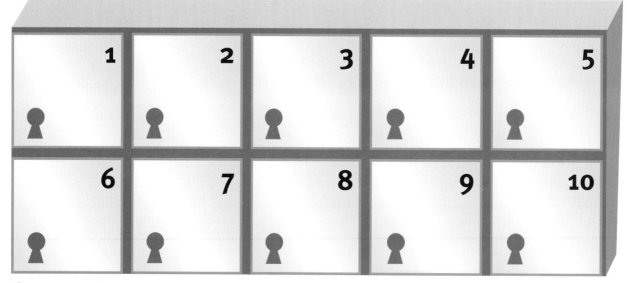

43 Frisky! | Level 3

This is just like the Tsunami puzzle on page 185—only a lot bigger and more difficult! For further instructions on solving it, please turn to pages 175–176.

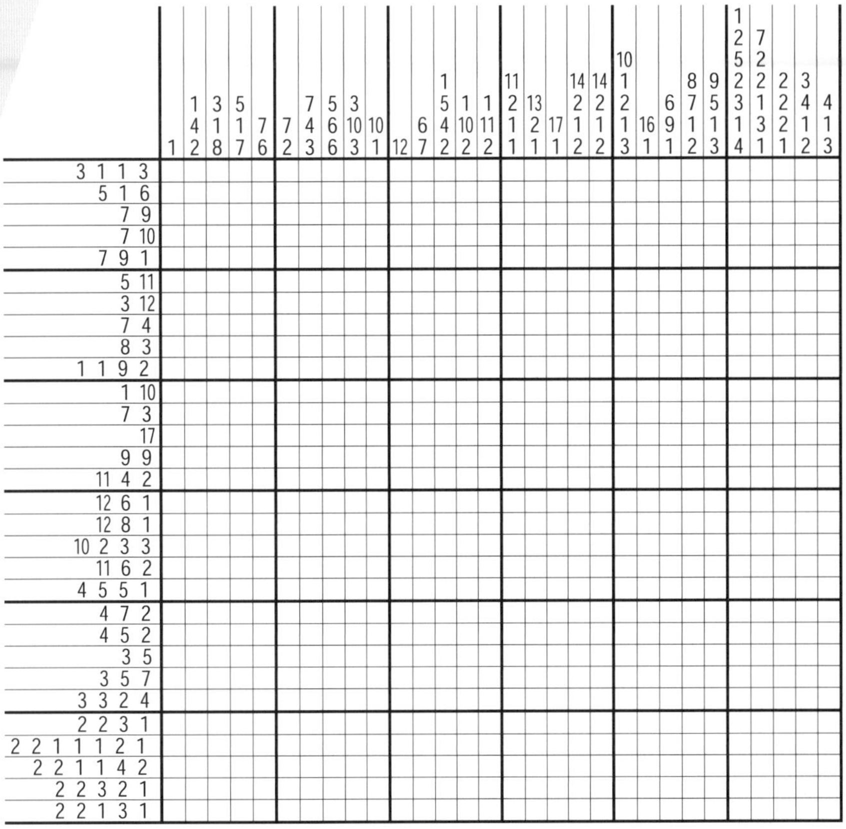
1
1 4 2
3 1 8
5 1 7
7 6
7 2
7 4 3
5 6 6
3 10 3
10 1
12
6 7
1 5 4 2
1 10 2
1 11 2
11 2 1 1
13 2 1
17 1
14 2 1 2
14 2 1 2
10 1 2 1 3
16 1
6 9 1
8 7 1 2
9 5 1 3
1 2 5 2 3 1 4
7 2 2 1 3 1
2 2 2 1
3 4 1 2
4 1 3
3 1 1 3
5 1 6
7 9
7 10
7 9 1
5 11
3 12
7 4
8 3
1 1 9 2
1 10
7 3
17
9 9
11 4 2
12 6 1
12 8 1
10 2 3 3
11 6 2
4 5 5 1
4 7 2
4 5 2
3 5
3 5 7
3 3 2 4
2 2 3 1
2 2 1 1 1 2 1
2 2 1 1 4 2
2 2 3 2 1
2 2 1 3 1

HINT:

If you feel you're getting stuck at any point during this puzzle, check one more time that you have cross-referenced every single row and column carefully to see if there is anything else you can fill in. The chances are you have missed something, and it may be that one extra shaded square that enables you to fill in many more.

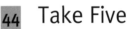

44 Take Five | Level 3

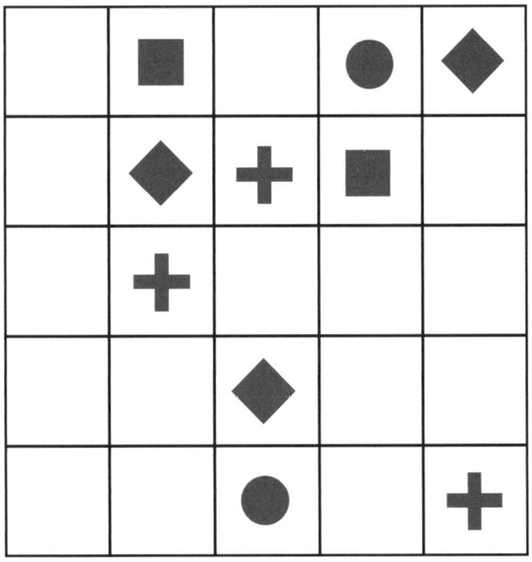

Can you complete the five by five block so that each of the symbols shown below appears in all vertical and horizontal lines?

SYMBOLS:

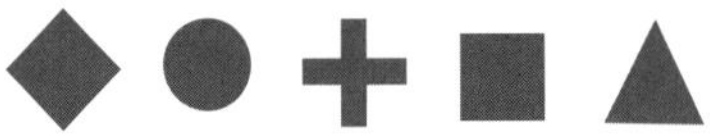

Answers on page 252

45

Queens High | Level 3

Gather eight counters or coins, or simply cut out eight small bits of paper, then use our chessboard to try an old puzzle. You must place the eight counters so no two are in the same line across or down or diagonally. If you choose, for example, A3, then you cannot put a mark in any other square in column A nor in row 3, nor in squares such as C1 or D6, which are in a diagonal line from A3.

Once you've done that, move on to the real puzzle! This is to choose eight squares, according to the rules above, so that the total of the eight numbers you mark is as high as possible. Just how many can you score with your eight queens on this numbered chessboard?

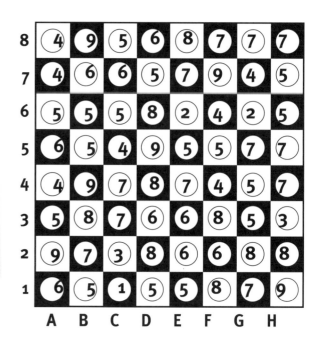

	A	B	C	D	E	F	G	H
8	4	9	5	6	8	7	7	7
7	4	6	6	5	7	9	4	5
6	5	5	5	8	2	4	2	5
5	6	5	4	9	5	5	7	7
4	4	9	7	8	7	4	5	7
3	5	8	7	6	6	8	5	3
2	9	7	3	8	6	6	8	8
1	6	5	1	5	5	8	7	9

46

Seascape III | Level 3

Another hunt is on for those hidden ships, but this time the puzzle is harder again. As usual, some parts of ships or sea squares have already been filled in, and a number next to a row or column refers to the number of occupied squares in that row or column. The ships may be positioned horizontally or vertically, but no two ships are in adjacent squares—horizontally, vertically or diagonally. This time, the part of a ship shown in a grid could be part of an Aircraft Carrier, Battleship or a Cruiser. We'll leave it to you to work out which!

HINT:
It may sound obvious, but remember that the Aircraft Carrier must be hidden in a row or column that's numbered 4 or above.

Aircraft Carrier

Battleship

Cruiser

Destroyer

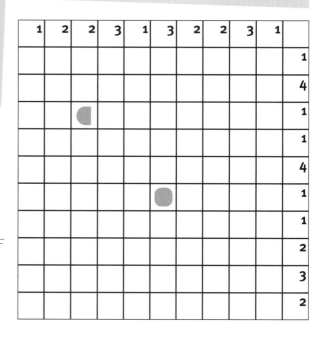

47 Pieces of Eight   Level 3

Can you carve this ornate cake along the lines of the hexagons to produce eight equal-sized sections? Each section must contain one piece of chocolate, one iced star, a dollop of cream and a strawberry.

= strawberry

= chocolate bar

= iced star

= dollop of cream

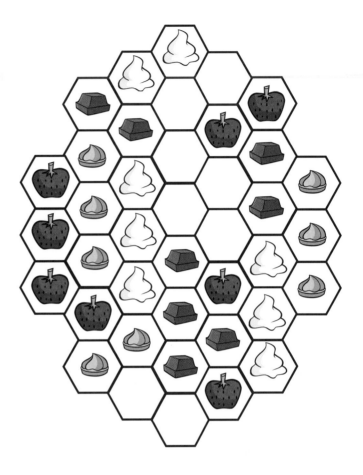

48 Pie-Eyed   Level 3

This circle represents a tasty apple pie, and eight hungry children all want a piece as quickly as possible! Can you work out how to divide the pie into EIGHT parts (not necessarily equal parts) with only THREE CUTS? No, pieces cannot be piled on top of one another!

HINT:
Not all of the cuts you make will necessarily make contact with the outside edge of the pie... think about it!

The idea here is that you must draw a line from number 1 to number 49, going through each and every one of the squares in the grid in the correct order. To show you what we mean, we've drawn a line as far as number 3. The square is number 3 because it's the third square that you have entered. So number 11 must be the eleventh square that the line reaches. Can you travel correctly all the way to square 49? We've put in a few numbers to get you started.

HINT:
This is one of those puzzles where it would be very wise to use a pencil—it may take you a few tries before you get the line completely right!

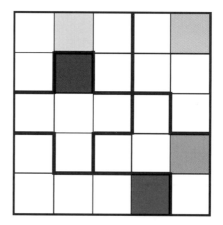

50 Logi-Squares | Level 3

These Logi-Squares are more difficult to solve than the earlier ones. As before, each line, across and down, must have one square shaded one of the five choices: this time, red, green, yellow, blue and purple. Each hue must also appear just once in each shape, shown by thick lines. Can you fill in the squares, or mark each square with its correct letter B, G, R, P or Y (for blue, green, red, purple or yellow)?

51

House That Again? | Level 3

Don, trainee real estate agent, has lost his write-ups on the houses on the Greenville estate. Luckily, he made plenty of notes on his few excursions. Now, a client has asked him what sort of house number 31 is, so he needs to get it right. Can you help Don give a detailed description of the house just by reading the notes he has made?

1. Houses with double-glazing have central heating.
2. Houses with red roofs have front gardens.
3. Odd-numbered houses have green doors.
4. Houses with iron gates have fierce dogs.
5. Houses with green doors have red roofs.
6. Houses with few visitors have white paintwork.
7. Houses without chimneys have leaded windows.
8. Houses with fierce dogs have few visitors.
9. Houses with plastic gnomes have double-glazing.
10. Detached houses have iron gates.
11. Houses with central heating do not have chimneys.
12. Houses with front gardens have plastic gnomes.
13. Even-numbered houses are detached.

52

Helping Hand | Level 3

Greg Slammer, entrusted with the beginners' section of the bridge club, gave the new recruits a little speech as follows: "To help you with your bidding, I shall give you some facts about my own hand's spades. From the eight facts I give you, it should be easy enough to deduce which spades I do or do not hold." Can you deduce what spades are in his hand?

1. If I have both King and Queen, I do not have the Jack.

2. If I have both Ace and King, I also have the Queen.

3. If I have the Queen, but not the Ace, I have the King.

4. If I have the King, but not the Queen, I have the Ace.

5. If I Have the Queen, but not the Jack, I do not have the King.

6. If I have the Jack, but not the Queen, I have the King.

7. If I have both Ace and Queen, I also have the King.

8. Of the four cards Ace, King, Queen, Jack, I have one at least.

53 Masters of Disguise | Level 3

Snuffy and his gang have been at it again. Casing the joint means, for them, adopting some outlandish disguise and working outside the bank. For one planned raid each member wore the uniform of a public service employee, adopting a foreign accent when spoken to. Suspicion was aroused by the dreadful accents, and each was taken to the police station to make a statement. The constable later admitted that it was a mistake not to have taken their names at the time and that he could only recall their overdone accents, so they were interviewed a second time. In the gang's usual attempt to obscure the truth with fiction, two of the men lied consistently and completely, and one told the truth. Can you work out which is which and identify each gang member's so-called occupation and nationality?

FIRST INTERVIEW
The Spaniard: Clogger was the Russian.
The postman was not Snuffy.
The Norwegian: The Russian was 'Arry.
The milkman was not Snuffy.
The Russian: The Spaniard was Snuffy.
'Arry was not the postman.

SECOND INTERVIEW:
'Arry: Clogger was the gasman.
The Spaniard was not the milkman.
Clogger: Snuffy was the gasman.
The Norwegian was not the milkman.
Snuffy: 'Arry was the gasman.
The Russian was not the gasman.

54 Domino Search | Level 3

Here is a bigger, tougher Domino Search puzzle for you. A set of double-nine dominoes has been laid out, using numbers instead of dots for clarity. But the lines that separate the dominoes have been left out. Can you draw in lines to show where each domino in the set has been placed? Use the check grid to tick off each domino as you find it.

5	8	0	1	0	3	4	0	1	6	3
6	7	4	5	2	0	8	5	8	9	0
6	9	4	6	0	6	2	1	2	4	7
4	7	4	2	3	1	4	0	8	7	5
4	8	5	9	6	8	0	3	9	7	2
4	3	7	4	7	1	9	2	1	3	2
6	2	5	1	0	6	1	6	1	3	6
7	8	9	7	0	2	7	8	3	8	3
0	9	1	2	3	5	5	3	9	8	5
7	9	4	2	9	6	5	8	1	5	9

0									
1									
2									
3									
4									
5									
6									
7									
8									
9									
	0	1	2	3	4	5	6	7	8	9

Two children have collected shells on the beach, and their mother encourages them to play a game. An odd number of shells are arranged in a row, and in turn each child could take one, two or three shells from the line and add it to his/her own store. When all the shells had been taken, the child with the odd number of shells would be the winner. Look at each of the games below, and find the winning move which gurantees the result of the game, whatever the other player does.

A
The player here whose turn it is next has a certain winning move. Whose move is it and what does she take?

B
Here, it is Karima's turn and she has a winning move—what is it?

C
It's Karima's first turn in this game, and she can be sure of a win with the right move. Which one?

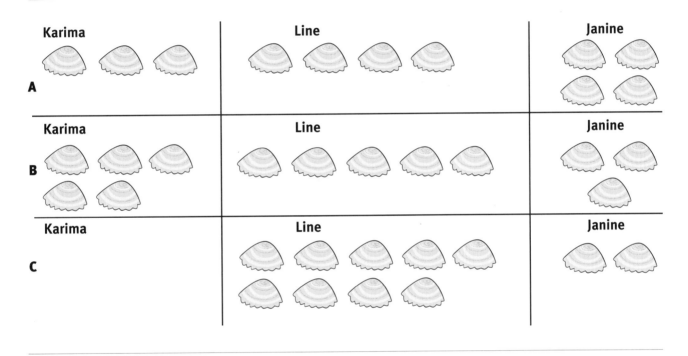

Each of the six people mentioned here has at least one sibling, and a spouse in the group. Each is a member of one of the professions mentioned. No one shares a profession with a sibling or a spouse. By reading the facts, can you identify the pre-marriage family groups, the marriages, and the profession of each person?

1. Neither Alice nor Dave is a surgeon.
2. Betty's sister's husband is an accountant.
3. Carol's husband's brother is an accountant.
4. Ed's wife is a surgeon, and so is Ed's sibling's spouse.
5. Frank's wife's brother is a lawyer.

57 Oh Rhett! | Level 3

This is another Tsunami puzzle; more difficult than before, but consequently more rewarding! For a reminder on how to solve this type of puzzle, turn to pages 176–177. With this particular Tsunami, you also need to use two pencils, one red and one black. The red numbers at the top tell you that these groups of squares must be shaded in red. The others should be shaded in black, as usual.

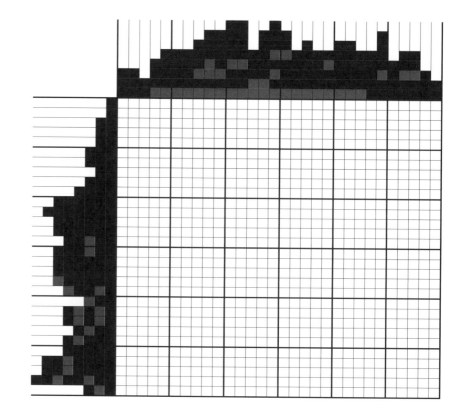

58 Easy as ABC | Level 3

Each line, across and down, is to have each of the three letters A, B and C appearing once each. So each line also has two empty squares. The letter and number given at the end of a line show you the first or second letter encountered along that line in the direction of the arrow. Note: C2 does not mean that C will be in the second square along, but that it will be the second letter you should come across in that row or column. From these clues alone, can you fill in all of the missing letters?

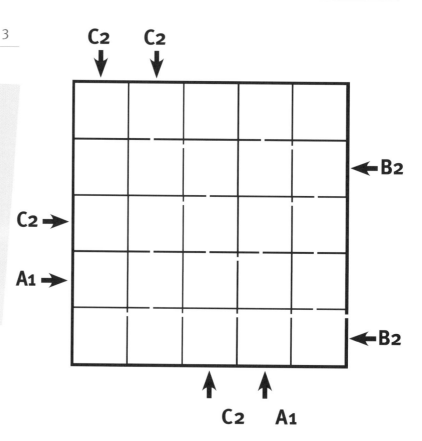

A local newspaper has made a complete mess of its ENGAGEMENTS column (shown below). In no line of the column does any name go with any other. Using the table opposite, can you identify the happy couples?

ENGAGEMENTS

Gloria Size—Andy Rest

Edna Clowds—Tommy Wrott.

Primrose Path—Wilf Hall.

Edna Player—Andy Case.

Edna Hare—Wilf Rest.

Joanna Hare—Jim Case.

Hedda Hare—Ed Case.

Joanna Player—Jim Karner.

Gloria Hare—Tommy Hall.

Joanna Size—Tommy Case.

Primrose Player—Ed Hall.

FORENAME	SURNAME	FORENAME	SURNAME
EDNA	CLOWDS	ANDY	CASE
	HARE	ED	HALL
	PATH	JIM	KARNER
	PLAYER	TOMMY	REST
	SIZE	WILF	WROTT
GLORIA	CLOWDS	ANDY	CASE
	HARE	ED	HALL
	PATH	JIM	KARNER
	PLAYER	TOMMY	REST
	SIZE	WILF	WROTT
HEDDA	CLOWDS	ANDY	CASE
	HARE	ED	HALL
	PATH	JIM	KARNER
	PLAYER	TOMMY	REST
	SIZE	WILF	WROTT
JOANNA	CLOWDS	ANDY	CASE
	HARE	ED	HALL
	PATH	JIM	KARNER
	PLAYER	TOMMY	REST
	SIZE	WILF	WROTT
PRIMROSE	CLOWDS	ANDY	CASE
	HARE	ED	HALL
	PATH	JIM	KARNER
	PLAYER	TOMMY	REST
	SIZE	WILF	WROTT

The following conversation took place in an office building, before the boss was due to fly away on business. Read it through, then work out exactly why Mr Attrick was fired.

HINT:
Think laterally on this one!

"Sir Arnold. Gerry Attrick wants to see you, sir."

"Who's he?"

"The nightwatchman, sir. He refuses to go home until he has spoken to you."

"Okay then, send him in."

An old and rather smelly man entered.

"Sir, I know you're going on a trip abroad today and I beg you not to."

"That trip's a secret—how did you know?"

"I had a dream last night—a plane crashed and you were on it. It's a warning, sir."

"Oh, don't be silly, that's rubbish. But thank you for staying on to tell me."

The businessman left on his trip and returned safely. He went straight to the office and called his secretary in.

"That Attrick man. Is he due on tonight?"

"Yes, sir."

"Call him—tell him he's FIRED."

61 Match Point | Level 4

Lay out 20 used matches or toothpicks as shown here. Now move three sticks to make SEVEN SQUARES all of the original size. How many different ways are there to do this?

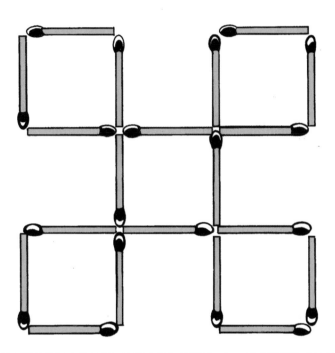

62 Not-So-Great Train Robbery | Level 4

Snuffy's gang have decided to attempt a train robbery, but as usual they get caught, this time as they attempt to make a getaway. On this occasion, the gang members have asked their wives to play a role in the robbery, so all six were questioned at the police station. As always, they tried to spread confusion by mixing truth with fantasy. One man told two lies, another two truths and the third one lie and one truth. Each loyal lady did the same, offering as much truth as her husband. Can you work out who did what, and just for the record, who's married to whom?

'Arry: Doris drove the van. Snuffy unloaded the goods from the train.

Beryl: Clogger got the keys from the guard. Wendy drove the van.

Clogger: Doris unloaded the goods from the train. 'Arry held up the driver.

Doris: Snuffy changed the signal. Wendy drove the van.

Snuffy: Beryl drove the van. Clogger changed the signal.

Wendy: Clogger loaded the goods onto the van. 'Arry held up the driver.

63 On Tap | Level 4

Mr Jones is proud of his ability to ferment a tasty wine from just about any natural ingredients. At the moment his small cellar contains six barrels. Read the clues below and try to work out which two ingredients (one from each list) are in which barrel, what the vintages are and what sort of wine is in each. On the barrels, the top sections show the different types of wine (DW=Dry White, etc), the middle sections show the six possible ingredients (AGL=Apple, grape, lychee), and the bottom sections the vintage. Cross or check these off to record your answers as you work out what each barrel contains.

Ingredients 1
Apple
Grape
Lychee
Peach
Raspberry
Sloe

Ingredients 2
Cucumber
Fig
Elderflower
Pea
Sprout
Turnip

1. The cucumber's vintage is more recent than the sprouts'. Every barrel of red is touching the other barrels of red. No barrel of dry, medium or sweet is touching another barrel the same as itself.

2. Only one pair of touching barrels contains consecutive vintages—the '89 and the '90.

3. The following are touching barrels, one item to each, which form a triangle (each line represents a different set of barrels):
    A. peach, pea and medium red
    B. apple, elderflower and the '86
    C. raspberry, turnip and the dry white
    D. sweet red, cucumber, sprout

The three straight lines of three barrels contain, not in any particular order, but one to each:
    E. sloe, grape and the '89.
    F. medium white, sweet white and dry red.
    G. elderflower, the '91 and the '87

4. The barrel numbers of the two mediums add up to six. The barrel numbers of the two drys add up to seven. The barrels with the grapes and the '91 vintage have numbers adding up to eight.

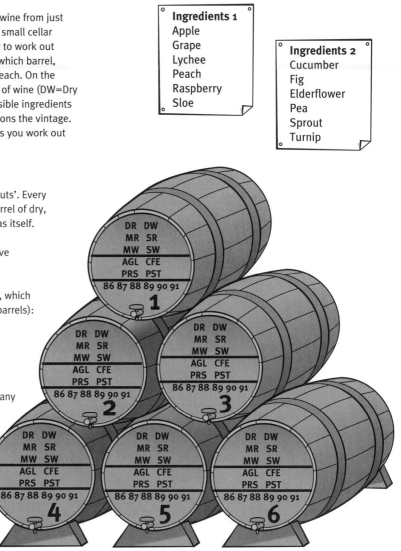

64 Logi-Square Six | Level 4

This is a particularly tough Logi-Square, as it has six squares to a section, rather than the usual five. Each square is to be filled with one of the six colors—blue, green, orange, red, yellow and white (represented by the W). All six should appear only once in each line, across and down. Also, every shape—shown by the thick lines—must have a square of each color in it. From those given, can you fill in the rest?

Here's your most tricky Seascape challenge yet. Your task is to find the vessels in the diagram. Some parts of ships or sea squares have been filled in as usual, and a number next to a row or column refers to the number of occupied squares in that row or column. The ships may be positioned horizontally or vertically, but remember that no two ships are in adjacent squares—horizontally, vertically or diagonally. Can you meet the challenge?

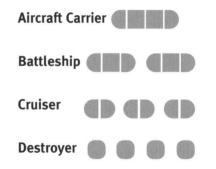

Aircraft Carrier

Battleship

Cruiser

Destroyer

Bill met three men. At first he got their names and occupations mixed up. Then, to try to help him remember, he wrote down the seven truths which are listed opposite.
But later he found that he couldn't figure out the real identities. Can you help him?

1. If Mr Arnberg is Basil, than Allan is not the attorney.

2. If Mr Cook is Basil, then the pharmacist is Mr Arnberg.

3. If Mr Cook is the pharmacist, then James is not the banker.

4. If Mr Arnberg is the pharmacist, then the attorney is Allan.

5. If Basil is Mr Cook, then Allan is not the attorney.

6. If Basil is not Mr Cook, then James is the banker.

7. If Mr Baker is Basil, then the attorney is not Allan.

67 Pot Luck

Level 4

At the village fete a plant stall had a display of 25 potted plants. Four customers each bought five plants—taking one from each row and each column. So with just 5 plants left, each was given a free gift of a plant type they hadn't already bought. One plant bought by each customer is shown. The chart indicates how many of some plants each purchased. The columns are counted from the left as you look on. Can you work out which pots each customer bought or was given free, and which plant was left on the table at the end?

HINT:
For non-gardeners, the begonia is yellow and the azalea pink!

	Azalea	Begonia	Cactus	Fern
Kevin	2			2
Len		2		2
Mary	3			
Jess			3	

68 Seeing Stars

Level 4

Can you name these two film stars? There's a tricky code involved!

HINT:
If you don't know where to start, think colors and numbers combined. This might help!

A

B

This is a Mosaic puzzle, so instead of looking at rows or columns of cells, here you must look at a square and those around it. Look at the explanation of how to solve It, then try to complete the large grid.

1. Using simple logic alone, it is possible from the numbers given to fill in the large grid and create a pixelated picture.

2. In a grid, most cells have eight neighbors, making a block of nine cells:

1	2	3
4	X	5
6	7	8

Cells along an edge have five neighbors and those in the corner only three.
The number in a cell tells you how many of it and its neighbors are to be filled in.

3. Here, five of these nine cells are to be filled in and four are to be empty, which you would show by marking with an 'X'.

0					3		3				1	
	3		3							3		0
				4		3			3		2	
3	4		3	3	3							
	3					5			3		2	
	3						3	2	1		2	
4				0		2				3		3	
	5				0		2			3	3		1
3		3	0					1		3		2	
					2		0		0		2		
3		3				4		0	1	1		3	
			2		5						1		3
3		2		4		2		1			2	3	
	5				4		3		5		4		
3				4		3		4				3	

This is a trickier version of the previous smaller puzzle of this type. Each row and column originally contained one A, one B, one C, one D and two blank squares. Each letter and number refer to the first or second of the four letters encountered when traveling in the direction of the arrow. Can you complete the original grid?

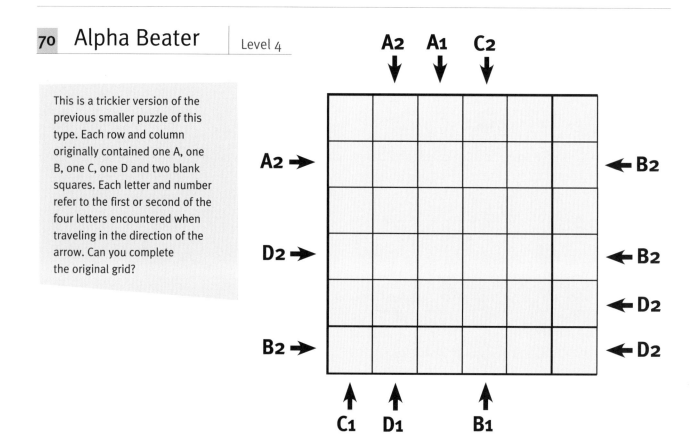

As with the previous Tsunami puzzles, the numbers tell you how many squares to shade in groups in any particular row or column. This one's tricky because it's so big—but it's a great one to dig into when you have some time to kill! If you need a reminder how to solve it, turn to pages 176–177 for a recap.

Row clues (top to bottom):
- 2 2 2 2 2 2
- 1 1 1 1 1 1
- 1 1 5 1
- 6 1 1
- 1 2
- 8 6
- 2 2 2 2
- 1 4 1 1 1 1
- 4 1 2 1 2 4 2
- 2 2 1 3 1 1 1
- 1 1 1 4 2 2 2
- 2 1 1 1 2 1 6
- 1 2 1 2 2 2 2
- 2 2 1 6 1 1
- 1 1 3 2
- 2 1 2 2 2 1
- 4 1 7 1 1 2
- 1 1 1 2 1 1
- 1 3 2 6
- 1 2 1 2 1
- 2 2 1 2 1
- 3 2 1 3 1
- 3 2 1 1
- 2 2
- 4

Can you take five letters away to leave one word?

| O | F | I | N | E | V | E | L | E | W | T | O | T | R | E | R | D | S |

73 On Course Level 4

Four employees at Hall-Thubbs Digital Co have recently taken work-related courses. From the clues given below, can you give a summary showing each employee's name, course and cost?

1. Martin's course cost $200 less than Charlie's, which cost $50 less than Holmes', which cost $200 more than was paid for Speedy Searching.
2. Connor's course cost more than Wexford's, which, at $400 per day, was not the cheapest.
3. Advanced Surfing cost $200 more than Brown's course, which cost $50 less than Tess' course.
4. Dalgliesh's course cost $50 less than Novice Newsgroups, which cost $250 more than Browsing for Beginners.

FORENAME	SURNAME	COST	COURSE
Connor			
Charlie			
Tess			
Martin			

74 Double Trouble Level 4

This is the toughest domino puzzle yet! A set of double-six dominoes has been laid out, using numbers instead of spots. The thick lines show the position of each domino. The numbers at the end of each row and column are the numbers that must be placed in that line. In each horizontal domino, the smaller number is always on the left. In each vertical domino the smaller number is always on top. Given that the shaded dominoes in the grid are the doubles, can you find the unique place for each domino?

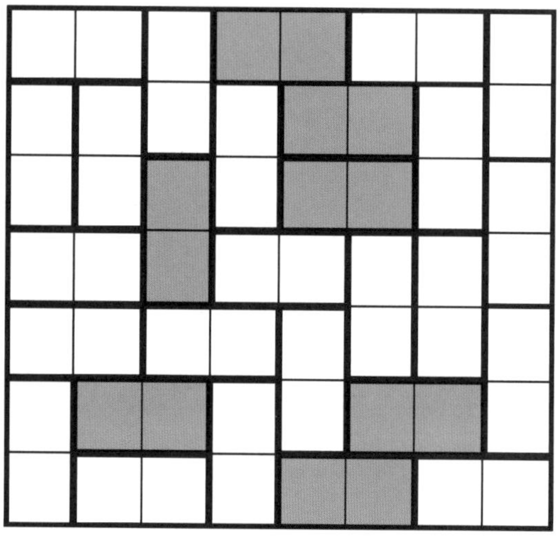

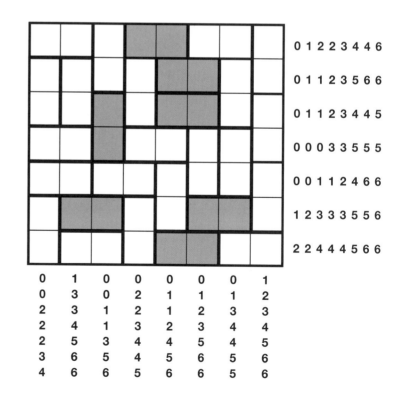

0 1 2 2 3 4 4 6
0 1 1 2 3 5 6 6
0 1 1 2 3 4 4 5
0 0 0 3 3 5 5 5
0 0 1 1 2 4 6 6
1 2 3 3 3 5 5 6
2 2 4 4 4 5 6 6

0	1	0	0	0	0	0	1
0	3	0	2	1	1	1	2
2	3	1	2	1	2	3	3
2	4	1	3	2	3	4	4
2	5	3	4	4	5	4	5
3	6	5	4	5	6	5	6
4	6	6	5	6	6	5	6

75 Dance On | Level 4

At a Fancy Dress Ball, five leading couples have cobbled together different costumes and stepped out, led in the foxtrot by the King and Queen. In the first four dances each had a different partner from among the five and nobody danced with his or her spouse. The reporter for the local magazine recorded, as best she could, the five couples for each dance (see table). By looking at this, can you work out the name of each couple and which costumes they were wearing?

FOXTROT	RUMBA	TWIST	WALTZ
JIM & THE QUEEN	MR ELLIS & WILMA	PIRATE & KAY	ALAN & MONK'S WIFE
MR CORY & NORMA	LEN & LION'S WIFE	FAY'S HUSBAND & MRS WALKER	FAIRY'S HUSBAND & ASTRONAUTS WIFE
TIM & MATA HARI	MR MORRIS & MRS STEVENS	KING & FLOWER GIRL	SNOW WHITE'S HUSBAND & PAM
BOB & MRS MORRIS	MR WALKER & SNOW WHITE	ASTRONAUT & MONK'S WIFE	LEN & KAY
LION & WILMA	PIRATE & MRS ELLIS	PAM'S HUSBAND & FAIRY	BOB & NORMA

76 Hidden Value | Level 4

In these two collections of shapes, each of the rectangles has a value between 1 and 9 (no two values being the same in one puzzle). When two or more rectangles overlap, their values are added together, and some of the sums have been done. In each case, can you work out the value of A-E?

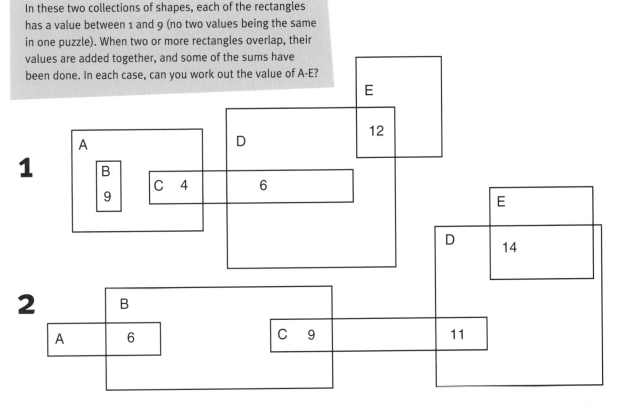

77

We Are Sailing | Level 4

Here's another Mosaic puzzle based on
looking at a square and those around it, rather than rows or columns of cells. It works just like the puzzle on page 212, where you'll find a detailed explanation of how to solve it.

HINT:
As you fill in squares with Xs (to show they're empty), keep the Xs light as you go along, so that numbers needed later are not blotted out by a layer of ink.

	5		5	4	3			3		4			
		6			3		3		4		5	5	
	5		3		2	3	3	2		3	4	4	
2		3		3	1	4			3	2		2		3
	1	1			0		6				1		
				3		3			4		1		
	5					5		5		6		1	
		9			6		5		6		6		1
	6		6		5		7		7		9		6
					5		6		5		6		3
	0		0			5			6				6
2		2		2		6		7		6		6	
	2		1		3		6		6		6		5
		4					5				5		2
	1		2		2		1		1				1

78

Alpha-Square | Level 4

We offer another tricky alphabet square to fill. Each row and column originally contained one A, one B, one C, one D and two blank squares. Each letter and number refer to the first or second of the four letters encountered when traveling in the direction of the arrow. Can you complete the original grid?

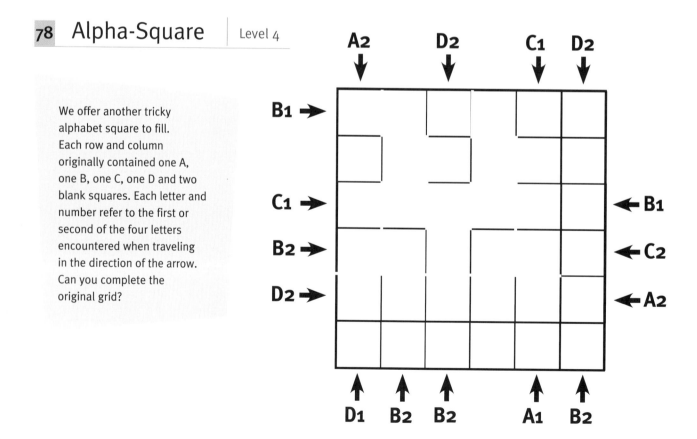

Five women are about to go overseas on holiday, but before leaving, they have to arrange for friends to look after their pets. Can you discover to which country each woman will travel, the type of pet she will be leaving and the name of that pet?

	CYPRUS	TURKEY	SPAIN	ITALY	THAILAND	GEMMA	HENRY	JOEY	KYLIE	MELISSA	BUDGERIGAR	CAT	DOG	HAMSTER	PARROT
MRS ABBOT															
MRS BRADY															
MRS CHARMER															
MRS DONKIN															
MRS EDWARDS															
BUDGERIGAR															
CAT															
DOG															
HAMSTER															
PARROT															
GEMMA															
HENRY															
JOEY															
KYLIE															
MELISSA															

1. Mrs Charmer is going to Cyprus but she's not the owner of Henry the parrot.
2. Gemma's owner is going to Turkey. Kylie the budgerigar does not belong to Mrs Abbot or Mrs Donkin.
3. Mrs Edwards owns the hamster. She is not going to Spain or Italy.
4. The cat's owner is going to Thailand but this is not Mrs Brady or Mrs Donkin, who does not own Joey or Melissa the dog.
5. Kylie's owner is not going to Spain or Cyprus.

OWNER	RESORT	PET NAME	PET TYPE

This is the very last logic puzzle, so give it your best shot! Simply divide the opposite grid into L-shaped pieces of the same size so that each piece contains exactly two pink circles. All the squares must be used. Sounds simple enough? Then go ahead, give it a try—you might find that it's a little tougher than it looks!

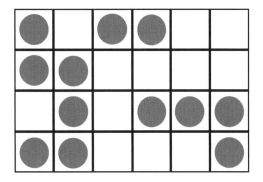

Keep It In Mind
Answers

LEVEL 1

1 – KIM'S GAME
a) 2 b) 8 c) rocket, plane, truck, snake, banana skin, telephone, dinosaur, car.

2 – WORD LINKS
a) 3: horse, rabbit, dog b) 2: cheese, biscuit c) 2: flute, guitar d) 3: shoe, jacket, hat.

3 – ME AND MY PA
a) Nancy Reagan b) Robert Redford c) Your answer here depends on the associations you have made. For example, you might connect Will Smith's father (refrigeration engineer) with Robert Redford's father (milkman). Alternatively, you might connect Nancy Reagan's father (car salesman) with Jerry Hall's dad (truck driver). Our preference is to link Elizabeth Taylor's father (art dealer) with Greta Scacchi's father (artist).

4 – BEFORE AND AFTER
a) Red patch on middle fish's eye has moved b) Direction of movement of isolated weed at right has changed c) Stone in bridge missing d) Bubble by big red fish's head missing e) Scales missing from orange fish at right f) Shadowy fronds present in background on second picture.

5 – FAMILY TREE
a) Teddy b) 29 c) 1 year d) Joel e) Joel f) Peter Tchaisky.

6 – JIMMY O'BRIEN AND THE KNOBLINGS
a) 8 b) 12 c) Herion High School d) Knoblings are ludicrous because they are bright pink e) The way to Herion is past "that tree" and through the park.

7 – COLORFUL WORDS
a) red b) blue c) orange d) rainbow. In England, the mnemonic for remembering the sequence of colors of the rainbow is: Richard Of York Gained Battle In Vain. The mnemonic, HOMES, is used to remember the Great Lakes: Huron, Ontario, Michigan, Erie, Superior.

8 – WHO AM I?
Madonna

9 – CLASSIC CINEMA
a) 25th b) One c) 8:00 d) 25th (otherwise the two films would clash) e) *Breakfast at Tiffany's*.

10 – SPOT THE DIFFERENCES
a) Number of sausages b) Direction moon is facing c) Hair on Punch d) Stripes on Punch's shirt e) Wrinkle on crocodile's nose f) Dot on bell at end of Punch's hat.

11 – NUMERACY
a) 2 b) 29493573745 c) 5.

12 – TITANIC TALE
a) Brock Lovett b) Cal Hockley c) 17 d) Rose said she didn't know what had happened to the diamond e) He won his ticket in a pub.

13 – THINGS FOR HENRY VIII TO DO
a) April 15, 1534 b) wild boar c) court jesters d) descant recorder e) varicose veins and overweight.

14 – THE ISLAND OF FREEWAY
a) right–hand lane b) route 1 c) 14.

15 – PICTURE SETS
a) ball b) horse c) alligator, ball, cow, dog, Elvis, flag, girl, horse.

16 – WHO AM I?
Abraham Lincoln

17 – CONVERSATIONS
a) dark blue b) Denim store c) Paul's wife d) a silver watch.

18 – SYMBOL ORDER
a) asterisk, star b) the positions of the third and fifth symbols, the triangles, have been switched.

19 – WHODUNIT?
a) pasta salad, blueberries, chocolate bar b) Nigel c) she claimed that she only wanted to eat unhealthy stuff d) Elliott's lunch was in a bag, Milo's lunch is in a bright blue box.

20 – DUCK SHOOT
a) green b) purple, with a blue beak c) four d) green.

LEVEL 2

21 – KIM'S GAME
a) 5: teddy, stopwatch, pizza slice, walkie talkie, radio b) cat, mouse, sheep, dog c) walkie talkie, radio, stopwatch d) 3: fish, rooster, hen e) crab.

22 – WORD LINK
a) house (greenhouse, doghouse, full house) b) case (notecase, suitcase, staircase) c) kin (Kinks, bikini) d) tree (Wall sTREEt).

24 – BAND PRACTICE
a) 3756 b) Number pages c) Give new reed for OC by Tuesday d) No, it's 432 5715 e) June 7.

25 – CRIME SPREE

26 – MONUMENT
a) 305'1" b) France c) 354 d) *Isere* e) Bedloe's Island f) Frederic Auguste Bartholdi.

27 – SHOPPING LIST
Quill repair kit, ink, paper, tights, apples, theatre tickets, fake blood, weekly entertainment review, dagger.

28 – NAME GAME
In the order in which they appear on page 24, the names are: Julie Kyoto, David Brains, Sarah Bland, Peter Davis, John Smith, Steve Jones.

29 – FAMILY TREE
a) Bubbles, Chocolate, Sadie b) Bubbles, Sadie c) Nixon, Belle.

30 – SPOT THE DIFFERENCES
a) White line from middle of road b) Box in back of yellow truck c) Bonnet of green truck d) Shadow under small blue car at far side e) Side of red truck's trailer has changed color f) Side window of furthest away purple truck missing.

32 – APARTMENT
a) utility room b) bathroom, bedroom c) living room, dining area d) The length of the bedroom.

33 – CHICAGO
a) In the jazz clubs of 1920s Chicago b) Fred Cassely c) Velma murdered her husband and sister d) Billy Flynn. He represents Roxie after receiving $3000 from Amos, her husband e) Kitty.

34 – HANDBAG HAUL
a) natural b) 3: gloves, address book, sunglasses c) scarlet d) 3: mascara, hairbrush, purse.

35 – NEGATIVE MEMORY
The coat, handcuffs, orange, butterfly and alarm clock are missing. They have been replaced by a feather, a key, a candle, a cup and a pipe.

36 – MATCH THE SEQUENCE
Sequence A: c
Sequence B reversed: a

37 – EXCHANGE STUDENT
a) Friday b) Football match c) Thursday on Oxford St and Bond St d) Heathrow e) Tuesday.

39 – BATTLESHIP
a) Hit b) B2–B4, D5–F5, E7–G7 c) D1.

40 – IDENTITY PARADE
The last face in the second row (blue, yellow background).

LEVEL 3

42 – SEQUENCE CHALLENGE
a) No b) Row 3 c) Cheese d) Row 1 e) Bath.

43 – SPORTS STARS
1. Mickey Rourke and Liam Neeson 2. Bill Cosby and Warren Beatty 3. Paul Newman 4. Gymnastics 5. Wrestling.

44 – SCHOOL DAYS
1. Math 2. Friday 3. Monday and Friday 4. Tuesday 5. Drama and Math 6. Spanish.

45 – HOUSE NUMBERS
1. Maddox 2. Calver 3. south 4.Maddox 5. south.

47 – TABLE SERVICE
a) 3: 1, 4, 7 b) 6 c) Medium d) 2: 3,8 e) No tomatoes f) 2: 1, 4.

49 – PAIRS
a) Penpal b) Tightrope c) Clocktower d) Pole position e) Hairpiece f) Curtain call g) Shoehorn h) Manhole.

50 – CONVERSATIONS
a) Hockey practice b) Kitty, Pete, Simon c) Train d) If the bus doesn't come soon e) He forgot his fare f) Cab g) Next week.

51 – SIX BLIND MICE
c (thumb missing from free hand).

52 – WHO AM I?
Nelson Mandela.

53 – FUNNY FAKES
The flowers, the green landscape, the abstract circle shapes, the long–nosed dog and the cat are all fakes.

54 – FAMILY TREE
a) 1734 b) Charles Carter and Anne Butler Moore c) 3 d) 1807 e) John Carter and Elizabeth Hill f) 1756.

55 – SPOT THE DIFFERENCES
6: Moon lower in the sky, eyebrow on caveman with hands in the air, star missing on right side of the picture under upraised arm, crescent shadow missing from top of cave, longer animal skin on caveman to the right of the picture, extra spots on front caveman's animal skin.

56 – BEING ERNEST
a) In the country b) to visit his rakish brother, Ernest c) Cousin d) Lady Bracknell e) In a handbag at Victoria station f) In order to woo Cecily g) They are both in love with the idea of Ernest h) They are brothers.

57 – MATCH THE SEQUENCE
a) Second row b) Blue with a red stripe c) Seventh column d) Paper clip e) Present f) Off g) Six h) Yes i) Lemon, orange, pineapple j) Rolling pin.

58 – BATTLESHIP
a) miss
c) B3

59 – PICTURES STRIP
C

60 – BARMAN!
a) 4 b) 1 c) With ice and a slice d) $55.

LEVEL 4

61 – MATCH THE SEQUENCE
No – in sequence 1, the third and fourth dice are the wrong way around. In sequence 2, the first and seventh dice should be swapped.

62 – VIRTUAL TOUR
a) Three b) Opposite the bathroom, at the front of the house c) The white house, the green door and the green potted plant d) Three; two on the porch, and one on the hall shelf e) Two; the main and guest bedrooms f) Seven; four dining chairs, two sofas and an armchair g) Blue h) Three; the door you enter from the living room, the patio door to outside and the sliding door to the kitchen.

63 – NUMBER CRUNCHING
a) 1 b) 14 c) Word (four instances, digit – three instances) d) 8 e) The "7 SEVEN 7" sequence should be "SEVEN 77".

64 – BEFORE AND AFTER
a) The girl is frowning rather than smiling b) The boy's left shoe has one less band on it c) There is a white dot missing beneath the boy's left foot d) The boy's scarf has a line missing e) There is a blue dot missing beneath the girl's right hand.

65 – MEMORY MAZE

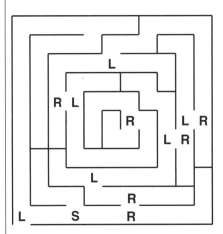

66 – WHODUNIT?
a) Major Sam Bartlett b) Clive, his wife June, and his mother c) Doctor, the billiards room d) Lockgear e) Dining room and reading room f) June to have a bath, Madame Richaux to fetch her diary g) George and Martin h) June.

67 – PICTURE PERFECT
a) Third b) Hat c) Hammer d) Right e) Fish f) Jug g) Yellow h) Flower.

68 – WHAT'S THE SCORE?
a) Salamanca is top, Cordoba is bottom b) Pamplona c) Burgos d) 20 e) Murcia f) 17 lose g) Valladolid h) 6:30 this evening.

70 – NON–WORD SEARCH

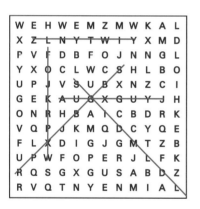

72 – PRESENT AND CORRECT?
Bob's big sister wanted an Anne Tyler, not Annie Proulx, novel, and Jim wanted Frommer's, not Fodor's New Zealand guide. The DVD should have been *Goldeneye*, not *Goldfinger*, and the flashlight and barbecue tools are going to the wrong men. His big sister's daughters are getting something pink, but the umbrella and coat sets are not "for the bedroom." His dad wanted A3, not M3 Tour, golfballs, and his Grandpa was expecting Jim Beam whiskey, not Jack Daniel's. The Estée Lauder perfume should have been Pleasures Eau de Parfum, not Beyond Paradise, and his Grandma wanted Tea Rose, rather than Rosewater, soap. Finally, he's forgotten the dangly silver earrings for Hannah.

73 – NEGATIVE MEMORY
Items missing: a) Present b) Lemon c) Bag d) Fork e) Brush.
New items: a) Aces b) Banana c) Hammer d) Bath e) Feather.

74 – BURGER BAR
a) MegaCola b) MegaBurger with cheese c) Salsa d) 10:24 e) MegaLemon f) No.

75 – FAMILY TREE
a) Rosey b) John Francis Fitzgerald and Mary Josephine Hannon c) 1832 – 1900 d) Mary Augusta Hickey e) Joseph Patrick Kennedy f) Mary Josephine Hannon g) 1835 h) James Hickey and Michael Hannon.

76 – TAKE YOUR CUE
Picture 3

77 – DINNER PARTY
Sarah, between Richard and Dean.

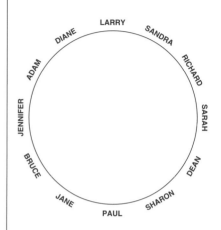

78 – WHAT'S ON
a) Black b) Robinson's Plastics (15, as opposed to Pinkerton Publishing's 10) c) Eye See Opticians Conference d) Tom Belton e) CTC Electronics Conference f) Three.

79 – BEDROOM BOOBY TRAP
The order is: A, F, C, E, D, B.

80 – CARD SHARP
J♠ 10♥ 7♦ Q♣ 2♣

Word Power
Answers

LEVEL 1

1 – ANAGRAM INITIALS
Beach, archer, droop, grieve, ebony, rustic.
The answer is BADGER.

2 – QUICK CROSS

3 – ODD ONE OUT
1. TURQUOISE (blue, the rest are shades of red) 2. STEP (the rest are parts of a shoe)
3. TUBA (brass, the rest are woodwind)
4. STAR (the rest are circular) 5. AZALEA (a shrub, the rest are trees) 6. POTATO (the rest are fruit).

4 – ARROWORD

5 – QUICK CROSS

6 – MATCH THE MEANING
1) D. Ghoulish 2) C. Tyrant 3) A. Relinquish
4) B. Regalia 5) D. Deceptive 6) C. Criticize.

7 – BIBLICAL BOOKS

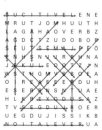

8 – VOWEL PLAY
1. France 2. Canada 3. Japan 4. Ethiopia
5. Albania 6. Croatia 7. Italy 8. Australia
9. Jamaica 10. Iceland.

9 – SLIM CHANCE

10 – TOTAL OPPOSITES
1) C. Misery 2) A. Foolhardy 3) D. Superfluous
4) A. Inertia 5) D. Impotence 6) B. Clumsiness.

11 – SOMETHING FISHY

12 – BRIGHT IDEAS
Mystic, allow, uplift, venom, earthy.
The answer is MAUVE.

13 – STARTER BLOCKS
1. CAN 2. MAN 3. CAR 4. PAT 5. SUN 6. DEN.

14 – ARROWORD

15 – BRANCH OUT

Whiten, impact, lumber, launch, orchid, watery. The answer is WILLOW.

16 – WORD LADDERS

A) BOOK, rook, rood, road, READ.
B) GIVE, live, like, lake, TAKE.
C) NAIL, fail, fall, fill, FILE.
D) CALM, palm, pale, page, RAGE.

17 – THE MISSING WORD

1. CARD 2. LIVE 3. ANTI 4. STAR 5. SENT 6. DEAL.

18 – PYRAMID

1) A 2) Ad 3) Lad 4) Lead 5) Dealt 6) Detail 7) Dialect 8) Delicate 9) Elucidate.

19 – ARE YOU GAME?

During, amateur, rancid, trouble, symbol. The answer is DARTS.

20 – STRAIGHT FORWARD

LEVEL 2

21 – WHO SAID WHAT?

1. Hives • Oboe 2. Assortment,
3. Loads • Nous 4. Loofah • New,
5. Eschew • Can 6. Banana • Hid
7. Effect • Hem 8. Right • Soon
9. Receptacle 10. Yours • Seat.
Quote: "It's for every nameless faceless woman of color that now has a chance because this door tonight has been opened." (Halle Berry)

22 – AMERICAN ANAGRAMS

1. Minnesota 2. Maryland 3. Nebraska
4. Pennsylvania 5. Vermont 6. Nevada
7. Washington.

23 – CODEWORD

24 – PATHFINDER

Pacific, Adriatic, Mediterranean, Atlantic, South China, Caribbean, Baltic, Norwegian, Barents, Ionian, Antarctic, Indian, Arabian, Tasman, Aegean, Yellow, Beaufort, Sargasso, Irish, Red, Bering.

25 – FACTFINDER

26 – ODD MAN OUT

1. COB (male, the rest are female animals)
2. PLINTH (column base, the rest are watch parts) 3. TIBIA (leg, the rest are arm bones)
4. MOTH (the others are swimming strokes)
5. ORANGE (the others are primary hues)
6. ATHENS (it's in Greece, the others are Italian cities).

27 – HAT BOX

28 – YOU WEAR IT WELL

1. Kate Bush 2. Cape Town 3. (US) Masters (golf) 4. Brian Hyland 5. Crimean War
6. Cyd Charisse 7. Denzel Washington
8. Leotard (Jules) 9. Svengali 10. Dr. Seuss.

29 – DILEMMA

30 – RIDDLE
The solution is GORILLA.

31 – MISSING LINKS

32 – ODD MAN OUT
1. THE CANDIDATE (Robert Redford, the rest are Michael Caine films)
2. EARTHLY POWERS (Anthony Burgess, the rest are Graham Greene novels)
3. SALOMÉ (Oscar Wilde, the rest are G.B. Shaw plays).

33 – FIRST THOUGHTS

34 – MATCH THE MEANING
1) A. Jaunty 2) B. Fraudulence 3) A. Ludicrous
4) A. Capricious 5) C. Instinctive
6) D. Motionlessness.

35 – SECOND THOUGHTS

36 – ODD MAN OUT
1. OPORTO (Portuguese city, the rest are Spanish cities) 2. MITE (arachnid, the rest are insects) 3. ESPADRILLE (footwear item, the rest are hats) 4. MANX (a cat, the others are all breeds of dog) 5. MIRROR (the others can all go after the word HAIR) 6. COCCYX (part of the spine, the others are all parts of the eye).

37 – CODEWORD

38 – COMMON BOND
1. *Goldfinger* 2. *A View to a Kill* 3. *Tomorrow Never Dies* 4. *Die Another Day* 5. *Moonraker* 6. *Live and Let Die*.

39 – WINE BOX

40 – OPPOSITES ATTRACT
1) D. Contraction 2) C. Destroy
3) B. Contaminate 4) B. Promising
5) C. Guiltless 6) A. Outspoken.

Answers

LEVEL 3

41 – JIGSAW CROSSWORD

42 – MUSICAL MIX
1. Beethoven 2. Sibelius 3. Tchaikovsky 4. Mendelssohn.

43 – WHO SAID WHAT?
1. Kitchen 2. Yam • Boo 3. Loathes 4. Ideas 5. Evasive 6. Mob • Sec 7. Iranian 8. Negate 9. Offbeat 10. Gobbets 11. Ugliest 12. Emotion.
Quote: "I have been getting a lot of grief about my backside. It seems to have become a national obsession." (Kylie Minogue)

44 – RELATIVELY SPEAKING
1. Warren Beatty 2. Ethan and Joel Coen 3. Simon 4. Graham Greene 5. Steve Martin 6. Dr. Hook 7. Whoopi Goldberg 8. American 9. Gemini 10. Guthrie.

45 – CONTINUITY

46 – ODD MAN OUT
1. BORROW (the rest begin and end with the same letter) 2. BLURB (the rest all derive from German) 3. CALL (the rest spell another word reading backward) 4. WIGWAM (the others only contain one vowel).

47 – CALL MY BLUFF
1)A 2) C 3) B.

49 – TWO TRICKY

50 – MATCH THE MEANING
1) A. Salty 2) B. Nous 3) D. Residual 4) A. Unrelated 5) C. Briskness 6) D. Necessary.

51 – HONEYCOMB
1. Convoy 2. Canyon 3. Apathy 4. Hockey 5. Kidnap 6. Inkpen 7. Impact 8. Karate 9. Radial 10. Menial 11. Covert 12. Votary 13. Oblate 14. Temple 15. Satire 16. Martyr 17. Gambol 18. Portal 19. Basset 20. Strive 21. Gargle 22. Eating 23. Novice 24. Cradle.

52 – TARGET
Demon, Deny, Done, Doyen, Dune, Dyne, Ends, Eponym, Mend, Menu, Meson, Money, Mound, Muon, Node, Nodus, Nome, Nope, Nose, Nosed, Nosey, Nosy, Nous, Nude, Omen, Onus, Open, Opens, Pend, Pends, Peon, Peony, Pond, Pone, Pons, Pony, Pound, PSEUDONYM, Puny, Send, Sends, Sonde, Sound, Spend, Spun, Syne, Synod, Undo, Undoes, Unposed, Upend, Upends, Upon.

53 – BACKWARD
CLUE NUMBERS (in order of clues on page)
Across 33, 19, 12, 37, 25, 10, 11, 21, 31, 22, 14, 13, 5, 34, 28, 17, 9, 23, 36, 35, 1.
Down 27, 18, 6, 32, 15, 5, 29, 22, 20, 4, 16, 31, 8, 2, 26, 7, 24, 14, 1, 30, 3.

54 – RIDDLE
The answer is OSTRICH.

55 – ODD MAN OUT
1. STEVENSON (senator, the rest were 20th century US presidents) 2. FORMENTERA (Balearic island, the rest are Canary Islands) 3. CURABLE (the rest contain a tree—ELM, ASH, OAK) 4. HILARIOUS (the other words each have a double set of letters in them) 5. DAUGHTER (the other words can all be preceded by the word HOUSE) 6. SIR (the other words read the same backward as forward).

56 – CRYPTIC CHALLENGE

57 – TWO TRICKY

58 – OPPOSITES ATTRACT
1) C. Sparse 2) D. Stringent 3) A. Veteran
4) B. Harmless 5) A. Insignificant
6) D. Iniquity.

59 – SKELETON

60 – THE NAME GAME
1. Henry Tudor 2. Henry Kissinger 3. Henry Ford 4. Henry Fielding 5. Henry Fonda
6. Henry Moore 7. Henry W. Longfellow
8. Henry Thoreau 9. Henry Hudson
10. Henry Thomas.

LEVEL 4

61 – TREBLE CHANCE

62 – CALL MY BLUFF
1. A 2. A 3. C.

63 – ELVIS LIVES
1. "Blue Suede Shoes" 2. "His Latest Flame"
3. "Return To Sender" 4. "Suspicious Minds"
5. "Crying In The Chapel."

64 – DINGBATS
1. Scrambled eggs 2. All in good time
3. Split second timing 4. Bags under the eyes.

65 – JIGSAW CROSSWORD

S	E	G	M	E	N	T		M	I	S	T	A	K	E
C		L		R	A	Y		T		N				N
A	V	O	C	A	D	O		T	H	O	U	G	H	T
M		S		S	A	T	C	H	E	L		L		R
P	I	S	C	E	S		L		R	E	M	E	D	Y
	G		L		H	O	U	S	E		O		E	
A	L	L	O	T		P	E	N		S	L	O	P	E
O		U	R	G	E		A	R	E	A		O		
R	O	U	T	E		R	K		G	R	A	T	E	
I		N		A	M	A	T	E	U	R		R		L
G	L	I	N	T		O		E	X	I	L	E		C
H		T		M	U	S	T	A	N	G		S		C
T	H	E	M	E		W		M		A	D	E	P	T
O			O	N	C	E		B	I	T	E		I	
S	T	O	U	T			D	O	E		E	T	H	O	S
E		S		H	E	A	R	T		E		U		
S	L	E	E	V	E		T		A	R	R	E	S	T
E		V		I	R	K	S	O	M	E		N		I
P	L	A	T	O	O	N		V	E	N	I	S	O	N
I		D		L		E	V	E		A		U		G
A	V	E	R	A	G	E		R	E	L	I	E	V	E

66 – INSIDE STORY

Sofa, Chair, Desk, Cabinet, Bed, Settee, Table, Wardrobe, Chest, Console.

67 – BRACER

1. Forest, frets, rest 2. Remain, Maine, mine
3. Maiden, named, dame 4. Veiled, lived, lied
5. Lacked, caked, deck 6. Wounds, sound,
dons 7. Israel, laser, sear 8. Tennis, tines,
sine 9. Sordid, Doris, Dors 10. Lagoon, along,
goal 11. Wangle, angle, lean.
The two features are:
ORIEL WINDOW and FAN VAULTING.

68 – SPIRAL

Pizzicato – Oliver – redbreast – trattoria
– Abraham – melody – yellow – worthless –
sensation – narrow – wireless – skied – dozen
– nib – bias – sheen – nylon – news – sir.
The two mollusks are:
PERIWINKLE and RAZORSHELL.

69 – OUTFIT

70 – THE NAME GAME

1. Jane Eyre 2. Jane Campion 3. Lady Jane
Grey 4. Jane Russell 5. Calamity Jane
6. Jane Seymour 7. Jayne Torvill
8. Jane Austen 9. Jane Fonda
10. Jane Krakowski.

71 – THREE–WAY CROSS

ACROSS: 1. Scope 6. Earl 10. Erie 11. Fatal
14. Ass 15. Arena 19. Esses 21. Pat 24. Naiad
27. Tsar 28. Gate 29. Brute.
DIAGONALLY L TO R: 1. Sores 3. Ore 5. Elf
6. Entracte 8. Rely 12. Date Line 13. Era 17.
Tee 21. Pease 22. Anna 26. Dub 27. Tau.
DIAGONALLY R TO L: 2. Co-ed 4. Priest 7. Ana
9. Learn 11. Feats 16. Eased 18. Caesar 20.
Slang 23. Erst 25. Ant.

72 – OPPOSITES ATTRACT

1) B. Generosity 2) D. Courageous
3) A. Slowness.

73 – CRYPTIC CROSS

74 – DINGBATS

1. Registered nurse 2. Bermuda Triangle
3. Beat about the Bush 4. Late in life
5. Crossroads 6. Lost in Space.

75 – ROUNDABOUT

RADIAL: 1. Style 2. Rates 3. Doses 4. Crane
5. Creel 6. Chess 7. Chest 8. Ruler 9. Elder
10. Ranks 11. Shear 12. Astra 13. Tiara 14.
Adore 15. Admin 16. Pried 17. Prate 18. Petal
19. Pearl 20. Bogie 21. Eider 22. Inane 23.
Seine 24. Kilts
CIRCULAR: 6. Sled 12. Assert 13. Tend 19. Ell
20. Brisker 25. Alien 26. Ones 27. Sulk 28.
Irish 29. Ate 30. Roe 31. East 32. Lee 33. End
34. Oat 35. Aim 36. Tag 37. Daily 38. Heard
39. Reinter 40. Scrape.

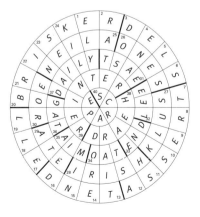

76 – ODD MAN OUT

1. TORRIDLY (the rest are anagrams of each other) 2. NEW (the rest all sound like numbers) 3. PROLONG (the rest contain three consecutive letters of the alphabet)
4. BORROW (the letters of the others are all in alphabetical order) 5. NOTICE (the vowels in all the other words are in alphabetical order) 6. SPEECH (the other words can each be split into two words of three letters, eg CAR and TON).

77 – ALPHA–RHYME

78 – MATCH THE MEANING

1) C. Cajole 2) B. Entanglement 3) B. Harmful
4) C. Suspension 5) B. Substantial
6) A. Gloomy.

79 – ARCANA

K	E	N	D	O	P	A	L	D	E	R	N
A	Q	M	E	M	O	V	A	I	S	Y	A
R	U	F	F	E	M	I	R	A	C	L	E
R	I	G	E	L	E	A	R	L	A	T	V
I	V	L	R	E	B	T	A	S	L	O	E
C	O	U	N	T	E	R	S	C	A	R	P
E	C	C	L	E	S	I	A	S	T	E	S
G	A	O	L	R	T	X	F	D	O	U	F
O	L	S	I	N	I	A	F	O	R	T	Y
A	P	I	C	I	A	N	R	E	M	I	T
T	I	D	I	E	R	C	A	T	S	C	T
S	U	E	T	T	Y	E	P	H	A	S	E

80 – FIGURE IT OUT

1. Blue Suede Shoes (Elvis) 2. Jack Nicholson
3. The Commodores 4. Nemo 5. "Revelation"
6. Andie McDowell 7. Brad Pitt 8. Paul Simon
9. Lily Tomlin 10. Tropic of Capricorn.

Expand Your Mind
Answers

LEVEL 1

1 – KNOTTY PROBLEM
No, the rope will not form a knot.

2 – RAMBLING SENTENCE
If you take the correct route, the maze spells out "This sentence is hidden."

3 – GLASS ACT
Move the middle match across so that the top right match points down at the middle of it. Move top left match diagonally down to the other side of the cherry.

4 – CIRCLE SIZES
The inside circles are exactly the same size. The size of the surrounding circles in comparison to the inner circles makes the circle on the left look bigger than the one on the right.

5 – GOING DOTTY
Move the four corner circles in toward the center so they are in the red positions below.

6 – CUBE CREATION
Cubes A, B, C and D can be made.

7 – CAMPING OUT
Divide the campsite up as follows:

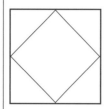

8 – SQUARING UP

9 – CROSS PURPOSES

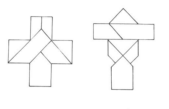

10 – COIN PUZZLE
Move coin D to position G. Move coin F to position B. Move coin E to position H. Move coin A to position C. (Steps 3 and 4 can be swapped.)

11 – COUNTING SKILLS
There's no solution to this question. The number of rods changes as you look at it —it's an optical illusion.

12 – THORNY MAZE

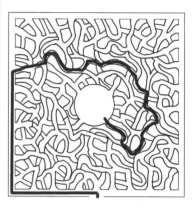

13 – EQUAL SHARES
Divide the area up as below (T=tree, H=house).

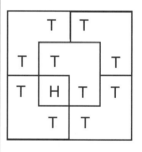

14 – TURN IT DOWN
Three discs need to be moved, as shown.

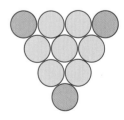

15 – STARS IN YOUR EYES

16 – NO RIGHT TURN

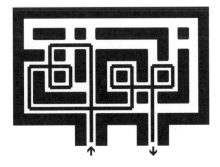

17 – SQUARING UP

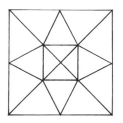

18 – SNAIL TRAILS

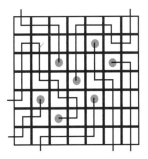

19 – GOING STRAIGHT

Although they look curved, the lines are straight—use a ruler to check!

20 – LETTER LINES

Go from E to B, then B to D, then D to C, then C to B, then B to A, then A to C, then C to E, then E to D.

LEVEL 2

21 – KNOT A PROBLEM?

Yes, it will make a knot.

22 – JUMP RIGHT IN

The moves are as follows. Note: "Jump blue" means that a blue counter jumps:

1 – Advance pink. 2 – Jump blue. 3 – Advance blue. 4 Jump pink. 5 – Jump pink. 6 – Advance pink. 7 – Jump blue. 8 Jump blue. 9 Jump blue. 10 – Advance pink. 11 – Jump pink. 12 Jump pink. 13 Advance blue. 14 – Jump blue. 15 – Advance pink.

23 – BRAIN TROUBLE

1) There are actually 11 letter Fs in this sentence. Chances are you found less than this on first count. Most people don't count the Fs in the word "OF," as our brains tend to skip over these short words quickly.

2) This paragraph is easy enough to read, but there are many repeated words within the box. Moving from line to line, our brain fuses these two words into one, as our expectation is that the words will only occur once.

24 – COUNTING UP

There are 46 squares in all.

25 – TWISTING TRIANGLE

Look at this triangle closely and you'll see that it is impossible to construct.

26 – DRIVING TEST

Here, there are 56 turns.

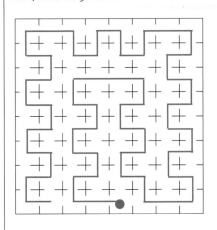

27 – CHOP AND CHANGE

Red lines show the new position of the moved matches.

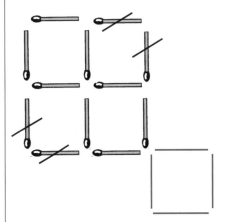

28 – 3–D DILEMMA

Cube D.

29 – COG CONFUSION

Weights 1 and 4 will fall, weights 2 and 3 will rise.

30 – STRAIGHT THROUGH

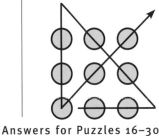

31 – BY THE LAKE

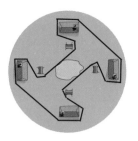

32 – BUILDING BLOCKS

33 – VICIOUS CIRCLE

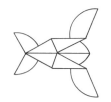

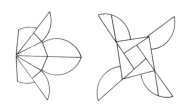

34 – FAIR AND SQUARE

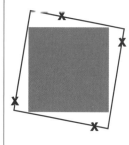

35 – IN AND OUT

36 – FITTING IN

Any square can be left empty, depending on your positioning of the tiles. Try it!

37 – WORD SQUARE

B	A	L	D
A	R	E	A
L	E	A	F
D	A	F	T

The words DEED and BRAT are spelled along the diagonals.

38 – FAIR SHARES

39 – PIZZA THE ACTION

18, 1, 15, 14, 17, 16, 19, 2, 4, 6, 7, 8, 9, 10, 5, 21, 3, 20, 13, 12, 11.

40 – CUBE CONFUSION

There is no answer to this question; the cube changes as you look at it.

Answers

LEVEL 3

41 – SHAPE SORTING

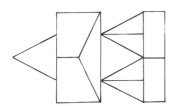

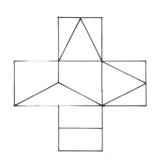

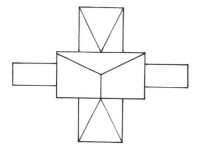

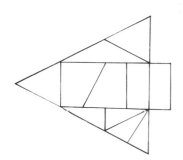

42 – STAR SEEKERS

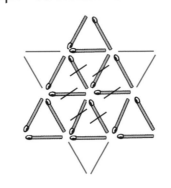

43 – ELEVENSES

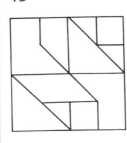

44 – MIDDLE GROUND

Although it doesn't look like it, the lowest of the three dots is at the center.

45 – PUZZLE PEOPLE

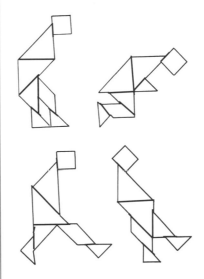

46 – DOUBLE SQUARED

Make cuts as follows:

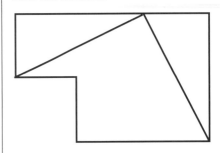

Then put together the square as here:

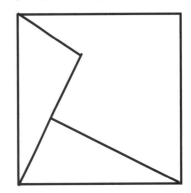

47 – CAT'S WHISKERS

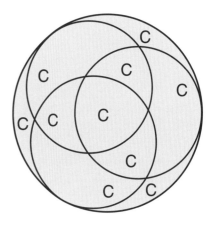

C=cat.

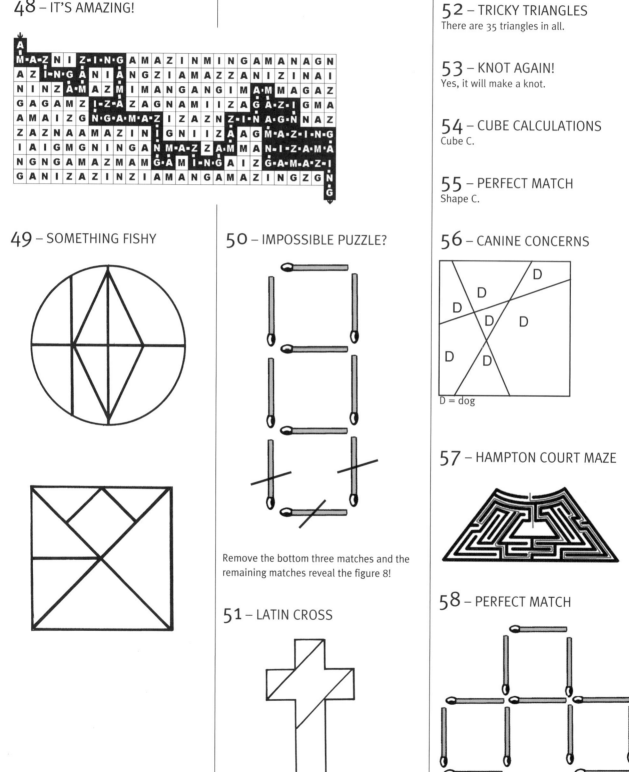

48 – IT'S AMAZING!

49 – SOMETHING FISHY

50 – IMPOSSIBLE PUZZLE?

Remove the bottom three matches and the remaining matches reveal the figure 8!

51 – LATIN CROSS

52 – TRICKY TRIANGLES
There are 35 triangles in all.

53 – KNOT AGAIN!
Yes, it will make a knot.

54 – CUBE CALCULATIONS
Cube C.

55 – PERFECT MATCH
Shape C.

56 – CANINE CONCERNS
D = dog

57 – HAMPTON COURT MAZE

58 – PERFECT MATCH

59 – GREEK CROSS
Make cuts as here:

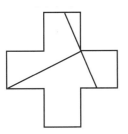

Then put the pieces together as here:

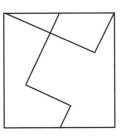

60 – BROKEN BOARD

LEVEL 4

61 – MOVING STAIRWAY
The stairway turns upside-down as you look at it. This means the dot may be at either the front or the back of the stairway at any time.

62 – WHERE TO CROSS

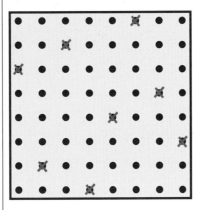

63 – HIP TO BE SQUARE
Smaller squares:

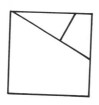

There are two possible solutions for the bigger square:

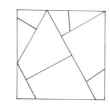

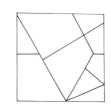

64 – CLEVER COGS
A must turn counterclockwise. B must turn clockwise.

65 – CHERRY PIE
C=Cherry

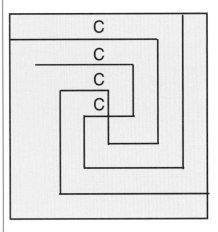

66 – PENTOMINOES

1

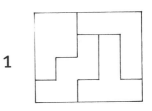

2

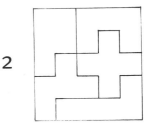

3

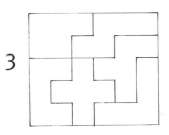

66 – PENTOMINOES (CONT.)

4

5

69 – TWISTS & TURNS

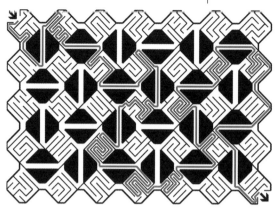

67 – THE HEXAGON

70 – FOUR THOUGHT

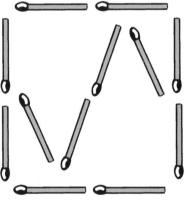

71 – BITS AND PIECES (CONT.)

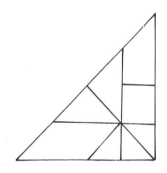

68 – SCHOOL'S OUT

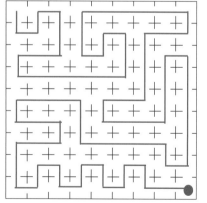

71 – BITS AND PIECES

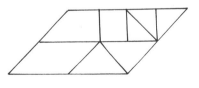

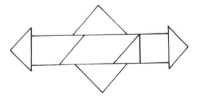

71 – BITS AND PIECES (CONT.)

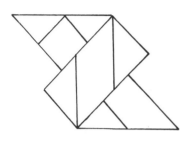

72 – TWO FROM ONE

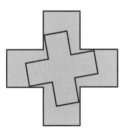

Cut out this shape inside the bigger cross, then the outer pieces will fit together to make another cross of a similar size.

73 – CONSTELLATIONS

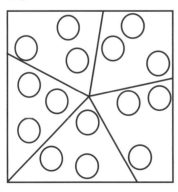

 = star

74 – FIVE CUBED

Cubes A and E can be made.

75 – MATCH IT UP

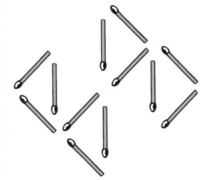

76 – FIND YOUR WAY

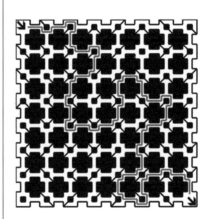

77 – KNOT OR NOT?

Yes, the rope will form a knot.

78 – HAPPY HOLIDAYS

1 can get to A,B,C.
2 can get to A,B,C.
3 can get to C,D.
4 can get to C,D.
5 can get to D,E,F,G,H.
6 can get to E,F,G,H.
7 can get to E,F,G,H.
8 can get to A,H.

Therefore, 1,2,3,4 go to C, and 5,6,7,8 go to H.

79 – LUCKY SEVEN

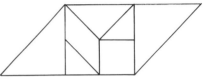

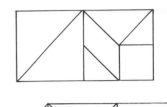

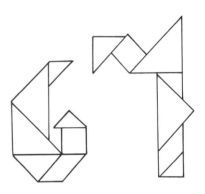

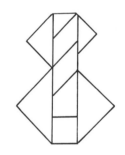

80 – MENTAL BLOCK

No solution – we'll just let you keep trying until you finally succeed!

Reason It Out
Answers

Answers

LEVEL 1

1 – WEIGHING UP
Six apples. Four cups balance five apples and four books balance one apple.

2 – AGE DIFFERENCE
Tony is 24, John is 15 and Carol is 9.
To work out using algebra, let's say Tony's age=t, Carol's age=c and John's age=j.

1) $(j+c) + t = 48$
2) $(j+c) = t$

So
$2t = 48$
$t = 24$.

So Tony is 24 years old. Then we can work out the other ages from the facts given. We know that in six years' time, Tony will be twice Carol's age. So when Tony is 30, Carol will be 15. So Carol must now be 9, as 15–6=9. If all their ages add up to 48, that must mean that John is now 15.

3 – WHAT COMES NEXT?
A) 50 (add 1, then 3, then 5, then 7, etc).
B) 16 (square numbers going down from 100.
C) 651 (first and second digit increase by 1 each time, while third digit decreases by 1 each time.

4 – CIRCULAR SUMS

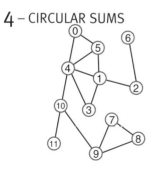

Note: numbers 7 and 8 are interchangeable.

5 – SECRET MESSAGE
The message is: I love you.
Each of the letters making up the message has a space after it, before the next letter.

6 – PLANET PLUS

```
    6  5  7  2
 8  9  1  3  2
 ─────────────
 9  5  7  0  4
```

7 – RED OR BLUE?
The odds are 1 in 126. The odds of picking a red ball first time are 1 in 2, then the odds of picking the second red one are 4 in 9, then 3 in 8, then 2 in 7, then 1 in 6. Multiply all of these together as fractions and you will get the result 24/6048, or 1/252 for picking five red balls. The odds of picking five blue balls are also 1/252, and so the odds of picking five balls of the same color are 1/252 + 1/252 or 1/126.

8 – SWAMP HOPPING

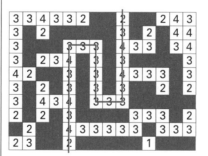

9 – LOST CAUSES
30% have their luggage, 25% have their tickets, 20% have their traveler's checks and 15% have their wallets. Therefore 90% have still got something, leaving at least 10% who have lost all of these items.

10 – PYRAMID

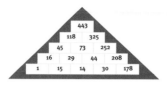

11 – THE KING'S SPEECH
The quotation is "I don't know anything about music. In my line you don't have to." The whole quotation reads backward, from bottom to top.

12 – WORD WONDER
A) ONCE (every word begins and ends with a vowel) B) BARD (every word spells another word when written backward) C) ROAST and STORE (each of the other words is an anagram of one of the other words in the list).

13 – KNOW YOUR NUMBERS
1) 8 apples 2) 18 peaches 3) 69 eggs
4) 25 laps 5) 3 boxes, 9 spare cookies
6) 18,000 seconds 7) 108 8) 3120 times
9) 172–158=14 10) 24 revolutions.

14 – STARSTRUCK

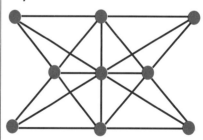

15 – URGENT MESSAGE
The message is: PLANNING TO SURRENDER. PLEASE HOLD FIRE.
Read the first letter top line, then first letter bottom line, then second letter top line, second letter bottom line, and so on.

16 – TO THE NINES
1) Dromedary 2) Labyrinth 3) Nostalgia.

17 – MOTHER AND DAUGHTER

The daughter is 20 years old, and the mother is 48.
To solve this using algebra, let's say that x=mother's age and y=daughter's age.

$x-6 = 3(y-6)$
$x+36 = 1.5(y + 36)$

So we know that:
1) $x-6 = 3y-18$ and
2) $x+36 = 1.5y + 54$

If we subtract equation 1 from 2, we get
$42 = -1.5y + 72$, so
$1.5y = 30$
$y=20$.
Then work out the mother's age from the facts given. If six years ago the daughter was 14, and at that point the mother was three times her age, the mother was then 42, which means six years later (ie now) she is 48.

18 – NAME THE DAY

The date is 06/17/1775, the date of the Battle of Bunker Hill.

19 – FIGURE-FIT

5	8	6	8	9	8	5	9	4	3	1	8	4	9	3	6
5	6	3	7	1	3	2	3	8	7	7	8	1	1	1	3
2	1	1	5	3	9	1	3	4	6	6	7	5	4	7	1
2	9	2	9	4	5	7	2	9	7	2	5	2	1	1	3

20 – ADD–A–NUMBER

a) 410 + 107 = 517.
b) 95 x 25 = 3225.
c) $6^4 \div 48 = 27$
($6^4=1296$)

LEVEL 2

21 – QUICK GETAWAY

The message is SHE KNOWS OUR PLANS. The right grid is a grille that must be placed on top of the letter grid to find the answer. Place it over and read the letters that can be seen from the top row down. Then turn the grille a quarter turn counterclockwise and do the same, then turn it again and so on.

22 – MAGIC SQUARE

10	16	20	4	15
3	23	18	19	2
11	7	1	25	21
24	13	14	9	5
17	6	12	8	22

23 – CODE AMONG THIEVES

The message is: smith is dead. there is no evidence against us. do not confess anything. Each letter is replaced by the one to its right on a standard keyboard.

24 – PYRAMID

				905				
			456		449			
		229		227		222		
	102		127		100		122	
36		66		61		39		83

25 – MASTER OF WORDS

The word is WAND.

26 – AGE CONCERN

James is 15 and Tom is 25.
Using algebra, let's name the number of years ago that the two met as x, James' age as j and Tom's age as t.

1) $t - x = 3(j-x)$
2) $j = t - x$

So
$j = 3j - 3x$
$3x = 2j$.
$j = 1.5x, t = 2.5x$
$j \div t = 1.5 \div 2.5 = 3 \div 5$, so $5j = 3t$

In 3j years' time:
$3j + (2j + t) = 100$
$5j + t = 100$
$3t + t = 100$
Therefore $t = 25$ and $j = 15$.

27 – CIRCULAR SUMS

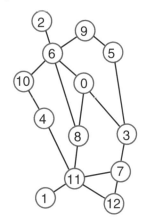

28 – OUTCAST

1) 7963 – every other number is divisible by the first number in its sequence, ie 8432 is divisible by 8, and 3972 is divisble by 3, and so on. 2) SUSAN. For each of the other names, the vowels are arranged in alphabetical order, ie A, E, I, O, U.

29 – KNOW YOUR NUMBERS

1) The Kruger National Park. (Convert square kilometers into acres, which is 20,000 km² x 247.105381 = 4,942,108 acres) 2) a 3) 15 of each type of Vogan. Add 3, 6, 7 and 10 = 26. Divide 390 by 26 = 15 4) b. 5) Sarah is 8, her brother is 12 6) $6
7) $28. Coffee costs $2 per cup and muffins are $1 each 8) The order is x, ÷, +.

30 – MAKING MAGIC

2	9	4
7	5	3
6	1	8

31 – NUMBER MAZE

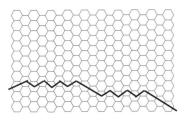

32 – ALL THE SQUARES

204 squares. First, there are obviously 64 1x1 unit squares on the board. If you then count the 2x2 unit squares, you'll find there are 7 rows of 7, making 49. Then, for the 3x3 unit squares, there are 6 rows of 6, making 36. Keep going this way and you'll find that all the square numbers from 64 downward are used, ie 8x8 down to 1x1. So the number of squares on the whole board is found using this sum: 64 + 49 + 36 + 25 + 16 + 9 + 4 + 1. The total is 204.

33 – RAY OF HOPE

By reading the third letter after every punctuation mark, Sir John discovered that the PANEL AT EAST END OF CHAPEL SLIDES. So he was able to flee the chapel and escape.

34 – FRUIT COCKTAIL

The chances are 3 in 34.
The first time, odds are 10 in 17, then 9 in 16, then 8 in 15, then 7 in 14. Multiply these all together as fractions to give you 3 in 34.

35 – SET SQUARE

6	x	3	÷	2	=	9
+		+		x		+
9	+	3	÷	4	=	3
–		–		÷		÷
8	–	5	x	2	=	6
=		=		=		=
7	–	1	–	4	=	2

36 – NUMBER JUMBLE

Simply allocate the numbers 1–26 to the letters of the alphabet, so that A=1, B=2 etc., and then use numbers to spell out the days of the week. Monday becomes 13,15,14,4,1,25 or 1315144125. So the next number in the sequence spells out Sunday, and is 1921144125.

37 – WEIGHT AND SEE

22 hats.
4 hats = 3 boots, so 16 hats = 12 boots.
1 snowman = 2 hats + 4 boots.
So 1 snowman – 2 hats = 4 boots.
So 3 snowmen – 6 hats = 12 boots, OR
3 snowmen = 12 boots + 6 hats, so
3 snowmen = 16 hats + 6 hats = 22 hats.

38 – HIDDEN WORDS

1. Tomato 2. Orange 3. Krona 4. Yen 5. Sage 6. Rosemary 7. Sweden 8. Germany 9. Drum 10. Cello 11. Chair 12. Desk.

39 – ROUND AND ROUND

The solution is: DID YOU FIND THE SPIRAL? Write out the letters in the direction of the spiral, so starting from the top left, write the letters OYDID in the direction of the spiral's first line, then write UTI downwards, still following the spiral's direction, and so on. When you've finished, read each row from left to right to find the message:

```
D I D Y O
U F I N D
T H E S P
I R A L ?
```

40 – NUMBER MASTER

1527, 7048.

LEVEL 3

41 – KNOW YOUR NUMBERS

1) 52mph 2) £153.66 3) $420.
4) 8,5 5) 147 pounds 6) $18 7) 382
8) He never reaches it!

42 – MAGIC SQUARE

17	24	1	8	15
23	5	7	14	16
4	6	13	20	22
10	12	19	21	3
11	18	25	2	9

43 – CRYPTOGRAMS

1. There are two kinds of directors in the theater; those who think they are God and those who are certain of it.
2. Jazz will endure, just as long as people hear it through their feet instead of their brains.

44 – MASTER OF WORDS

The word is BORN.

45 – ARROW NUMBER

46 – NUMBER MASTER

26189; 05263.

Answers

47 – LOGI–FIT

48 – BEN AND JEN
Ben was 78 and Jen was 64.
78^2 = 6084 and 64^2 = 4096.
6084 – 4096 = 1988.

49 – MULTITALENTED
The number is 9376. You can find this using a calculator, with a trial and error system. First, you must work out that the last three digits must be the same as one of the three–digit solutions (376 and 625). Then, starting with 376, you can try 1376, then 2376, then 3376 and so on. When you get to 9376, you'll discover that its square is 87909376.

50 – WHAT COMES NEXT?
1) A (April; the letters represent the months of the year, starting with August) 2) Uruguay (the countries in the list all start with the vowels in order: A, E, I, O, so the country to finish the sequence must begin with a U.) 3) 20 (replace each number with its appropriate letter of the alphabet (so A=1, B=2 and so on). Do this and the sentence reads: WHAT COMES NEX?. So the final number is 20, or the letter T, to complete the phrase WHAT COMES NEXT, the title of this set of puzzles.

51 – SECRET SOCIETY
The code says: There is only one quality worse than hardness of heart and that is softness of head. (F Roosevelt)

The keyword is SECURITY. Write out SECURITY followed by the remaining letters of the alphabet, in order, underneath the alphabet from A to Z, as below. Simply work out the message by comparing the coded letter with its standard alphabet counterpart.

52 – SUM WAY DOWN

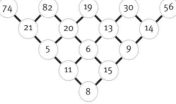

Digits of circles 'C' and 'E' can be reversed, for example 19 could be 91 and 56 could be 65.

53 – OUT OF THIS WORLD

5	8	8	5	2	4	7	2
3	3	3	3	2	3	3	3
4	6	7	6	4	6	6	4
1	2	3	5	7	2	8	6
4	2	3	1	1	1	5	2
5	5	7	7	7	7	5	5
1	2	6	5	8	3	7	4
4	4	4	2	1	2	2	2

54 – BRIEFCASE BLUNDER
The number is 78432.

55 – EVEN ODDS

93	24	45	51	72
60	66	87	33	39
27	48	54	75	81
69	90	21	42	63
36	57	78	84	30

56 – MISFITS
A) 3646 (in every other number, the digits add up to 14, eg 5+4+3+2=14). B) 8197 (in every other number, the last two digits can be multiplied together to give the first two digits, eg 9x6=54).

57 – PAN MAGIC

25	32	14	16	23
19	21	28	30	12
33	10	17	24	26
22	29	31	13	15
11	18	20	27	34

58 – WINE WONDER

```
      1 8 7
    1 2 3 8
  9 4 6 5 8
  ─────────
  9 6 0 8 3
```

59 – SET SQUARE

84	+	10	=	94	–	22	=	72
÷		+		–		–		–
6	+	32	=	38	–	12	=	26
=		=		=		=		=
14	+	42	=	56	–	10	=	46
+		÷		–		–		+
52	–	7	=	45	÷	5	=	9
=		=		=		=		=
66	÷	6	=	11	x	5	=	55

60 – HOW OLD?
The father is 45, the mother is 37 and the son is 18.
To work this out using algebra, let's say d=dad, m=mother, s=son.
1) d+m+s = 100
2) d+9 = 2(s+9), so d+9=2S+18, so s=d-9/2
3) m+9 = d+1, so m = d–8

Substitute 2) and 3) into 1), giving:

d+(d-8) + (d-9) / 2 = 100
2d+2d-16+d-9 = 200
5d = 225
d = 45

Using 2), s = (45-9) / 2 = 18
Using 3), m = 45-8 = 37

LEVEL 4

61 – THE MISSING LINK

S	A	I	L	O	R	B	K	N	O	C	K	E	R
T	S	T	E	P	W	A	N	T	P	I	X	Y	T
A	S	S	Y	E	S	R	E	Q	U	A	T	O	R
G	U	S	E	N	H	N	W	S	S	I	L	T	A
E	U	P	K	E	E	P	V	T	A	C	H	I	P
K	E	Y	S	R	D	R	E	A	R	Y	A	N	Y
I	O	B	I	E	R	O	T	I	C	F	L	O	E
S	W	A	P	T	E	N	O	R	S	O	F	T	L
S	E	C	H	U	N	T	E	R	S	B	E	L	L
S	A	K	E	I	A	O	S	E	T	T	L	E	F
I	G	A	M	P	L	O	F	A	R	S	K	Y	R
D	A	Y	W	E	A	R	I	R	O	O	F	R	O
E	L	A	Z	E	Z	E	R	O	K	N	O	B	N
H	A	N	D	L	E	S	E	R	E	J	E	C	T

P	T	Z	O	A	X	L	F	J	C	V	W	Y
S	R	B	G	E	M	K	U	N	D	I	H	Q

62 – CREATE-A-SUM

```
   7  6  5
   1  4  3
   2  8  9
-----------
 1 1  9  7
```

Note: there are alternative solutions, but numbers must remain in the same columns.

63 – NUMEROCROSS

1	2	3	■	1	■	3	4	5
0	■	1	4	0	2	8	■	0
8	1	7	■	5	■	5	3	0
■	7	■	2	3	4	■	6	■
2	0	0	■	■	■	1	0	0
■	4	■	2	5	2	■	2	■
1	1	7	■	1	■	5	8	5
4	■	6	4	6	2	0	■	4
3	4	2	■	7	■	8	1	6

64 – COOKIE CRUMBLES

Katie had 6 cookies. Tommy had 5 cookies. Sam had 4 cookies. Brad and Jack each had 3 cookies.

Using the initials of their names to represent the amount of cookies each person ate, we know that:

1) $k=b+j$
2) $s=k-2$
3) $t=s+1$

We know that neither Katie nor Tommy ate the least number of cookies. So the two who had the least cookies are two of either Brad, Jack or Sam. As nobody ate more than six, the two who had the least number had no more than three each. So we can use trial and error on all the possibilities of who those two were and how many cookies they ate, using the equations above, in order to finish up with the above answers.

65 – MUSICAL NOTE

Using the hint S=7, T=7, U=7. For example, ABC numbered 1 (as below), DEF numbered 2, GHI numbered 3 and so on. The message says: BE AT THE JAZZ CLUB SATURDAY AT TEN.

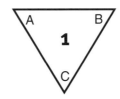

66 – NUMBER CROSS

1	3	4	2
5	6	■	0
1	■	1	1
5	6	5	6

To solve this puzzle, it will certainly help if you can answer the historical clue, 1616, reading down the shaded squares. But if you don't know the exact date that Shakespeare died, you will at least know that the date must begin with a 1, so the top left square is a 1. You therefore know that the answer to 1A must be less than 2000, in which case you can work out that 5A must be less than 16 (since we know that 122 x 5A = 1A). We also know that 5A is a prime number, so it must either be 11 or 13. However, the solution to 122 x 13 contains an 8, and we know from our extra clue that the numbers 7, 8 and 9 do not appear in the solution. So the answer to 5A must be 11. Therefore the answer to 1A is 1342. We now know that 2D begins with 3, and the clues tell us it is a square number, so the answer must be 36 (the only square number in the thirties). Next, we know that 2D x 4A = 3D, and both 2D and 4A end in a 6, therefore 3D must also end in a 6. So we now know the solution to 3D is 2_16, and by using a calculator you can quickly work out that the only possible digit to fill the gap and give an answer ending in 6 (as 4A must do), when the four–number digit is divided by 36, is 0 (ie, 2016/36 = 56). So the answer to 3D is 2016, and 4A is 56. We know that 6A is a result of 101 x 4A, or 101 x 56, which gives us the answer 5656. 1D is the result of 101 x 5D, which we now know is 101 x 15, giving us our final result of 1515.

Answers

67 – CIRCULAR SUMS

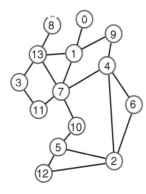

68 – NUMBER MASTER

48132; 08156.

69 – KNOW YOUR NUMBERS

1) $26.40. 2) $1125; $875. 3) 17–25.
4) $24.90 and $30, so the first is better
by $5.10. 5) 26 and 6. 6) 92 cents. 7) 45
handshakes. 8) 43.

70 – WEIGHT BEARING

9 marbles.

1 car + 3 blocks = 12 marbles.
1 car = 1 block + 8 marbles, so
1 car + 3 blocks = 4 blocks + 8 marbles.
So: 12 marbles = 4 blocks and 8 marbles.
So: 4 blocks = 4 marbles, or 1 cube =
1 marble. So: 1 car = 9 marbles.

71 – NUMBER SQUARES

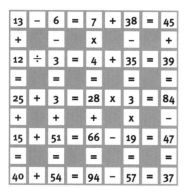

72 – MASTER OF WORDS
The words are GNUS and BELL.

73 – ARROW NUMBER

74 – MISSING NUMBERS
Each number is a result of the previous
number's digits being multiplied together, so
in the first sequence: $6 \times 9 \times 2 \times 8 \times 2 = 1728$.
Then $1 \times 7 \times 2 \times 8 = 112$. So for row B,
missing number is 945, and for row C,
missing numbers are 1764 and 168.

75 – LOGI–FIT

G	R	E	A	T		T	I	M	E	S
R		I		R		I				I
A	1		G	O		2				L
S		V	E	N	U	E				L
S	U	G	A	R		T	A	C	K	Y
		U		3		S				
G	A	U	L	T		V	E	N	U	S
R		T	O	N	A	L				P
A	4		P		G		5			I
Z		I		U						L
E	T	H	I	C		E	Q	U	A	L

76 – WORD ADDITION
One solution:

```
  7 6 2 1 8
4 5 6 2 1 8
5 3 2 4 3 6
```

The second possible solution:

```
  7 2 4 3 1
8 9 2 4 3 1
9 6 4 8 6 2
```

77 – SUM WAY DOWN

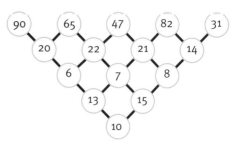

Digits of circles 'C' and 'E' can be reversed, for
example 19 could be 91 and 56 could be 65.

78 – CRYPTOGRAMS
1. Money won't buy happiness, but it will pay
the salaries of a large research staff to study
the problem.
2. More than one newspaper has been ruined
by the brilliant writer in the editor's chair.

79 – EACH WAY

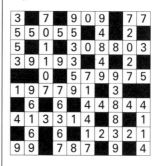

80 – HANG–MATHS

```
    2 5 7
      2 3
  ———————
  7 7 1
5 1 4 0
  ———————
5 9 1 1
```

Think Logically
Answers

Answers Think Logically • Puzzles 1 – 10

LEVEL 1

1 – EXPLORERS
James Cook did not explore Australia (1), or the River Niger (4), but New Zealand. This was not in 1828 (1), or 1795 (2), but in 1769. Park explored the River Niger (4), so Sturt explored Australia. This was not in 1795 (2), but in 1828, so he was not Mungo (3), but Charles, leaving 1795 as the year of Mungo Park's exploration.

In summary:
Charles Sturt, Australia, 1828.
James Cook, New Zealand, 1769.
Mungo Park, River Niger, 1795.

2 – DRINK UP!
Whisky goes with soda and it can be eliminated for Sam (1), Tom (3) and Lisa (2) so it must be for Julie. Elimiate vodka for Tom (3) and gin (2) so he has brandy with his ginger ale (3). So Sam has vodka. With Lisa's gin eliminate tonic (2), ginger ale (3) and soda (1) so it has bitter lemon. This leaves vodka and tonic for Sam.

In summary:
Julie, whisky and soda.
Tom, brandy and ginger ale.
Lisa, gin and bitter lemon.
Sam, vodka and tonic.

3 – IN CONCLUSION I
A. No conclusion. The athletic football players may or may not be ballet dancers. We have no way of telling.
B. Some people we trust are liars. (Or, equivalently, some liars are people we trust).
C. 1. All successful students are old (ie not young) 2. All young students are not successful.

4 – DOMINO SEARCH

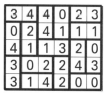

5 – SEASCAPE I

6 – HEDGE YOUR BETS

7 – TRUTH WILL OUT
Case One
'Arry took the sweets. Basher was the lookout. Snuffy distracted the shopkeeper. If 'Arry is telling the truth then Basher distracted the shopkeeper. But that means Snuffy is also telling the truth—Basher was not the lookout. So Basher is a liar. If Snuffy is telling the truth then 'Arry distracted the shopkeeper but that means Basher is also telling the truth saying he did not do that. So Snuffy is the second liar. So Basher is telling the truth. 'Arry took the sweets and he (Basher) did not distract the shopkeeper so he was the lookout and Snuffy distracted the shopkeeper.

Case Two
'Arry both took the bag and ran off with it.

From the lads' statements, whichever of them is lying completely (and one of them is) 'Arry must have taken the bag. Either Snuffy saying he took the bag is a lie or 'Arry saying Snuffy took the bag is a lie. So the witness' first statement is the true one and therefore her second statement is a lie and Snuffy did not run off with the bag – so 'Arry did. This makes Snuffy the complete liar and 'Arry the half–truth teller.

8 – FILM BLUFF
Ava Gardner K24, David Nivea K25, John Wane L25, Clint Eastward M26, Jack Lemon N26, Meryl Streak N27.

9 – MATCH POINT

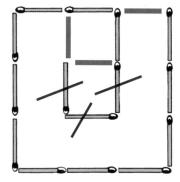

10 – CLOSE CALL
Jodie won, Michelle was second, Katie third and Susan fourth. If Judge B was right about Jodie being second then Judge A was wrong about Jodie winning and also wrong about Susan being second. But he had one place right, so Judge B was wrong about Jodie, so

248 Answers for Puzzles 1–10

he was right about Katie being third. So Judge C was wrong about Katie and therefore, right about Michelle being second. So Judge A was wrong about Susan and must have been right about Jodie winning.

11 – IT'S YOUR MOVE

Mentally divide the board into mirror halves and play symmetrically opposite to player X's every move. If you (Noughts) are about to fill a square that would give you three in a line then the other player has just done that in his/her last move and has already lost the game. If Crosses knows you will use this strategy (and not using it could be fatal), he/she can only try to play so as not to get any three Xs in any line—and the game would end in a draw. Either way Noughts cannot lose the game.

12 – ACE IN PLACE

KD, 9D, QC, JC, KH
9S, TC, TH, JH, 8S
TS, JD, KC, 9H, 9C
JS, 8D, 8H, AH, KS
QD, 8C, QH, QS, TD.

13 – SNUFFY'S GANG

Snuffy chopped the tree down, Basher stripped the bark and Clogger collected the resin. This makes Clogger the complete liar and Basher the half–and–half liar.

If Basher is the truth teller then Clogger stripped the bark, Snuffy chopped the tree down and so Basher collected the resin. But this would lead to both Clogger and Snuffy telling one truth and one lie. But we know one of the three lied twice. So Basher is not the truth teller. If clogger is the truth teller then Basher collected the resin, Clogger chopped the tree down and so Snuffy stripped the bark. But that would lead to both Basher and Snuffy telling two lies each and we know somebody told one lie and gave one true statement. So Snuffy must, for a change, be the one who told the truth.

14 – CONE–FUSION

Rachel bought hers from Rico's (1) so Penny bought hers from Luigi's (4) and is vanilla (1). So Rachel is the girl who chose chocolate (3). Alec's is not mint (2) but coffee and so Vince had the mint. Alec did not buy his from Antonio's but Benito's so Vince was the customer of Antonio.

In summary:
Alec, coffee, Benito's.
Penny, vanilla, Luigi's.
Rachel, chocolate, Rico's.
Vince, mint, Antonio's.

15 – STONE ME!

Put three on the ground to form an equilateral triangle then dig a hole to put the fourth one the same distance from each of the others. If you don't want to have holes in the garden—pile the earth up to make a pyramid and put the stone on top.

16 – COBRA

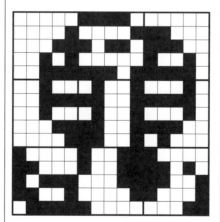

17 – COFFEE

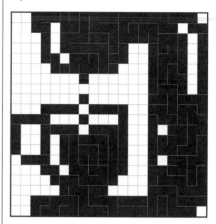

18 – COURT ORDER

From left to right:
K of Spades, Q of Spades, K of Clubs, K of Hearts.
There are these three pairs to be found among only four cards: KK, KQ, QK. The only way to achieve this is KQKK. Similarly, the suits form these three pairs: SS, CH, SC. And these lead to SSCH. Finally there is one known suit/card pair SQ. So the first card is the King of Spades and the rest following the order named.

19 – PICK ONE

The left box cannot have the yellow flowers if you pick a yellow, so it must be the box with yellow and red. So the right box must have yellow and the center box red. If you had picked a red flower from that left–hand box, you wouldn't be able to tell which box had which flowers.

20 – PICK–POCKETS

'Arry faked the slip. Snuffy took the wallet. Clogger ran off with it.

If 'Arry told the truth both times, so did Snuffy and vice versa. Therefore Clogger was the truth teller. So 'Arry told one truth and one lie and Snuffy was the complete liar.

Answers

LEVEL 2

21 – WHOOPS!
Monday's breakage in the lounge was not the vase (3) or the ornamental glass (1) or the ashtray (2) but the lamp. It was not 10 years old (4) or 5 years old (3) or 50 years old (1) but 100 years old. The 50-year-old article broken on Tuesday was not the ornamental glass (1) or ashtray (2) but the vase. The ashtray was broken on Thursday (2) so the ornamental glass was broken on Friday in the dining room (1). The ashtray was not broken in the hall (2) but the study, so the vase was broken in the hall. The article in the dining room was not 10 years old (4) but 5 years old so the ashtray was 10 years old.

In summary:
Monday, 100-year-old lamp, lounge.
Tuesday, 50-year-old vase, hall.
Thursday, 10-year-old ashtray, study.
Friday, 5-year-old glass, dining room.

22 – HOW FEW?
Four. A sister and her brother, both married. One has a son and the other has a daughter.

23 – FERRY NICE
Call the boys A, B, C. The girls a, b, c.
A's girlfriend is a and so on.
TR = crossing to restaurant.
RR = returning from restaurant.

1. bc TR.
2. b RR then ab TR.
3. a RR then BC TR.
4. Bb RR then AB TR.
5. c RR then bc TR.
6. A RR then Aa TR
OR
6. b RR then ab TR.

24 – STALL ORDER
ROW 1:
RADISH, LYCHEE, BROCCOLI, DATES
ROW 2:
BANANAS, CAULIFLOWER, FIGS, WATERCRESS
ROW 3:
TURNIP, CHERRIES, YAMS, APPLES
ROW 4:
KUMQUAT, PEAS, GRAPES, ONIONS.

25 – SEASCAPE II
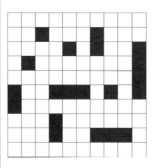

26 – GRAVE NEWS
The lady dies on the Monday and her body was then flown across the International Date Line to a place where it was still Sunday for immediate burial.

27 – PETTY CASH
Clarissa took the cash. Larissa took the gold pen. Melissa took the stamps.

If Melissa's first statement is the true one then Melissa took the cash; Larissa took the stamps (because she did not take the pen) and so Clarissa took the pen. But this would make both of Melissa's statements false. This contradiction with the introduction means that Melissa's first statement is a lie and her second statement is true: Larissa took the pen. So Melissa took the stamps and Clarissa removed the cash.
Note: Larissa's statement is not needed to solve the puzzle.

28 – CUBE ROUTE
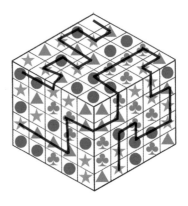

29 – IN CONCLUSION II
A. Some tedious songs are not Jerry Holler's.
B. None but purple-haired boys have rings through their noses. In other words:
All those with rings through their noses are purple-haired boys.
C. No politicians are fit to serve on a jury.

30 – DOMINO SEARCH

3	6	1	0	4	0	6	3
0	2	5	3	6	1	1	2
0	4	6	6	2	5	3	1
5	3	3	6	0	4	6	4
1	4	1	2	0	2	4	5
0	2	5	4	4	2	3	5
3	5	1	0	1	2	6	5

31 – DIE SPOTTING
9. Each line is the sum of the numbers on the face opposite to the one you can see. On standard dice, the opposite faces have a total of 7; thus the first row is 4 (opp 3) + 6 (opp 1) + 2 (opp 5) = 12. Second row is 3 (opp 4) + 2 (opp 5) + 1 (opp 6) = 6. So for the bottom row the sum is 4 + 3 + 2 = 9.

32 – IN A JAM

Sonia is making raspberry jam (3) but she is not making the caramel sponge (1) or the lemon (2) or the vanilla (3) but the orange sponge. So she is also the fudge maker (2). Audrey is not making the caramel sponge (1) or the lemon sponge (2) but the vanilla sponge. So she is also making the coconut ice (3). Jane is making the lemon sponge (2). So Kelly is making the caramel sponge and also plum jam (1). Jane is not making blackberry jam (2) so Audrey is and Jane is making strawberry jam. Kelly is not making nougat (1) but toffee and so Jane is making nougat.

In summary:
Kelly: plum jam, caramel sponge, toffee.
Audrey: blackberry jam, vanilla cake, coconut ice.
Jane: strawberry jam, lemon cake, nougat.
Sonia: raspberry jam, orange cake, fudge.

33 – EQUAL MEASURES

9	2	2	0	6	9	9	5	5
0	7	3	5	5	5	5	5	5
6	6	6	6	0	0	1	1	5
0	0	4	4	4	1	0	4	0

34 – LOGI-SQUARES

B	G	Y	O	P
P	Y	O	G	B
G	B	P	Y	O
Y	O	B	P	G
O	P	G	B	Y

Y	G	P	B	O
B	P	O	Y	G
G	O	B	P	Y
O	B	Y	G	P
P	Y	G	O	B

35 – IN CONCLUSION III

A. Punks do not want to get a job.
B. Some boasters do not deserve rewards.
C. Jenkins is not sober.

36 – DRAGON

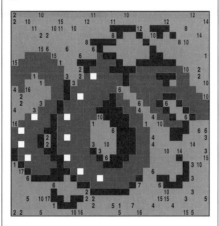

37 – TENTACKLE

A. Andy & Glen B. Gary & Joe
C. Bill & Kevin D. Freddie & Tom.

38 – TAKE ROUTE

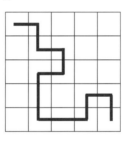

39 – PER-LEASE STATE!

Ben was on the bicycle.
John was in the car.
Dennis was the pedestrian.
Aaron owned the apple-cart.

If we assume Ben's first statement to be his true one then he owned the cart and John did not drive into it. But this makes two of Dennis' statements true: Ben is lying and Dennis is not the cart owner. So Ben's first statement is not true. If John's first statement is true then his third statement is false and he is the cart owner. This makes Dennis' third statement true and so he is lying in his first statement. Which means Ben is telling the truth about John being in the car. But he cannot be both the owner of the cart and the car so his first statement cannot be true. So Ben is not the pedestrian.

If Ben drove the car then, from his own statements, Aaron owned the bicycle. So John could only be the pedestrian, as he would be telling the truth about not being the cart owner. This means Dennis is telling the truth about Ben lying and also telling the truth about John being the pedestrian. So Ben did not drive the car and therefore he must have been the bicycle rider.

From Ben's statements we now know that only the second one can be true and so John is the car driver.

Of Dennis' statements – the first is a lie, so the second is a lie and the third is true – he did not own the cart. So Dennis is the pedestrian and Aaron owned the cart.

40 – SEAT YOURSELF

With Mrs A in place, the sex of the diner at each place is easily determined using the first two rules. The exceptions are 6 and 12 which can be M/F and F/M depending on where Mr A sits in relation to his wife. The two adjacent ladies (Mrs D and Mrs F) are at 11/12 or 6/7. Trying the former will lead to Mrs C not being opposite Mr B so Mrs D is at seat 6 and the rest follows:
1. Mr B 2. Mrs B 3. Mr E 4. Mrs E 5. Mr D
6. Mrs D 7. Mrs F 8. Mr F 9. Mrs A 10. Mr A
11. Mrs C 12. Mr C.

Answers

LEVEL 3

41 – BERET TRUTH
If Henri wears red they are all telling the truth – which they clearly are not! – so Henri wears blue. If Pierre wears red then all the others are lying, but Claude would then agree with Pierre and also be telling the truth – so Pierre wears blue. As Henri and Pierre wear blue, Jacques must be lying and so also wears blue. If Francois is wearing blue then Claude would be lying and Pierre telling the truth. Thus Francois wears red and so does Claude.

42 – TAKE YOUR PICK
1. Jam 2. Holiday 3. Coffee mug 4. Boat 5. Dishcloth 6. Apple 7. $500 8. Camera 9. Foot spa 10. Golf ball.

43 – FRISKY!

44 – TAKE FIVE
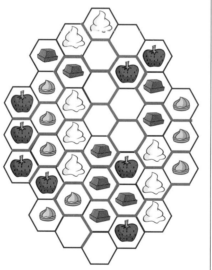

45 – QUEENS HIGH
57 points can be scored by placing the queens at: A2, B7, C3, D6, E8, F5, G1, H4.

46 – SEASCAPE III
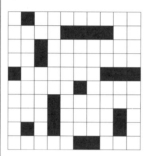

47 – PIECES OF EIGHT
Red lines show cuts.

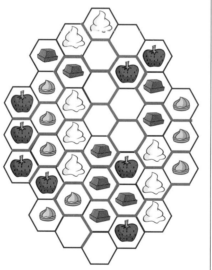

48 – PIE-EYED
First, make a circular cut somewhere between the center and the edge right around the pie. This will divide it into an inner circle and an outer ring. Then make two cuts right across from edge to edge and this will divide the circle and the ring into four parts each.

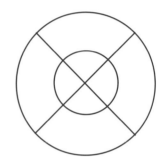

49 – COUNTING UP
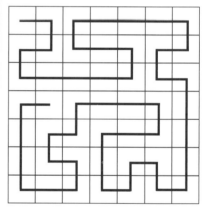

50 – LOGI-SQUARES

Y	B	G	P	R
B	R	P	G	Y
P	G	Y	R	B
G	Y	R	B	P
R	P	B	Y	G

B	Y	R	P	G
G	R	P	Y	B
P	B	Y	G	R
Y	G	B	R	P
R	P	G	B	Y

51 – HOUSE THAT AGAIN?

Using just initial letters, such as DG (not bold) for double glazing and **DG** (bold) for NOT double glazing the clues can be charted as follows:

1. DG——CH 2. RR——FG 3. ON——GD and so on. Now form the longest chain of linked facts: clues 1 and 11, for instance, give DG——CH——**C**, which says that houses with double glazing have central heating and do not have chimneys. Number 31, being an odd numbered house, gives this chain: ON——GD——RR——FG——PG——DG——CH——**C**——LW

3 5 2 12 9 1 11 7 (clue numbers)

So number 31 has a green door, red roof, front garden, plastic gnomes, double glazing, central heating, no chimney and leaded windows.

52 – HELPING HAND

Let **A** (bold) stand for "I hold the Ace" and A (not bold) stand for "I do not hold the Ace" and similarly for K, Q, J. Statement 1 can be taken as "I do not hold KQJ" and we write KQJ=0. Similarly we can state all the remainder, as

1. **KQJ**=0. 2. A**KQ**=0. 3. AK**Q**=0. 4. A**KQ**=0.
5. **KQJ**=0. 6. KQJ=0. 7. **AKQ**=0. 8. AKQJ=0.

There are 16 possible solutions, which can be written

AKQJ **AKQ**J **AK**Q**J** **A**KQJ **A**KQJ **A**KQJ **A**KQJ **A**KQJ
AKQJ A**KQJ** A**KQ**J A**K**QJ AK**QJ** AK**Q**J AKQ**J** AKQJ.

Delete those including **KQJ** (for statement 1), and similarly for the other seven. Only one possibility is left, namely **A**KQJ. That is, "I hold the Ace, but not King, Queen or Jack".

53 – MASTERS OF DISGUISE

If 'Arry and Clogger were the two liars then the milkman would be both the Spaniard and the Norwegian. So one of them must be the truth teller. Snuffy is definitely a liar. The Russian was not the gasman. So in the first set of statements the Norwegian must be a liar so Snuffy was the milkman. So Clogger is a liar saying Snuffy was the gasman so the Norwegian was the milkman. So 'Arry must be the truth teller. So the Spaniard was the postman. The Russian is a liar by this first statement so 'Arry is the postman and Clogger the Russian gasman.

In summary:
'Arry is the Spanish postman
Clogger is the Russian gasman
Snuffy is the Norwegian milkman

54 – DOMINO SEARCH

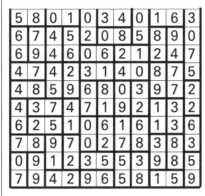

5	8	0	1	0	3	4	0	1	6	3
6	7	4	5	2	0	8	5	8	9	0
6	9	4	6	0	6	2	1	2	4	7
4	7	4	2	3	1	4	0	8	7	5
4	8	5	9	6	8	0	3	9	7	2
4	3	7	4	7	1	9	2	1	3	2
6	2	5	1	0	6	1	6	1	3	6
7	8	9	7	0	2	7	8	3	8	3
0	9	1	2	3	5	5	3	9	8	5
7	9	4	2	9	6	5	8	1	5	9

55 – SHELL WE PLAY?

Game A

Janine has the winning move – take three and leave the last one for Karima. Karima has no chance of winning – if she takes one, Janine takes three and wins. If she takes two, Janine takes one and leaves the last for Karima. If Karima takes three, Janine takes the last one and wins again. Having an odd number and leaving four shells is fatal.

Game B

Karima takes one and leaves four. If Janine takes one, Karima takes three and wins. If she takes three, Karima will take one and win and if she takes two, Karima will take one and leave the last one for Janine. But with a moment's thought, it will be obvious that this situation does not only work for Karima having six and leaving four. It will work if she has any even number and leaves four. She will always be able to take 1 or 3 and finish with the odd total.

Game C

Karima must take one and leave eight. Whatever Janine does, Karima can then be sure to form an even number on her next turn and leave either four or five. What she needs to take is beginning to look familiar: Janine takes one—Karima takes three. This leaves four. Janine takes three—Karima takes one. This leaves four. Janine takes two—Karima takes one. This leaves five.

56 – PROFESSIONAL PARTNERS

Betty has a sister (2) but she cannot be Carol (2&3) but Alice. So Alice cannot be an accountant (2) nor is she a surgeon (1) but a lawyer. Frank's wife has a brother (5) and Carol is the lady with a brother so she is married to Frank (5). Ed's wife is a surgeon (4) so she is not Alice, the lawyer, but Betty. So Alice is married to Dave. He is an accountant (2). Carol's brother is not Dave (5) but Ed, who must be a lawyer (5). Frank must be Dave's brother ((3). So Ed's sibling's spouse (ie Carol's husband, Frank) is the surgeon. Carol cannot be a surgeon (husband) or lawyer (brother) but is an accountant.

In summary:
Betty, surgeon, and Alice, lawyer, are sisters. Frank, surgeon, and Dave, accountant, are brothers. Carol, accountant, and Ed, lawyer, are siblings. Marriages are: Betty and Ed, Alice and Dave, and Carol and Frank.

57 – OH RHETT!

58 – EASY AS ABC

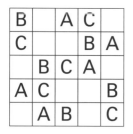

B		A	C	
C			B	A
	B	C	A	
A	C			B
	A	B		C

59 – DISENGAGED

Numbering the announcements down the columns 1 to 11 we find that Ms Hare is not Edna (5), Gloria (9), Hedda (7) or Joanna (6) but Primrose. Her intended is not Case (6) nor is he Joanna's (6), Hedda's (7) or Edna's (4) but Gloria's. So she is not Player (4) nor is Joanna (8) or Edna (4), so Hedda is. Joanna is not Size (10) nor is Gloria (1) so Edna is. Gloria's Mr Case is not Andy (1), Ed (7), Jim (6) or Tommy (9) but Wilf. He is not engaged to Ms Path (3) so Gloria is Ms Clowds and that means Joanna is Ms Path. Primrose Hare is not engaged to Ed (11), Jim (6) or Tommy (9) but Andy. Joanna Path is not engaged to Jim (6) or Tommy (10) but Ed. Edna Size is not engaged to Andy (4) or Tommy (2) but Jim. So Hedda is engaged to Tommy. Jim is not Rest (5) or Wrott (2) or Karner (8) but Hall. Hedda Player is not engaged to Wrott (2) or Karner (8) but Rest. Joanna Path is not engaged to Karner (8) but Wrott so Andy is Karner.

In summary:
Edna Size – Jim Hall.
Gloria Clowds – Wilf Case.
Hedda Player – Tommy Rest.
Joanna Path – Ed Wrott.
Primrose Hare – Andy Karner.

60 – FLIGHT OF FANCY

He was fired for sleeping while on duty. As the nightwatchman he should have been awake and not having a dream!

LEVEL 4

61 – MATCH POINT

Take three from any corner square and complete the square next door and two of the opposite squares. There are eight distinct ways – two answers for each of four squares. An example is given below.

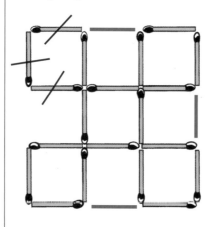

62 – NOT-SO-GREAT TRAIN ROBBERY

Clogger and Wendy both told the truth each time. Snuffy and Doris told one truth. 'Arry and Beryl told two lies. Which means: 'Arry held up the driver. Beryl drove the van. Clogger loaded the van. Doris unloaded the goods from the train. Snuffy changed the signal. Wendy got the keys from the guard.

If 'Arry is the truth teller then Beryl told one truth and one lie (Wendy drove the van) and so Wendy told two truths. Beryl's true statement would have to be Clogger getting the keys. But Wendy's (true) statement says Clogger loaded the goods. This contradicts the introduction, which says each played only one part. So 'Arry is not the truth teller. If Snuffy is the truth teller, then Beryl drove and Clogger changed the signal. But these two "facts" mean that at least one of Beryl's statements is a lie. So is one of Doris' and so is one of Wendy's. But one of the ladies must be a truth teller. So Snuffy is not the truth teller. So Clogger must be the honest soul. We now know that Doris unloaded and 'Arry held up the driver. These facts make both

of 'Arry's statements false. So he is the complete liar and Snuffy does the half–and–half job. Wendy has therefore told at least one truth. If Doris is the truth teller then Beryl also told at least one truth – that Wendy drove. So Doris cannot be the truth teller. The same argument applies to Beryl. If she tells the truth then Doris tells at least one. So Beryl is not the truth teller and Wendy is – which makes her Clogger's wife. And he loaded to goods onto the van. As we know Snuffy told one truth it must be that Beryl drove the van, otherwise Clogger would have had two jobs. This makes Beryl the complete liar and therefore 'Arry's partner, leaving Snuffy's with Doris. Her true statement must be that Snuffy changed the signal. All of which leaves Wendy teasing the keys from the guard.

63 – ON TAP

There are four possible ways to arrange for the three red barrels to be touching but only one of those also has two whites in a straight line of three as required by item F. This is with the three whites in barrels 1, 4 and 6 and the reds in 2, 3 and 5.

In summary:
1. Medium white lychee and elderflower, '88.
2. Sweet red, apple and turnip, the '91.
3. Dry red peach and sprout, the '86.
4. Dry white sloe and fig, the '87.
5. Medium red raspberry and cucumber, the '89.
6. Sweet white grape and pea, the '90.

64 – LOGI-SQUARE SIX

B	W	O	Y	G	R
W	G	R	O	Y	B
G	O	Y	R	B	W
Y	R	G	B	W	O
O	B	W	G	R	Y
R	Y	B	W	O	G

65 – SEASCAPE IV

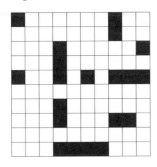

66 – WHO'S WHO?

Allan is not the attorney. This is the logical result based on the fact that you get it no matter what Basil's family name actually is. If Basil is Mr Arnberg (1), if he is Mr Cook (5) or Mr Baker (7). Mr Cook is not Basil (2&4). James is the banker (6), so Allan is the pharmacist. So the attorney is Basil. Thus the pharmacist is Mr Baker since he is not Mr Arnberg (4) nor is he Mr Cook (3), and he is Allan. So the attorney is Mr Arnberg and the banker is Mr Cook.

In summary:
Basil Arnberg, attorney.
James Cook, banker.
Allan Baker, pharmacist.

67 – POT LUCK

The begonia in the middle of the top row was left. Looking at the five rows of plants, they were purchased or given as follows:

Jess, Len, Begonia left, Kevin, Mary.
Mary, Len given, Jess, Len, Kevin.
Len, Kevin, Mary, Kevin given, Jess.
Jess given, Jess, Kevin, Mary, Len.
Kevin, Mary, Len, Jess, Mary given.

68 – SEEING STARS

A. Diane Keaton. B. Hugh Grant.
The code is very simple once you know it!
Three red stars means use the third letter of RED (eg D), and so on.

69 – RABBIT

70 – ALPHA BEATER

B	A		C	D	
D	A			B	C
	C	D	A		B
A	D	B	C		
B		C	D	A	
C			B	D	A

71 – FLOWERY

72 – TRICKY TEASER

Take away the letters of FIVE LETTERS and they will leave the letters of ONE WORD.

73 – ON COURSE

From clue 1 we can deduce that Martin's course was $50 cheaper than Speedy Searching, which was $150 cheaper than Charlie's, which was $50 cheaper than Holmes'. This gives us all four courses in order of cost, lowest to highest.
Wexford cannot be Martin (2) so Connor's cannot be the second cheapest course (2) nor is his third (that's Charlie), so he is Holmes. So Tess, the other forename, took Speedy Searching. So Martin is Brown (3) and Charlie took Advanced Surfing (3). Martin did not take Novice Newsgroups (4) but Browsing for Beginners (4). So Connor took Novice Newsgroups. So Charlie is Dalgliesh (4) and that means Tess is Wexford. Her course costs $400 so Martin's is $350, Charlie's is $550 and Connor's is $600.

In summary:
Connor Holmes, Novice Newsgroups, $600.
Charlie Dalgliesh, Advanced Surfing, $550.
Tess Wexford, Speedy Searching, $400.
Martin Brown, Browsing for Beginners, $350.

74 – DOUBLE TROUBLE

2	6	1	4	4	0	3	2
0	1	5	2	6	6	1	3
2	3	0	5	1	1	4	4
3	5	0	0	5	3	0	5
0	6	1	2	0	6	4	1
2	3	3	3	1	5	5	6
4	4	6	4	2	2	5	6

75 – DANCE ON

Numbering the couples in each dance column one to five. Len is not the Lion (Rumba 2) so he is not the man in couple Foxtrot 5 so he must be Mr Cory—the only other first name left in the foxtrot list. So Alan (Waltz 1) is the fifth male and he is the Lion. In the Rumba column only one male surname is missing and that name is Stevens (Rumba 3 lady). So the Pirate is Mr Stevens (Rumba 5). Kay is not the Astronaut's wife (Waltz 3) or the Monk's (Waltz 1), or the Pirate's (Twist 1) or the Lion's (Rumba 2 and waltz 4) but the King's. Pam is not the Monk's wife (Waltz 1), Astronaut's wife (Waltz 2), Pirate's wife (Twist 1 & 5) but the Lion's. Norma is the not the Monk's wife (Waltz 1) or the Astronaut's (Waltz 2) but the Pirate's therefore Mrs Stevens. Pam's husband (Twist 5) is the Lion, so Fay's husband is the Monk (Twist column). So Wilma is the Astronaut's wife (Waltz 2). Wilma is not Mata Hari or Queen (Foxtrot column), or the Fairy (Waltz 2), or Snow White (Rumba 1 & 4) but the Flower Girl. Snow White is not Wilma (Rumba 1) or Pam (Rumba 2) or Norma (Rumba 3) Or Fay (Rumba 5 and Twist 1) but Kay (Rumba 4). Len Cory is not married to Norma (Foxtrot 2), Pam (Rumba 2), Kay (Waltz 4) or Fay (Mrs Ellis), but to Wilma. So he is the astronaut. Kat is not Mrs Walker (Twist 1 & 2), so she is Mrs Morris and Pam is Mrs Walker. So Alan is Mr Walker. This means Norma is the Fairy (Twist 5—only forename left). The only surname left for a man in the Waltz column is Ellis so he must be Bob (Waltz 5), and he is the Monk married to Fay. Jim is the King (introduction) so he is married to Kay Morris. So Tim is married to Norma Stevens and he is the Pirate. Fay is not Mata Hari (Foxtrot 1 & Rumba 5) but the Queen and Pam Walker is Mata Hari.

In summary:
Alan & Pam Walker, Lion & Mata Hari.
Bob & Fay Ellis, Monk & Queen.
Jim & Kay Morris, King & Snow White.
Len & Wilma Cory, Astronaut & Flower Girl.
Tim & Norma Stevens, Pirate & Fairy.

76 – HIDDEN VALUE

PUZZLE 1
We know that the following is true:
A+B=9, A+C=4, C+D=6, D+E=12.
If A+C=4, then C must be either 3 or 1 (it cannot be 2 because no two values are the same, so A and C cannot both be 2). But we know that C cannot be 3 because C+D=6, and again, no two values are the same.
So C must be 1 and A must be 3. You can then work out the remaining values using the equations above.
Solution is therefore:
A–3, B–6, C–1, D–5, E–7.

PUZZLE 2
We know that the following is true:
A+B=6, B+C=9, C+D=11, D+E=14.
If A+B=6, then A must be either 1, 2, 4 or 5.
So if we try out each of these possibilities against the other equations, we find that:
A cannot be 1, because that would make both D and E equal to 7.
A cannot be 4, because that would mean D must also be 4.
A cannot be 5, because that would make E equal 11, and it must be 9 or below.
Therefore A is equal to 2, and the solution is:
A–2, B–4, C–5, D–6, E–8.

77 – WE ARE SAILING

78 – ALPHA-SQUARE

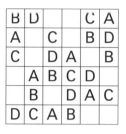

79 – HOME AND AWAY

Mrs Charmer is going to Cyprus (1). She is not the owner of the parrot (1), the budgerigar (2&5), the hamster (3), or the cat (5). So she owns the dog called Melissa (4). Kylie the budgerigar (2) has an owner who is not going to Turkey (2), Thailand (4), Spain or Cyprus (5) but Italy. Her owner is not Mrs Abbot or Mrs Donkin (2), or Mrs Edwards (3), or Mrs Charmer (1) but Mrs Brady. Mrs Edwards is not going to Spain (3), or Thailand (3&4), but Turkey. So she is the owner of Gemma (2). Mrs Donkin is not going to Thailand (4) but Spain. So Mrs Abbot is going to Thailand and is the owner of the cat (4). So Mrs Donkin owns Henry the parrot (1) and Joey must be the cat.

In summary:
Abbot, Thailand, Joey, cat.
Brady, Italy, Kylie, budgerigar.
Charmer, Cyprus, Melissa, dog.
Donkin, Spain, Henry, parrot
Edwards, Turkey, Gemma, hamster.

80 – L FOR LAST

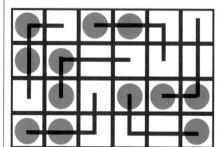

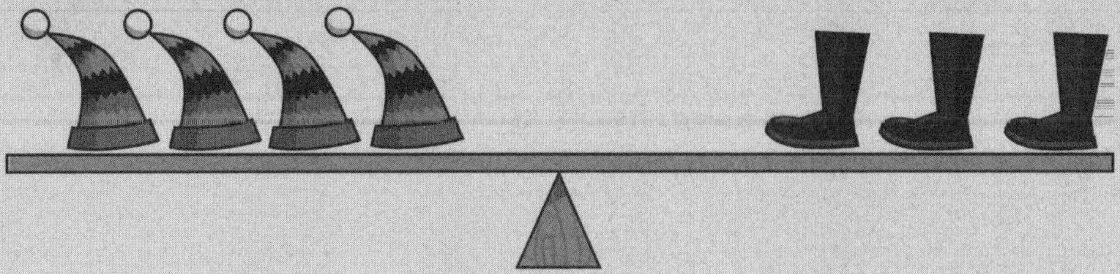

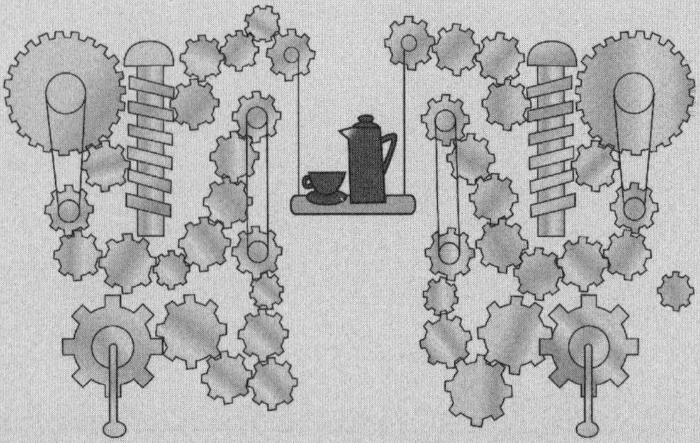

	16			
				2
17		12		22

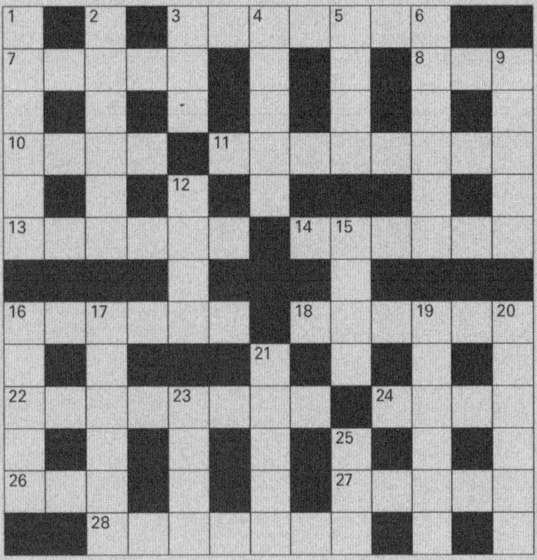

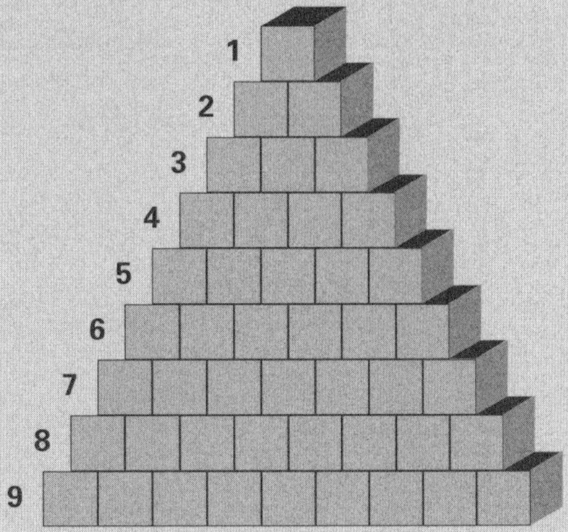
1
2
3
4
5
6
7
8
9

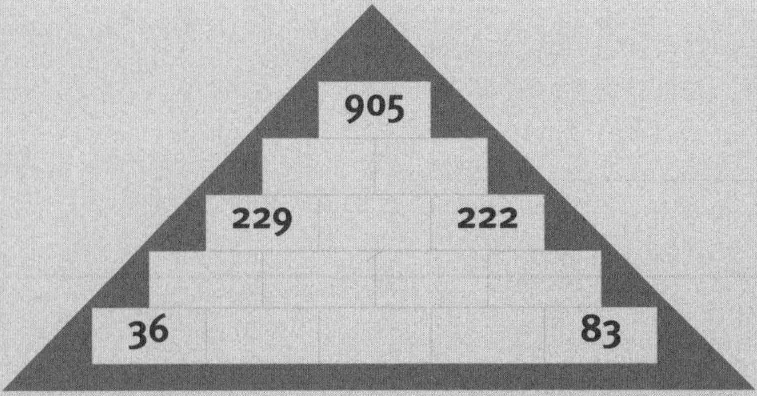
905
229
222
36
83

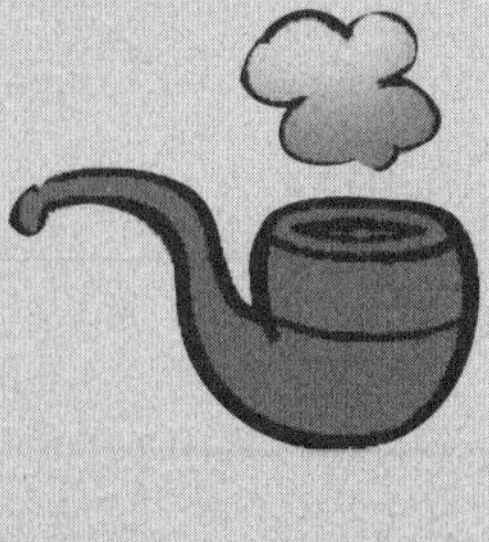